Dances of Death

Dances of Death

The Group Theatre of London in the Thirties

MICHAEL J. SIDNELL

faber and faber
LONDON·BOSTON

First published in 1984
by Faber and Faber Limited
3 Queen Square London WC1N 3AU

Filmset by Wilmaset, Birkenhead, Merseyside
Printed in Great Britain by
Redwood Burn Ltd, Trowbridge, Wiltshire

British Library Cataloguing in Publication Data

Sidnell, Michael J.
Dances of death.
1. Group Theatre — History
I. Title
792'.09421   PN2596.L7G7

ISBN 0–571–13321–5

for Felicity

Contents

Illustrations

Acknowledgements

During the writing of this book many people have helped me: searching memories and records; answering my questions in person and by correspondence; giving me access to documents; and drawing on their own research to aid mine. It would be too much to hope that the result is at all worthy of the generosity, patience, and encouragement I have received. I am particularly indebted to some former members of the Group Theatre named below and I am conscious of not being able to do justice to the energy and talent they put into the making of it. I ask their indulgence for what must be, to some degree, the shortcomings of any book that concerns itself with the most ephemeral of the arts. I must also note, sadly, that some of those whom I thank for their help have died since it was given.

One of the pleasures of my investigation of the Group Theatre was to hear many recollections laced with amusing anecdotes and extending well beyond the scope of this book. The only deep reticence I encountered had to do with political affiliations; on all other matters my informants were concerned to give a full and accurate account of the Group and their association with it.

Among the memorable occasions associated with the writing of this book was one on which Nella Moody sang songs from *Out of the Picture* and brought home to me the character of that work and her feeling for it. On another signal day, John Allen, Ormerod Greenwood and Alan Rolfe sang for me the songs from *The Dance of Death*, in which they had performed in 1934 and 1935. This was made possible by the kindness of Carolyn (Murrill) Evans, who provided me with a copy of her father's score, and of John Glofcheski who accompanied the singers. Then, I had the good fortune to be in England when Donald Mitchell staged songs from *The Ascent of F6* at the Aldeburgh Festival. And I thank the composer, Rod Taylor, and all those who helped me get inside *The Dog Beneath the Skin* with a production of the play at Hart House Theatre in Toronto.

As well as John Allen, Ormerod Greenwood, Nella (Burra) Moody and Alan Rolfe, whom I have mentioned, I thank other ex-members of the Group Theatre who helped me to understand it: William Alwyn, Peter Bennett, Vivienne Bennett, Jean (Richardson) Berkoff, Mervyn Blake, Sir William Coldstream, Peter Copley, Robert Eddison, Christopher Isherwood, Isobel (Scaife) Jenke, John Johnson, Hedli (Anderson) MacNeice, John Piper, Oliver Reynolds, Jean Scott Rogers, Audrey Russell, Vera (Poliakoff) Russell, Mary Skeaping, Stephen Spender, Lady Summerson (Elizabeth Allison), Doris Thelluson, the late Selma Vas Dias, the late Roy Walker, Desmond Walter-Ellis, Robert Wellington, and Joan White. I am especially indebted to John Moody for recollections and materials drawn from his long and active association with the Group Theatre and for his very helpful advice. In the earlier stages of my research Robert Medley spent many hours recalling the Group Theatre and answering my questions. At a later date he kindly offered corrections to my manuscript but since this was finished and delivered before the publication of his *Drawn from the Life: A Memoir* (Faber and Faber, 1983), I was unable to make significant use of the personal and documentary account of the Group Theatre that he gives in that book.

Other people whose help I gratefully acknowledge are: Alan Andrews, Sir Frederick Ashton, Jennifer Aylmer, Gisela E. Bahr, Andrew Blackwood, Barry C. Bloomfield, Bram Bootman, Sally Brown, the late E. Martin Browne, Ronald

Bryden, Penelope Bulloch, Patrick Carnegy, Humphrey Carpenter, Norman Claridge, Susan (Kehrer) Clausen, John Cole, Nancy Copeland, the late E. R. Dodds, Eric Domville, Ellen Dunlap, Valerie Eliot, John Evans, Alan Filewod, Brian Finney, James Forsyth, Sir Alec Guinness, David Halliday, Denis Halliday, Denis Johnston, Ann Jones, Bruce Kidd, Pia Kleber, Sally Leach, Heather MacCallum, Ruth-Ann MacLennan, Donald Mitchell, Don Moggridge, the late Allardyce Nicoll, Myfanwy Piper, Alice Prochaska, the late Dame Marie Rambert, Herta Ramthun, Jack Reading, Denis Rice, George Rylands, Rosamund Strode, Ann Tucknell, John Willett, Erika Wilson and Basil Wright.

Included above are members of the staffs of various libraries and museums. I would like to thank, also, unnamed helpers at the following institutions: Akademie der Künste der DDR; BBC Sound Archives; the Humanities Research Center of the University of Texas; the Karl Marx Memorial Library; the Library of King's College, Cambridge; the Library of King's College, London; the Library of Swarthmore College; the London Theatre Museum; the Marshall Library, Cambridge; the Theatre Museum of the Victoria and Albert Museum; the New York Public Library, especially the Berg and the Theatre Collections; the Toronto Metropolitan Library; and the University of Toronto Library.

I thank Dr Lola Szladits, Curator of the Berg Collection of the New York Public Library, for her unfailing helpfulness, advice and encouragement; and, indeed, for getting me started in the first place. Dr Edward Mendelson, a stalwart friend to this project and to me, has been a mine of information most freely given. To Valerie Eliot I am indebted for supplying extracts from T. S. Eliot's correspondence; to Donald Mitchell for his help and for quotations from the diaries of Benjamin Britten.

The following have kindly allowed me to quote copyright works: the Estate of W. H. Auden—the 'Epilogue' to *Lancelot of Denmark* and extracts from letters, prompt copies, and other works; Valerie Eliot—letters from T. S. Eliot and extracts from *The Superior Landlord* and from an unpublished lecture; Mr Dan Davin—letters and prompt copies of Louis MacNeice; Faber and Faber—extracts from published works of Auden, Auden and Isherwood, Eliot, MacNeice and Spender; Ormerod Greenwood—letters to Gordon Craig; Robert Medley—sketches and designs; Michael Yeats and A. P. Watt and Sons—letters of Yeats; Donald Mitchell —extracts from the diaries of Benjamin Britten. These copyright materials are not to be reproduced without written permission of the copyright holders.

For copies of photographs and stage designs reproduced in this book I am very grateful to: John Moody (nos. 2, 5, 6, 14); the Enthoven Collection of the Victoria and Albert Museum (no. 7); the Department of Prints and Drawings of the Victoria and Albert Museum (no. 33); the National Portrait Gallery (no. 10); and the Henry W. and Albert A. Berg Collection, the New York Public Library, Astor, Lennox and Tilden Foundations (nos. 1, 4, 8, 13, 15–32, 34, 35). I am most grateful too to Anne Day, who photographed illustrations in the Berg Collection. It has not been possible to identify the original photographer in every case. Any oversights in this respect or with respect to unlocated copyright holders I will attempt to make good as opportunity arises.

I owe a particular debt to Robert Medley, Henry Moore and John Piper, whose design sketches are reproduced here with gratitude.

I offer my thanks to the Master and Fellows of Corpus Christi College, Cambridge, for having me as a visitor for a year during the writing of this book; to the Social Sciences and Humanities Research Council of Canada for financial support; to the University of Toronto and to Trinity College, Toronto, for freed time and material help.

It is partly to acknowledge my wife's immense contribution to this book that I dedicate it to her.

M.J.S.
December 1983

Foreword

It is over fifty years since the theatre group whose activities are described in this book was founded. For those of us who were deeply involved in the Group from the start it was a far more intense experience than might be gathered from Michael Sidnell's admirable account of an enterprise that suffered throughout from uncertain artistic policies and lack of entrepreneurial experience. There had been and were other 'alternative' theatres, as they are now called, but the Group, through the vision of Rupert Doone, was the only one which saw the necessity of forming a permanent company on the basis of an intensive training of the actor. I do not know to what extent Rupert was influenced by the Compagnie des Quinze, whose first visits to London took place during our formative years, and I do not think he was aware of the extent to which he was developing the approach to the theatre which had been enunciated by Jacques Copeau in 1912 – the bare stage, the poetic text and the highly trained actor. In some respects he was a more original teacher than Michel St Denis. He established the Group Theatre without previous experience either as an actor or as a director and without a long period of gestation such as Saint-Denis had had with his uncle Copeau in Burgundy. It was therefore ironical that in 1936, when the Group was faltering, Saint-Denis should have been able to establish (at the London Theatre Studio) the very kind of school that Rupert had envisaged. Yet, as Michael Sidnell perceptively points out, the Group Theatre exerted a considerable influence on the poetic drama, while the London Theatre Studio did nothing for the drama but transformed the approach to acting.

What, then, were these teaching methods on which Rupert Doone so heavily relied? His first achievement was to adapt the principles of classical ballet to the training of the actor. Thus the five positions, turn-out, elevation, the proper placing of the torso on the pelvis and general co-ordination became the basis not for a classical style of movement but for a strong, flexible and well-placed body which (in theory) we could adapt to the demands of any theatrical style. Teachers of classical ballet tend to be shocked when I say that we found something natural within the severe demands of the classical style – natural, that is, within the discipline of expressive movement. Of all the many teachers of classical ballet whom I have seen, Rupert Doone was virtually unique in one crucial respect: his insistence that no movement or gesture must be made, and no part of the body held in position in an inexpressive manner. This was a matter not of the nature of the movement or the position of the limb but of the sensual awareness that must run through it. Many teachers recognize that gesture and movement must emanate, as it were, from the diaphragm or spine, but few insist that at the same time the mind must be wholly involved. Thus if concentration was primarily on the legs, and the arms were held out in what dancers call *port-de-bras*, this sensual awareness – I can think of no other term and I have forgotten how Rupert described it – must run through the arms in stillness as much as the legs in motion. It was, I think, by insisting on this total expressive quality of movement rather than on its physical correctness that Rupert effected a modulation from the training of the dancer to that of the actor.

In evolving this new style of training for actors Rupert Doone was greatly helped by his familiarity with the so-called Central European school of dance. (He had known Kurt Jooss and Rudolf Laban since 1927.) This provided us with the sense of flow that is so often missing from classical ballet. Floor-work was an important part of the training and one that many of us remember with particular anguish in view of the amount of time we had to spend actually scrubbing the floor of our premises in 9, Great Newport Street.

In the following pages there is a recurrent suggestion that the poets – Auden and Eliot in particular – found the quality of our verse speaking suspect. This was a fair judgement. Throughout the years of which I am writing (1932–6) Rupert did not succeed in finding a voice teacher who could adequately supplement his own work on the body. I can recall three voice teachers, all excellent in their own ways, who worked on wholly conventional lines. It was Rupert himself who initiated a great deal of choral speaking, using passages from *The Waste Land* and *Murder in the Cathedral*; but in spite of an inadequate understanding of the physical basis of speech he had a sharp intuitive sense of how to point a phrase and give the verse a dynamic that was in refreshing contrast to the elocutionary ideals common at the time.

In improvisation our work was fumbling. We studied animals and improvised certain characters, but I do not think that Rupert saw clearly the particular qualities of observation, recall and resourcefulness that improvisation can develop and that were richly exploited by St Denis; nor did Rupert ever use it as a production method. On the other hand we developed what may now seem to have been a strange obsession with music-hall, a form which, though dying, was still far from dead. Some of us paid frequent visits to the Granville Theatre of Varieties, Walham Green, where many of the great stars such as Max Miller and Little Tich still topped the Bill. Music-hall satisfied at least two of our ideals. One was to escape from the social naturalism and superficial psychology of the contemporary theatre and to find means of establishing a direct relationship with the audience. In theory this may sound a pretentious ideal but in practice it was something very precise. Several of us are agreed that the most 'exciting' performances we gave were not in theatres but in venues where actor–audience contact was much closer: *Fulgens and Lucrece* played in the round (or rather the square) in the great hall of King's College in the Strand; *Sweeney Agonistes* played in the corner of our room in Great Newport Street, and the sequence of carols and Irish–Scottish folk songs simply but stylishly choreographed by Tyrone Guthrie (referred to in the text as *The Group Theatre in Songs, Dances and a Play*).

For a young actor in the early 1930s the Group Theatre provided an unforgettable experience. It provided us with a base from which, with the perennial scorn of the young for established ways, we could express our contempt for the commercial theatre (on which, of course, we depended for a living). We tended to dismiss anyone over thirty as 'old hat' – Craig, Stanislavsky, Yeats and Eliot were exceptions. I can only revert to the over-used word 'excitement' to convey the fervour and the ferment in which we lived. But it was not an easy life. Even while the Group was dominant in our minds, it came second to earning a living. Many of us were playing in the commercial theatre while attending classes at Great Newport Street in the late afternoons and rehearsing at weekends. Classes were at five o'clock so that we would not have to miss them on matinée days. I myself was a member of the Old Vic company for two seasons (1933–4–5) while the Group was at its most demanding. After Rupert's exacting classes we would gather in the Express Dairy across the road (rechristened by Rupert the 'Excess Dreary' because of its unvarying bill of fare), where conversation was often as stimulating as the classes had been.

Rupert Doone was the central figure of the Group Theatre; it was his achievement and it reflected closely his strengths and weaknesses. Everyone, from W. H. Auden to the newest recruit from among the spear carriers at the Old Vic, found him infuriating, incoherent, tyrannical, but also, far more important, inventive, imaginative, productive, convincing, with that natural originality which he shared with Wystan Auden. Having worked with Reinhardt, Cocteau and Diaghilev himself, he dragged us into the mainstream of European culture, while the list of Group Theatre members

(Appendix C) shows the extent to which we were supported by many of the outstanding young painters, poets and musicians of the day. Rupert was a hard-bitten professional, but he was able to exploit the qualities of the young – freshness, persistence, unconquerable enthusiasm. Group Theatre productions became established and controversial avant-garde events. Members of the Comédie Française and the Compagnie des Quinze attended our occasional parties, while the following pages give details of collaboration of one kind or another with Eliot (whose support was of the most generous kind), Spender, Auden, Yeats, Piper, Britten, Herbert Murrill, Brian Easdale, William Alwyn and many others. The calm loyalty of Robert Medley, Rupert's lifelong companion, soothed many clashes; Tyrone Guthrie, then rising to eminence, gave judicious support; and the Group Theatre's secretary, John Ormerod Greenwood, made a contribution over a number of years without which I doubt whether the Group Theatre would have survived as long as it did. It is for me a matter of the deepest personal regret that circumstances prevented a lasting relationship between Rupert and his closest collaborators. He was near to creating the most interesting theatrical ensemble Britain has seen this century.

JOHN ALLEN
March 1984

1
Introduction

The exploitation and incidental destruction of the
divine gift of the public entertainer by
prostituting it to the purposes of financial gain
is one of the worser crimes of present-day
capitalism.

JOHN MAYNARD KEYNES, 1936[1]

In the years following the end of the Second World War, the
English theatre was transformed. Before the war the theatre
had become so fragmented artistically and so hard pressed
economically, so thoroughly unnerved by competition from
cinema and radio, that a theatrical (if not a social) revolution
seemed necessary to arrest its steady decline in popularity and
significance. It was not revolution but the outbreak of war that
resolved most of the old feuds within the theatre and put it on a
new social footing. Wartime exigencies made state support of
the theatre expedient and politically tolerable. CEMA (the
Council for the Encouragement of Music and the Arts) and
ENSA (the Entertainment National Service Association) were
created to sustain the morale of civilians and the armed forces
and to engage performing artists in the war effort. The most
powerful proponent of CEMA, and its second chairman, was
John Maynard Keynes, who had been active in various
attempts to overcome the financial obstacles to theatrical
initiatives in the pre-war years. He used—and exceeded—the
authority vested in CEMA to such good effect that government subsidy for the arts was accepted as no less relevant to
social reconstruction after the war than to the winning of it.
The establishment of the Arts Council in 1946, under Keynes's

chairmanship, entrenched the principle of continuing state support for the theatre (and other arts) and, after a period of dubious experiment in which commercial theatres were among those subsidized, the partly state-funded, professional but non-commercial theatre that we have grown accustomed to began to evolve.

The years immediately following the Second World War saw the collapse of touring companies, the closure of theatres and very little in the way of new English plays or theatrical techniques, but state subsidies helped to keep the theatre going and, as the level of support increased, began to have far-reaching effects. Local government took its cue from Westminster and much of the ground lost to the touring companies was occupied by civic theatres, some with their own companies. Eventually, the so-long-advocated National Theatre itself appeared, constructed and operated on the grand scale, even though a national theatre in all but name, the Royal Shakespeare Company, was already in operation.

Today, well-established opera, ballet, and dance companies have their own buildings and organizations coexisting, without rivalry (or collaboration), with the theatres. Subsidized theatres have assumed the artistic leadership. Their mixed economies of dependence on both the box office and grants have internalized the old conflict between commerce and art. The 'commercial theatre' brings added opportunities for actors and playwrights who are not wholly dependent on it. Commercially backed productions may run for months, or years, and even become permanent tourist attractions but the scope for breaking new ground in any unsubsidized theatre, apart from the very smallest 'fringe' operation, is derisory. The much-diminished commercial sector is unvexed by would-be reformers, though conservationists have not always prevented it from doing away with parts of itself in order to redevelop valuable sites for non-theatrical uses.

Censorship, though so obviously incompatible with a subsidized national institution in a democratic country, lingered on after the war but was at last abolished in 1968. The

Theatres Act signified the end of a long era of official suspicion and control. More practically, official approbation has brought with it the development of a whole gamut of publicly funded paratheatrical activity: training programmes for actors, designers, directors and all manner of theatre professionals on a scale scarcely conceivable before the war; and the study of the theatre as an academic subject in schools and universities.

Theatregoing has become, almost by definition, a middle-class recreation and since the theatre is by no means a pervasive medium like television, its power to enhance life, to educate minds and emotions is limited. On the stage the 'working class' is more frequently, more knowledgeably and more sympathetically portrayed than ever before but for audiences in which it is scarcely represented. This anomaly makes playwrights and producers uneasy, and it is indeed ironical that large-scale subventions for the theatre came about only after it had ceased to be 'popular' entertainment. In the light of the 'invisible income' the theatre earns from tourism, subsidy is readily understandable, though how this important factor may affect the theatre in other than economic ways is more obscure. What is certain is that, at whatever price, the English theatre has achieved a high level of artistic accomplishment and prestige and a definite sense of its social role. In these ways, and in its economic stability, it contrasts markedly with the pre-Second World War theatre.

Nor is it just by comparison with the troubles and dissensions of the 1930s that the English theatre now appears extraordinarily stable and secure. The theatre was in a condition of continuous and intensifying revolution for virtually the whole period from about 1890 to 1939, during which it was subject to fundamental economic, social and technological changes and was beset by wave on wave of would-be reformers intent on restoring its grasp on reality, its communal role, and its vitality as a literary medium and as a confluence of the arts.

Before the turn of the century, a literary avant-garde that had knocked at the managers' doors and found them firmly shut, was looking for ways to circumvent the established theatre. Alternatives such as Grein's Independent Theatre and the Stage Society—to name but two of many play-producing groups—were founded to give 'serious' new drama the hearing that managerial conservatism, abetting official censorship, denied. The efforts made to produce new plays by Ibsen and other European dramatists were not notably successful and offered little encouragement for aspiring English playwrights. George Bernard Shaw managed to build his audience through the medium of print, and his prominence as a published-but-unperformed playwright was a clear indication to others, as well as to himself, of the theatre's shortcomings. He occupied the crumbling citadel but, long after his plays had been proved good theatre and good business, the inability or disinclination of the established theatre to accommodate new playwrights with intellectual ambitions remained a justified grievance against it. Indeed, it was not until the mid-fifties that the English Stage Company broke the ice by giving not unprecedented but singularly effective encouragement to innovative young playwrights. It is doubtful, though, that the ESC's efforts would have come to much had they not coincided with the immense increase in the demand for new plays that accompanied the development of television broadcasting. The work of a new generation of playwrights nurtured by television became available to the theatre, and the theatre, having now the opportunities and obligations brought by state subsidy, became more receptive to new plays than it had been for many years.

The agitation for 'serious' drama that gathered head in the 1890s was no threat to the theatre managements but the growing popularity of the music-halls was. In the early years of the century, the theatres attempted to meet the competition by adding variety turns while the halls, for their part, put short plays on their bills and enticed stars from the 'legitimate' theatre to play in them. This mixture of genres had interesting implications beyond the purely commercial ones. The spectacle was not as ludicrous as it seemed to the rhymester who foresaw the day,

> *When theatres to song and dance*
> *Are quite completely dedicated,*
> *And when the halls the home will be*
> *Of tragedy and comedy.*[2]

The rivalry between theatres and halls for a place in the sun, and the efforts to get new drama in from the cold, were soon complicated by the advent of the cinema. While the movies were still dumb they could be regarded as a supplement to variety entertainment. With the arrival of the talkies, the devastation of the music-halls was assured and that of the theatres seemed imminent. It became a matter of urgency for the theatre to define its function and its art.

In 1920, when the picture palaces had already begun to displace the music-halls, T. S. Eliot looked to the moribund techniques of the latter for a form that might revive the theatre. It was not the 'seriousness' of naturalism and realism that he wanted but poetry, which, he thought, might somehow be grafted on to the old theatrical stock of the halls:

> The Elizabethan drama was aimed at a public which wanted *entertainment* of a crude sort, but would *stand* a good deal of poetry; our problem should be to take a form of entertainment and subject it to the process which would leave it a form of art. Perhaps the music-hall comedian is the best material.[3]

As Eliot must have been aware, something of the kind had already been attempted by Jean Cocteau, in *Parade* most notoriously. Eliot's taste for the music-hall was part of his *literary* inheritance from such poets of the 1890s as Arthur Symons and John Davidson. Cocteau was also in this line of development from the 'decadent movement', with its longings for a robust, sensuous theatrical complement to poetry. But Cocteau's approach was very different from Eliot's.

Cocteau was not looking specifically for a way to make verse viable on the stage. His 'poetry' embraced dance, music and the plastic elements of staging, as well as words. Through the combination of the arts of the theatre he tried to liberate it from the tyranny of mere words and to reassert the creative independence of performance. The audience might look *through* the most inadequate presentation of *Romeo and Juliet* to the reality in Shakespeare's words. There was no looking through the *danced* performance of Cocteau's *Roméo et Juliette*, since the execution itself, the dancers' performance, was of the essence. At one extreme, the actor was merely the vehicle of the text; at the other, the dancer was the primary artist without whom there was no art. Cocteau concentrated on dance, without restricting himself to it.

Ideally, in the Coctellian view, the actor and dancer would be one, as in certain non-European theatres, and the actor-dancer would be a singer, too. The designer and writer would collaborate intimately with these performers to create a poetry of the theatre in which the presentation itself and the object represented would be inextricable. Such collaboration required a permanent ensemble in which, necessarily, the director-writer or theatre poet, responsible for the basic conception, would be the key figure. W. B. Yeats and Bertolt Brecht were, like Cocteau, theatre poets of this kind and André Obey and Michel Saint-Denis, working as a pair with the Compagnie des Quinze, had much in common with them. And, in England, W. H. Auden had the opportunity and, for a time, the inclination to assume the role of theatre poet working in collaboration with Rupert Doone and the Group Theatre. These were exceptional cases, however. Generally the writers stayed, or were kept, out of the way of the performers and it was the director, interpreting the words of others, who came to occupy the commanding position that had once been held by the actor-manager.

In the early years of the century, Edward Gordon Craig was the great promulgator of the idea of a *creative* theatre, proclaiming the priority of the dancer over the playwright, of plasticity and movement over words and, above all, the absolute authority of the director as the presiding genius. Since the English theatre was so out of joint that such artistic control was impossible, unless for a rich man with his own theatre, Craig chose to make himself a living and potent symbol of the director in exile from his art, as well as his country.

Unlike Craig, William Poel was an interpreter of drama drawing on theatrical history for his methods but he probably did more to establish the authority of the stage director. For Poel it was the necessary condition of the attempt to revive the essential elements of Elizabethan staging. The play was the thing and the director was the dead playwright's theatrical executor. The acceptance of this idea nicely prepared the way for the director to become also the trustee of the theatrically incompetent—as he was usually supposed to be—living playwright. Among Poel's artistic heirs were Harley Granville-Barker, Nugent Monck and Tyrone Guthrie. Their work in Shakespearean and other productions and the work of Theodore Komisarjevsky, E. Martin Browne, Michel Saint-Denis and Rupert Doone cleared the way, in England, for the rise to supremacy of the director. They were sometimes called 'stage directors' but more commonly 'producers', a significantly ambiguous term that served also to designate the men who hired them and their casts. In the name of art, these first 'directors' laid claim to control over all facets of production, though, unlike some of their European counterparts, they usually lacked the means to assert it thoroughly. Only after the Second World War did Guthrie and a clutch of younger men, with Peter Brook foremost among them, begin to dominate major theatrical enterprises in something like the way that Craig had thought they should.[4]

It was shortly after the appearance of Craig's *On the Art of the Theatre*, in 1905, that some of its precepts were realized by Sergei Diaghilev and the artists he brought into the scintillating theatrical collaboration of the Ballets Russes. Diaghilev revitalized the theatre but not in a manner that Craig or his followers could approve. Dancers came into their own, there was collaboration of the arts and a sovereign artistic director. But Diaghilev's principle genre was traditional, if not archaic, ballet, the very genre that those most interested in the reunification of dance and drama were intent on displacing.

In 1926, Terence Gray, disciple of Craig, apostle of 'dance-drama', and owner of the Festival Theatre in Cambridge, violently contrasted the Diaghilevian and the dramatic modes:

> The Russian ballet still has a vogue ... for the very wealthy patronize it freely and employ it regularly to assist them in the process of digestion, stipulating only that in return they shall not be required to think or feel anything, but be allowed just to sit very still with half-closed eyes and be dimly conscious of a kaleidoscope of pretty, harmoniously moving colours and pleasing musical vibrations. It also has a following of a certain type of degenerate artist, and a sprinkling of vital and intelligent admirers who recognize in it isolated qualities of greatness such as the superlative technical attainment of its dancers, individually and in mass movement, and in some of the musical and pictorial material which it employs. But of serious dramatic quality it has nothing whatever, and as a factor in the development of the art of the theatre it is as dead as the *commedia dell'arte*. Its ballets are meaningless and without form or coherence, it has lost touch altogether alike with reality and with dramatic art, and its standard of production looked at from the standpoint of contemporary culture can only be described as belonging properly to the nursery.[5]

In fact, Diaghilev had a considerable influence on the dramatic theatre, though the main contribution of dance came from another quarter.

Just as writers such as Shaw, Cocteau and Eliot had quite distinct ideas about the regeneration of the stage, so did the dancers; particularly the devotees of classical ballet on the one hand, and those of 'modern dance' on the other. One of the dancers and choreographers who worked for Gray in the twenties (and who was a former member of Diaghilev's company) was Ninette de Valois. She also danced for Yeats and set up a ballet school at the Abbey Theatre at his request. But this involvement with drama was a brief departure from her chosen work of laying the foundations for classical ballet in England. She had a strong aversion to the more radical forms of dance, which tended to subvert classical ballet and ally themselves with drama, and were, as she put it, 'based on a primitive form of "jungle agility"'. It was not a purely artistic issue. She saw dangerous political implications in the 'drum-tapping, leaping dervishes from Central Europe'. The outstanding company of 'dervishes', that of Kurt Jooss, gave her 'the uncomfortable feeling that in everyday life they may possibly wear a uniform and answer to numbers instead of names'.[6] Such perceptions of the connections between theatrical style and politics were to be vitally important in the theatre of the thirties and had the strongest bearing on the ways in which dance and drama were, and were not, combined.

Mary Wigman, Rudolf Laban and Kurt Jooss, leaders of the radical 'Central European School', sought a revolution not only in dance itself but throughout the theatre and even more generally than that. 'Young actors of today', declared Wigman, 'scorn the superficial make-believe of the present theatre. . . . The new dance is close to the expression the theatre must eventually accept'.[7]

Yeats was one poet-playwright in sympathy with this theatrical objective without conceding any politically Leftist claim on it. His *Plays for Dancers*, of which the first appeared in 1917, had resulted from his discovery, he said, of an adequate theatrical model. Ostensibly this model had nothing to do with the European theatre—it was the Japanese Noh—but Yeats's long and admiring association with Craig had predisposed him to attempt to combine dance and words; and it was characteristic of the ageing poet to arrive, by an obscure route, alongside the young avant-garde. It was Yeats's need for actor-dancers that drew him to Rupert Doone and the Group Theatre, even though he thought of them as Communist sympathizers.

Doone, a devotee of Diaghilev, was the dancer-choreo-grapher of the time most interested in the dramatic theatre. In 1930, just as he was refocusing his attention from ballet to drama, he encountered Tyrone Guthrie and their protracted discussions were the preliminaries to the foundation, in 1932, of the Group Theatre as well as to Guthrie's *Theatre Prospect*, published in the same year.

In this manifesto, Guthrie argued forcefully for the restoration of music to the dramatic theatre and ingeniously for its incorporation of dance. Nigel Playfair's 1920 produc-tion of *The Beggar's Opera* had been an excellent beginning in these respects but it had led only to pale imitations, not to further development. 'To bring music back into the theatre would not be hard,' Guthrie supposed, but with dance he had difficulty in choosing from its distinct forms those most readily adaptable to drama. Ultimately the folk-dance tradition should prove the richest source, he thought, but for the moment it had become too isolated by pedantry and too infected by amateurism. Ballet was rootlessly aristocratic and Guthrie saw few possibilities of adapting it:

> The Camargo Society may yet do something more than blow upon the dying embers of the Diaghilev ballet, but it is doubtful whether it will ever look with favour upon a drawing together of dancing and acting, and it is doubtful whether training in classical ballet, except in its earliest rudiments, is desirable for an actor.

Ballroom dancing was 'too negroid and amorphous to fit happily into a classical framework, too refined for experi-ments in modernity'. Better than ballet or ballroom dancing was the example of Isadora Duncan, and better still the 'proletarian' dance of Wigman and Laban. But Guthrie had his suspicions about the German dancers who derived 'too much from the East' and 'too much from primitive sources' to be suitable models for the English theatre. So, Guthrie concluded,

> Until we can found a school of movement based on our own folk-dances . . . actors can be taught by a method

that derives something from the exact science of the classical ballet ... something from the freedom and rhythmic energy of the revolutionaries. ... An actor trained in such a school could readily acquire, under direction, types of movement to enable him to appear adequately in Sheridan or Toller, *Everyman* or some experiment in an untried form.[8]

For the short time that they were jointly responsible for the artistic direction of the Group Theatre, Guthrie and Doone adopted this eclectic approach.

Between the First and Second World Wars, the symptoms of decay in the theatre were obvious and many remedies were prescribed: new plays, new dramatic forms, new audiences, new methods of acting and the training of actors, fundamental changes in theatre architecture and scenic design. The prescriptions were legion but there was a strong consensus about the diagnosis: commercialism was the cancer at the root of the theatre's ills. The 'commercial theatre', as it was so frequently and contemptuously called, purveyed to an undiscriminating bourgeoisie the 'culinary' entertainment of make-believe complacencies, decked out in tinsel and focused on 'stars'. As the supreme obstacle to the recovery of the seriousness and art in the theatre, commercialism had somehow to be circumvented or destroyed.

Professional actors, by definition, worked in the 'commercial' theatre but some worked the other side of the street, too. The distinction between the 'commercial' and the 'other' theatre was not so hard and fast as that between professional theatre and the rest now is. Some professional actors, intent on art or reform, habitually joined forces with amateurs, supposing that, in one way or another, artistic excellence and the reform of the theatre depended heavily on those who did not, or could not, earn a living from it, or were willing to do unpaid work from time to time. In any case, not a few actors were paid at a level that hardly distinguished them, economically, from amateurs.

As for the amateurs, some of them were trying to make the theatre serve political or religious causes that placed them as far above mere professionalism in motive as they might fall short of it in skill. The causes themselves attracted audiences and stimulated new techniques and a few professionals joined the amateurs in trying to endow propaganda or worship with the status of art. And, whether by this or other means, many reformers envisioned a professional but non-commercial theatre that would satisfy their artistic ambitions and also provide their daily bread. Professional but not commercial was almost a contradiction in terms, but for many performers, the ultimate goal of theatrical reform was an artistic institution which could provide them with a living other than by the prostitution of their talents.

In the thirties, the English theatre's accumulated difficulties were compounded by the general social and political unrest. Its ills were frequently diagnosed as the secondary symptoms of a sick society. The theatre might be used as the instrument of a new social revolution and its restoration might follow therefrom, but it could not be considered in isolation. Bodies such as the Trades Union Congress, the Labour Party and the Church of England began to see the theatre as a means of affirmation and propaganda and this attention was recipro-cated by those who, for the theatre's own sake, wanted it to tap new or ancient springs.

One of the most radical of the reformers, having the utmost contempt for the professional stage, was certain that play-wrights would have to find new social bases if their work was to be significant:

I doubt whether there is anything to be done with the contemporary theatre-going public: you have got to assemble a new audience.

The young dramatist to-day, however, does not want to write a play merely to please a small audience of poetry-lovers many of whom he will know, and the faces of the rest of whom he remembers having seen before and is tired of seeing. The best opportunity that presents itself seems to be the opportunity to appeal to those who are interested in a common cause which the poet and dramatist can also serve. Only a cause can give the bond, the common assumptions between author and audience which the serious dramatist needs. . . . There are only two causes now of sufficient seriousness, and they are mutually exclusive: the Church and Communism.[9]

When this statement appeared, in October 1934, its author was writing a commissioned play for the Canterbury Festival and also involved in planning a season of poetic plays for a small audience. Moreover, the next production of his work would be by the Group Theatre, which was more closely associated with Communism than with the Church, though cleaving to neither. Confusingly, political and religious drama often had much in common in motive and techniques. Hence Auden's equivocally Marxist *The Dance of Death* and Eliot's unequivocally Christian *The Rock* were bracketed together as products of a new school of playwrights. Such were the complexities of the theatrical, religious and political situation that Eliot was trying to unravel.

The two common causes cited by Eliot had been developing theatrical offshoots from the early years of the century. The impetus for a new wave of religious drama had come from the revivals by Poel, Monck and others of medieval plays. Although the ecclesiastical authorities were slow to recognize drama as an adjunct to religious observance, amateur groups associated with churches discovered audiences not only for revivals but for new biblical plays modelled on the supposedly naïve 'mysteries'. And on a rather more exalted literary plain, Laurence Housman, John Masefield, and D. H. Lawrence as well as Yeats, Eliot and Auden were among the writers influenced by the movement.

Religious drama received a powerful boost in 1929, when George Bell, the Dean of Canterbury, founded the Canterbury Festival with Nugent Monck as its first Director. Shortly afterwards, when Bell was elevated to the bishopric of Chichester, he appointed a Director of Religious Drama for the diocese, the first such appointment ever made. In the same year, 1930, the Religious Drama Society was formed with Bishop Bell as its President. The Bishop and his Drama Director, E. Martin Browne, drew T. S. Eliot into the theatre, with the ultimate consequence that poetic drama and Christian apologetics became inextricably linked in England. Religious drama arrived at its apogee after the war when plays by Eliot and Fry received full-scale production in the West End, but the 1935 production of *Murder in the Cathedral* was the first significant advance from the sanctuary to the commercial theatre. Apart from the merits of the play itself, it was the entrepreneurial skill of Ashley Dukes in the deployment of his Mercury Theatre company that accomplished this feat.[10]

Proponents of the other cause mentioned by Eliot also found a precedent in the play cycles presented by medieval trade-unionists. 'What the drama was able to do for the Catholic Church, the Guilds, and the ruling class, it can do for the working class,' wrote one of the leaders of the Workers' Theatre Movement. Shaw was the 'John the Baptist' of Socialist theatre, which now awaited its real founder.[11] In this evolutionary view, the communal, celebratory and propagandist functions of medieval drama, and some of its techniques, were to be revived with a new content.

The Workers' Theatre Movement was founded in 1910 and, after a period of torpor, was totally reorganized in 1928. In this second phase, its productions were distinguished chiefly by their revolutionary, Communist politics and by 'agitprop' techniques. The WTM groups,

> rejected what they called the 'theatre of illusion' and instead put forward a theatre of ideas. . . . They performed not full-length plays, but sketches and satires, or montages of mime and song. Instead of individualistic characterization ('the basis of the bourgeois stage') they

concentrated on types, and employed the simplest possible devices as signifiers. 'If you wanted to represent the boss you put a top hat on, and if you wanted to be a worker you put a cloth cap on.'[12]

Other characteristics of WTM performances were simple words, strict choreography and a bare stage.

The last feature was one that the WTM productions had in common with those of Jacques Copeau at the Théâtre du Vieux Colombier. Copeau's *tréteau nu* let the audience 'see' the verbal poetry, demanded physical virtuosity of the actors and was a purification of a theatre surfeited with luxurious, inartistic, bourgeois naturalism. The WTM's somewhat different rationale for the use of the open platform was given in a working paper for its First National Conference in June 1932:

> So to enable the message of the Workers' Theatre to reach wide masses of the workers, and to give a much more flexible and dynamic picture of society than is possible on the curtained stage, a new form is being evolved. This form, which is known in Germany as the agitprop style, needs no elaborate stage, but an open platform. No scenery that is not easily carried about by hand; no make-up; and a minimum of costume. In a word, the propertyless class is developing the 'property'-less theatre.[13]

The actor as creative artist and the worker as dispossessed propagandist were approaching, from their different directions, a 'poor', anti-bourgeois theatre. In England, Auden's *The Dance of Death* was a point of convergence.

Throughout the thirties, the interplay of theatrical technique with political or religious ideas was often bewildering, even to those most immediately involved. Was ensemble acting a Socialist method or an apolitical technique? Were episodic structures and the interpolation of song and dance into dialogue Leftist merely by convention or was there an ideological basis to such dramaturgy? Did parable and doggerel point to the Left, symbolism and poetry to the Right? How was a workers' chorus distinct, formally, from a liturgically derived one? What were the ideological connotations of the basic usages 'theatre' and 'drama'? Why did nobody speak of religious or poetic *theatre*, or, conversely, of workers' or political *drama*?

Among those who wrestled with these questions, and kept a very close watch on each other's technique, were the three outstanding poets of the time. Yeats served as an example for both Eliot and Auden. Auden, as a beginning dramatist, took cues from Eliot's essays in *The Sacred Wood*. Eliot noted the originality of *Paid On Both Sides* and *The Dance of Death* and was alert to the possibilities of the Group Theatre. Auden again was influenced by the resounding achievement of *Murder in the Cathedral* as a poetic drama; and Eliot by the way in which Auden and Isherwood sought spiritual value in strictly contemporary dramatic terms. It is fascinating to observe, through the thirties, Auden converging on Eliot, Eliot borrowing from Auden, Auden and Isherwood attempting to finesse Eliot's new Christian dramaturgy, and Yeats, at one point, offering to join the dance.

As the particular strand of the pre-war English theatre that the following chapters attempt to unravel, the Group Theatre is especially interesting in that it was acutely responsive, even to the point of opportunism, to the artistic aspirations and social pressures of its time. This was partly because it was not so much an organization with fixed—some might say *any*—principles as a nebula of young and gifted individuals whose personal development collectively determined that of the Group Theatre. When Keynes was arranging for *On the Frontier* to be presented at the Cambridge Arts Theatre in 1937, he was much put out to discover that the Group Theatre, which was to produce the play, not only had no money but 'had no real business existence', either.[14] He had reason to be surprised since the Group Theatre had been active for several years and its productions included a recent one in his own theatre. By various expediencies, the Group Theatre had managed to get by without any formal provision for business dealings and without many of the other attributes of a theatrical organization. In fact, the Group Theatre habitually defined itself in terms of what it was *not*: not a club; not a management; not a building; not an organization specially devoted to the production of new, classical, verse or political plays. As to what it was, at any particular moment, its protean transformations can be divided into three main phases.[15]

The organization founded in 1932 stressed co-operative training and had a certain arts-and-craftsy innocence. Its major models were Copeau's Théâtre du Vieux Colombier and Michel Saint-Denis's Compagnie des Quinze. Its most successful productions were an 'experimental reading' of *Peer Gynt* and the first modern revival of the Tudor interlude *Fulgens and Lucrece*.

The second phase opened with the production of Auden's *The Dance of Death*, in 1934, which gave the Group Theatre a Leftist inclination, and ended with its biggest success, *The Ascent of F6*, in 1937. In these years, the Group Theatre achieved a *succès d'estime* with its small-scale production of *Sweeney Agonistes* and mounted a full season which included *The Dog Beneath the Skin*. It became known for radical methods of presentation but also acquired something of a reputation for sloppiness and lack of principle.

In 1937, the Group Theatre reorganized itself as a small group of performers, poets and other artists, nominally supported by several hundred ordinary members. In this third phase, the plays written for the Group Theatre—Louis MacNeice's *Out of the Picture*, Stephen Spender's *Trial of a Judge*, and *On the Frontier* by Auden and Isherwood—were its main reason for existence but its 'theatre' extended beyond the theatre building. It declared an interest in a broad front of artistic activity and (before the term was invented) staged 'happenings' that served as self-identification, self-promotion and expressed a generally anti-totalitarian attitude. The career of the Group Theatre in the thirties as successively an actors', directors' and playwrights' theatre is the epitome of the wasteful conditions, insincerities and great visions of the time. As such it is essential to the understanding of that period in broadly historical terms. More particularly its theatrical experiments anticipated major developments in the English theatre that were to come much later. And, like that of Goethe's *Wilhelm Meister*, the history of the Group Theatre illustrates some of the perennial artistic and moral problems that confront those who are intrepid or foolhardy enough to apprentice themselves to the theatre.

2
Rupert Doone and the Foundation of the Group Theatre

Item, we leave our old friend Rupert Doone
Something dynamic and his own theatre
And a setting of his Unconscious on the bassoon. . . .[1]
W. H. AUDEN AND LOUIS MACNEICE, 1937

It was largely the ambition and energy of John Ormerod Greenwood that brought the Group Theatre into being and it was he who did most of the spade work in the early days.[2] Auden, who joined the Group Theatre a few months after its foundation, immediately began to shape its artistic character and was a determining force in its later development. Tyrone Guthrie, for a moment, was poised to become the leader of the Group and to make of it an English equivalent of Copeau's Théâtre du Vieux Colombier. T. S. Eliot, who became a member in 1934, was helpful in practical ways and influenced the plays written for the Group, as well as being chiefly instrumental in publishing them. Greenwood, Auden, Guthrie, Eliot and others helped to make the Group Theatre what it was—though that was not, by any means, what any of them wanted it to be—but from first to last, for good and ill, it was the talent, will and temperament of Rupert Doone that fashioned and dominated the enterprise.[3]

Doone's leadership of the Group was his second career in the theatre. His first had come to its crisis in 1929, when he was engaged by Diaghilev and danced several roles with the Ballets Russes. Anton Dolin was the only other English male dancer to achieve this distinction. For Doone it came too late:

his first season with Diaghilev was Diaghilev's last. Like other members of the company—Alicia Markova, for instance — Doone was staggered by the impresario's death; the more so for having held, so briefly, a rather makeshift place that should have led to better things in the coming seasons that never came.[4]

Doone's career as a dancer had begun in true picaresque fashion. At the age of 16 he had run away from his home in Redditch, West Midlands, where his father was a needle-maker and he himself an apprentice draughtsman, to seek fame and fortune in London. The boy survived in the city by becoming a male model until he was befriended by a musician with whose help he began to transform himself from Ernest Reginald Woodfield, a runaway apprentice with artistic longings, into the dancer known by the more romantic name of Rupert Doone.

He attended the classes of the Duncan-inspired pioneer of free dance, Margaret Morris, and went on to join Serafina Astafieva's school at 'the Pheasantry', where Anton Dolin and Alicia Markova were fellow pupils. A short, powerful-looking man, he was a dancer noted for his energy and flair. Marie Rambert thought his physique ugly and Lydia Lopokova called him 'the potato', but his talent was recognized by them and others.[5] His first professional engagement was as understudy to Edouard Espinosa at His Majesty's Theatre. Touring with Cléo de Mérode in the South of France was another early one; and this was followed by an engagement, which Doone did not complete, with the Swedish Ballet in New York. In 1924 he was engaged by Count Etienne de Beaumont to dance in Cocteau's *Roméo et Juliette*. The rehearsals were turbulent and de Beaumont saw Doone as a source of trouble. No doubt he was, since his associates frequently found him at least 'difficult' and sometimes 'impossible'. On this occasion, Cocteau (who was Doone's lover) urged de Beaumont to keep Doone on for his ability as a dancer, despite his personal faults, but de Beaumont was not to be persuaded and Doone was dismissed.[6]

Back in England in 1924 Doone became Léonide Massine's pupil. Massine, not yet reconciled with Diaghilev, was working for Cochran at this time and also teaching dancing according to Enrico Ceccetti's famous method. From Massine Doone learned Spanish dancing and exhibited his skill in this métier to excellent effect as dancer-choreographer for Playfair's 1924 revival of Sheridan's *The Duenna*. Some thought that the contribution of 'Rupert Doone and his Spanish dancers' overbalanced the production, but Playfair himself considered that the dancing 'was perfectly in keeping with the picture, and was so good in itself as to be a continual delight'.[7] Doone found special satisfaction in a production that combined dance and drama.

Further engagements came through Massine. He danced to his teacher's choreography in *On with the Dance* (1925) and in the Coward-Cochran revue, *Still Dancing*. In 1926 also Doone danced with Anton Dolin at the London Palladium and took tuition from Vera Trefilova. Then in her fifties, Trefilova made Doone her partner for several performances in Berlin. Robert Medley attributes to her a considerable development of Doone's technique as a classical dancer. Without her help, says Medley, Doone might not have attracted Diaghilev's interest. In 1927 he joined Phyllis Bedells's little troupe at the Palladium, and in the following year he was engaged by Ida Rubinstein for her season at the Paris Opéra. Her opening production was attended by Diaghilev, who saw nothing good in it but the dancing of Doone. The 'very pleasant young English boy, whom we have known for some time' was 'the best dancer by far,' said Diaghilev. This was Doone's cue. He wrote to the impresario asking to be taken on, and Diaghilev agreed to fit him into his forthcoming English season.[8]

Doone's uneven progress as a dancer was hindered by his volatility and assisted by his charm, but these were only the qualifying features of an irrepressible talent and will that had to find expression where they could. Unluckily, in many ways, Doone began as a dancer ten years before the real beginnings of classical ballet in England. There was work to be found in music-hall, revue, the occasional extravaganza like *Cairo* or operetta such as *The Duenna*, and Doone tried them all. On the Continent there were established ballet companies and of these Doone had some experience too. Although he was never professionally associated with the modern dance movement he was sympathetic to it (as might be expected of one of Margaret Morris's former pupils) and was apparently invited by Kurt Jooss to become an instructor at the Central Laban School.[9]

According to his own account, Doone had a profound respect for classical ballet but also held the conviction that new work had to break with tradition, in an informed and deliberate way, so as to reflect the 'attitudes and opinions of the times'.[10] This Terpsichorean version of 'tradition and the individual talent' he probably imbibed from Cocteau and Diaghilev; at any rate, his confidence and sense of artistic direction came from experience and an acute sensibility rather than from any grand vision of a theatre of the future.

Left stranded by the death of Diaghilev, Doone began to explore the possibility of making a career in the dramatic theatre. A fellow dancer put him in touch with Anmer Hall, who was then presenting a season at the Festival Theatre, Cambridge. Hall went to see Doone dance and offered him a place in his company.[11] On the stage Doone danced memorably—and stole the show some thought—in *Tobias and the Angel*: offstage he confided to Hall's stage director, Tyrone Guthrie, his ambition of forming an acting ensemble. Another of his confidants was Isobel Scaife, an actress in her first professional season. She became his consistent supporter, one of the founders of the Group Theatre and a regular performer for it.[12]

When he joined Hall's company, Doone had taken a step away from ballet but not a decisive one. After the season in Cambridge (and after the foundation of the Group Theatre), he remained active as a dancer. He appeared in the first (1931) and later seasons of Marie Rambert's Ballet Club, with the Camargo Society and with the Vic–Wells Ballet. In 1931, the

regular columnist of the *Dancing Times* constructed a
hypothetical English national ballet, in which Dolin, of course,
would be the first male dancer to be hired and Doone would
get the next contract, 'because, not only is he an excellent
dancer, but he always takes the stage with the air of an old
hand, and is essentially an artist in his work'.[13] This was the
world of make believe. There was no national ballet company
and Rupert Doone, who was then 28 years old, could scarcely
hope for stardom as a dancer. It was possible, though, that he
might become an outstanding choreographer, and it was in
this capacity that he became increasingly active.

The most important of Doone's choreographic works was
The Enchanted Grove, presented by the Camargo Society in
1931 and in the opening season of the Vic–Wells Ballet in the
following year. This exotic piece, based on the music of
Ravel's *Le Tombeau de Couperin*, was about the interruption
of a Chinese court entertainment by the arrival of a Japanese
courtesan and her suite. The bold introduction of a pantomime horse—'a Ming version of the Griffiths Brothers'
famous steed',[14] as one reviewer called it—probably owed
something to Cocteau's equine character in *Orphée*. Markova, Dolin, de Valois and Doone himself danced in *The
Enchanted Grove* and Duncan Grant created an ill-received
décor. The first audience was enthusiastic but the critical
reception was unfavourable and Doone's ballet was soon
dropped from the Vic–Wells repertory. Phyllis Bedells thought
it 'rather a muddle' and Arnold Haskell said much the same,
though his criticism was tempered. Doone's choreography
lacked 'the simplicity, musical and dramatic sense of de Valois,
or the wit, elegance and plastic knowledge of Ashton' but as
Doone learned to refine and control his experiments, said
Haskell, he should do the important work of which he was
capable.[15]

Had *The Enchanted Grove* been better received, or had
Doone realized his hope of following this ballet with one based
on a scenario by Auden, his career would probably have taken
a different course—and there might have been no Group

Theatre. As it was, Doone did no further choreography for the developing classical ballet companies in England, though he did find some choreographic work outside the Group Theatre.

In 1933 he was appointed to revive Massine's choreography for *Die schöne Helene* in Berlin, and he arranged ballets for Basil Dean's production of *Hansel and Gretel*. In the same year he was stage director and choreographer for Ashley Dukes's production of *Jupiter Translated*, which included an interpolated ballet, or *intermède*. This was the first dramatic production at Dukes's tiny Mercury Theatre, where both ballet and drama were to flourish, though not, as on this particular occasion, in combination. 'The Marriage of Hebe', as Doone's *Jupiter* ballet was called, was danced by Pearl Argyle and Antony Tudor. The production pleased but rather mystified the critics, unused as they were to such a mixture of forms. They would become more accustomed to it with Doone's Group Theatre productions, several of which incorporated ballets.

One of the important features of Doone's complex artistic make-up was that though he was neither well educated nor very articulate he was a voracious reader of poetry. For a moment, indeed, he had some aspirations as a writer but sensibly recognized that writing was not his medium. Not being himself a poet, one of his passions became the *performance* of poetry and he brought to it the conviction — one that comes more readily to dancers than to actors—that performance is always in itself real, hazardous and creative, never a matter of mere interpretation. In 1935, he would contest more literary views of poetic drama with the insistence that there was 'no such thing as an interpretative art: the actor does not interpret the poet's words, he recreates them'.[16] In practice this meant that Doone, and consequently the Group Theatre, aspired to collaborate in the primary theatrical creation and were much more interested in the vocal performance of poetry, especially choric poetry, than in mimetic speech and characterization. Doone developed this dancerly view of poetry gradually and in the course of his work with the poets who wrote for the Group, but he had always been convinced that performers were more than interpreters and it was in this conviction he and a few young actors from the Westminster Theatre formed the ensemble that was to become the Group Theatre.

When it opened in 1931 as London's newest theatre, the Westminster had the potential to be either a radiant source of new theatrical life or the unobtrusive hobby of a wealthy theatrophile. Which way it would go was a vital matter for Tyrone Guthrie and some of the actors engaged for the opening season.

A. B. Horne, the owner of the Westminster, Anmer Hall, its manager, and Waldo Wright, an actor who sometimes played there, were one and the same man. Hall (to use his best-known style) was nearly 60 when, running counter to the common commercial practice of the time, he brought the St James's Picture Theatre and converted it into a 'legitimate' theatre. A wealthy man of liberal mind, Hall had behind him a considerable record of theatre management running from the opening of the Scala Theatre in 1905, in association with Johnston Forbes-Robertson, to the management of the Festival Theatre, Cambridge, in 1929–30. Well-made comedies, like those of the Quintero brothers, pleased him and, in a more adventurous spirit (in which he was encouraged by the actress Gillian Scaife), he also produced works by such modern masters as Luigi Pirandello and Eugene O'Neill. For such work he made the new Westminster Theatre a decent, civilized, not unconventional setting.[17]

The nucleus of Hall's first company there came from the 'close and friendly little brotherhood'[18] he had assembled at the Festival Theatre. It included Tyrone Guthrie, who was making his London début as a director, Gillian Scaife, Flora Robson, Robert Eddison, Evan John, Isobel Scaife and Joan White. All of these, and Anmer Hall himself, would take out memberships in the Group Theatre in its first few months, though not all as active participants.

James Bridie's *The Anatomist* was the company's first and
very successful production. It enjoyed a long run, in the course
of which some of the younger actors began to form groups for
co-operative training and playreading. Among the most
dedicated and ambitious of them was Ormerod Greenwood.
Just down from Cambridge, where he had been President of
the Mummers, Greenwood was 24 years old, a Quaker, a
devotee of Edward Gordon Craig and an idealist imbued with
a strong sense of mission to the theatre. From his lowly
position, he saw Hall as fudging a great opportunity. This new
theatre, with a strong company, an outstandingly talented
young director and actors eager to dedicate themselves to
some high objective, was merely drifting. Not to be fobbed off
with a theatre on the lower slopes of Parnassus, Greenwood
opened his heart to Gordon Craig:

> The Westiminster Theatre exemplifies, in a small way, the
> thesis you have always held about the collaboration of
> business man and artist. . . . The fault of this theatre is
> that it is hopelessly conservative (even reactionary) in
> policy, and most anxious not to be branded as 'exper-
> imental'. In time this is bound to kill it unless things
> alter—but for the moment it is just enough ahead of
> people for them to like it. . . .[19]

For the moment Craig did not respond and Greenwood and
his collaborators were left to their own devices. With
Greenwood as its chief organizer, a coherent group began to
form and Rupert Doone, who was not a member of the
Westminster company, joined it and began to conduct the co-
operative classes.

In the first, formless, group activity various plans and
policies were canvassed. Selma Vas Dias, an actress with more
experience than most of the others involved, wanted to form a
Socialist troupe which might be a professional counterpart to
the Workers' Theatre Movement.[20] Rivalling Doone for the
leadership of the little group, she found no followers. Two of
the other young but relatively advanced professionals, Joan

White and Robert Eddison, favoured an actor's workshop in which they could systematically develop their skills when they were not in rehearsal. They opposed Greenwood's idea of mounting a production and using it to demonstrate their talents to invited managers and directors. Greenwood's sights were set particularly on Harcourt Williams of the Old Vic.

It was this production group that eventually, and with mixed motives, formalized its existence as the Group Theatre. Its members' long-term objective was to train together and create an ensemble based on sound artistic principles. They were also alive to the possibility that on their pilgrimage they might be seduced into Lilian Baylis's company or even lured into the unregenerate commercial theatre.

Some of the discussions about aims and methods took place among the '8 Group'.[21] 'Group' signified the transcendence of individualism, competitiveness and the 'star' system. '8'—though their number soon grew—reflected the admiration of the first would-be ensemble for Michel Saint-Denis's Compagnie des Quinze, who had visited England earlier in the year with productions of *Noé* and *Le Viol de Lucrèce*. The refined simplicity of Saint-Denis's fifteen, the disciplined virtuosity of their movement and gesture, the poetry of their speech and the vitality they created on a sparsely furnished stage made a radical and purifying contrast to West End tinsel. John Gielgud reports that he encountered a radically new style of acting when he took the lead in Saint-Denis's English production of *Noah* in 1934 and Tyrone Guthrie, in retrospect, saw in the Quinze a return to ritual and religion in the theatre.[22] In the early thirties, there was no English equivalent to the French company and it was the aim of '8 Group' to make good that deficiency.

The group's dedication to training was qualified by its eagerness to get on with performance. A proposed production of Leonid Andreyev's *Katerina* fell by the wayside, but in November 1931 Sir John Vanbrugh's *The Provok'd Wife* was put into rehearsal under Doone's direction. John Moody, a young actor who had also trained as a painter and a singer,

came over from the Old Vic to join the cast.[23] Another very
valuable recruit was Herbert Murrill, a schoolmaster recently
down from Oxford.[24] Murrill had already made a beginning
in the theatre with a short opera, *Man in Cage*, which had run
for nine weeks at the little Grafton Theatre. Arranging the
music for *The Provok'd Wife* was the first of his many
contributions to the Group Theatre.

Training and rehearsals took place in a dirty, hired room in
West Street, off Cambridge Circus. The new group worked
there for some five months, in the course of which, in February
1932, the Group Theatre was founded with thirteen members.[25] None of the founders knew that another 'Group
Theatre' had recently been formed in the United States: this
was a piece of information that T. S. Eliot imparted later.[26]
There was nothing at all businesslike about the new
organization. Business, indeed, was the last thing the Group
Theatre was concerned with. What it aimed for was,

> to develop a simple way of acting that is flexible and
> easily adaptable to any play, whether ancient or modern,
> that it may wish to produce. And by improvisation to
> bring the actor to use his own powers of invention and rid
> him of self-consciousness. It emphasizes movement as the
> beginning of training and approaches it through dancing;
> and in the same way voice production through singing.

The Group Theatre hoped that

> by continually playing together and by using its own
> producers, playwrights, painters, musicians, technicians,
> etc., to produce a company which will work like a well-
> trained orchestra.[27]

In April, *The Provok'd Wife* was at last staged, at the
Everyman Theatre. A note in the programme diffidently
explained that this first 'demonstration performance' was to
be taken as an experiment in method, not as representing the
standards it aimed at. In extenuation of the inadequacies of the
performance it cited the illness of the musical director and the

absence, in the final stages of rehearsal, of the director (who had been engaged by Max Reinhardt in Berlin). The ensemble character of the performance was emphasized by the absence of the actors' names from the programme.[28] But they made no greater impression collectively than they did as individuals. Still, the Group Theatre had begun and if clouds of amateurishness clung about it there was at least a gleam of great dedication.

After this modest inauguration, the Group continued with training and undertook a second production. For this they chose *The Man Who Ate the Popomack* by W. J. Turner. The play had been presented with great success by Terence Gray at the Festival Theatre and had frequently been revived there. The Group expected that it would be a suitable piece to put on for two weeks at the small Kenton Theatre in Henley, for the amusement of the summer visitors. Once again Doone left the production in its final stages and Oliver Reynolds, another recruit from the Old Vic, took over as director. *Popomack* opened in Henley in late July, flopped and, after five days, expired.

While the Group was wilting in Henley, Doone was in London dancing for the Camargo Society, having by no means relinquished his ambitions as a classical dancer. And it was shortly after this that he and Robert Medley were visited by Medley's old schoolfriend, W. H. Auden. The poet had come, Medley recalls, specifically in response to their invitation to him to join in the work of the Group Theatre; though it appears that Doone wanted him to write a scenario for a ballet. Given Auden's interest in the stage, the existence of an ambitious, raw, newly formed group of actors that had need of a poet must have seemed providential and a great deal more interesting than a purely balletic collaboration with Doone. At any rate, as will be seen, he decisively interested himself in the Group's affairs.

No less promisingly, Tyrone Guthrie, who had taken a distantly benevolent attitude to the co-operative efforts of the young actors at the Westminster—borrowing costumes on

their behalf for *The Provok'd Wife*, for example—began to
take their new organization seriously. If anything, he was even
more frustrated than they were by Anmer Hall's vague
management of the Westminster: 'We have become just an
ordinary "commercial" theatre, only our manager is as
unbusinesslike as our position geographically is obscure and
our programme informed by no policy whatsoever,' he wrote
to a friend.[29] While the founders of the Group Theatre were
pressing ahead with training and their first productions,
Guthrie wrote his *Theatre Prospect*, which could be described
as, in effect, a prospectus for a co-operative theatre company
and an oblique letter of advice to Anmer Hall.

Drawing on the examples of the Volksbühne, the New York
Theatre Guild, the People's National Theatre, the Scottish
National Theatre Society (with which he had worked), the
Embassy Theatre Club and Komisarjevsky's Independent
Theatre Club, Guthrie proposed a scheme for a new theatre
supported by subscribers and supporting a regular company.
By contrast with the theatrical democracy that the founders of
the Group Theatre favoured, he proposed an artistic consul-
ship of two directors, since he thought it better 'to risk the
dangers of an autocracy than of democracy or oligarchy'. The
directors would be subject to 'the sanction of the box office' if
they proved inadequate; if not, there was the hope that one of
them might become a new 'Granville-Barker, a Jacques
Copeau or a Diaghilev'.[30]

Guthrie's hypothetical theatre would have a school attached
to it in which great emphasis would be given to music and
dance. He also envisioned 'laboratory production' in which
'author, designer, director and actors are all working in close
co-operation, in a technique they have evolved together'. The
theatre would join the revolt against the naturalism of the
'bourgeois' theatre but on no account would it be political in
the Russian or German manner. It was to be rooted in English
tradition and, said Guthrie—with Irish fervour—'a revival of
romance'. Having laid out a scheme which implied a Guthrie
and a Doone jointly training a company within a well-planned

organization, and having sounded his warnings against artistic democracy and political engagement, Guthrie joined the Group Theatre and shortly became, with Doone, one of its two 'Intendants'. He was, as Auden said, 'quite a "cop"'.[31]

Chastened but not overcome by the reception of *Popomack*, the Group engaged in a short period of intensive training. Just as writers of the day had the habit of 'going away' to work, the Group thought that some form of rustication would be conducive to its artistic development. There were excellent theatrical precedents for this, of course: Konstantin Stanislavsky, Copeau and Saint-Denis had taken their companies into rural retreats. Although the Group could not afford a lengthy sojourn out of town, they could at least inaugurate a policy they hoped to adopt on a full scale later. They found accommodation at a school in Suffolk and for two weeks in August they immersed themselves in a 'Summer Study' consisting of classes in dance and movement, singing and verse speaking and experiments with masks, conducted, mostly, by Doone.

In these sessions, as in the earlier ones, Doone was a demanding instructor, requiring of his trainees great imaginative and physical exertion. He taught the basic ballet positions and, to the beat of his tambour, endeavoured to instil flexible, rhythmic movement in the ensemble. Mannerisms, stereotypes and inhibitions had to be discarded—the masks being used partly for this purpose. Ruthlessly, and with more imperious conviction than system, Doone insisted on complete dedication to theatrical creation. His own undoubted sincerity, his experience and his precise intuition earned him obedience for the most part, but he met obdurate opposition when, at times, he treated his trainees too much as though they were accomplished dancers, acrobats or just plain martyrs to art. As Robert Medley, the painter and the Group's chief designer, who lived with Doone for many years, admitted, 'it required devotion and patience to work with or for him.'[32] In the early years of the Group Theatre especially, Doone received that devotion from actors who saw in him a genius and drive that more than compensated for a 'difficult' personality.

In October 1932 a new schedule of classes began in town.
Doone taught movement and Geoffrey Dunn, who was in
charge of operatic production at the Royal Academy of Music,
taught voice.[33] The active members trained for two or three
sessions a week and took pride, some of them, in humble tasks
such as scrubbing the 'studio' floor—such was their zeal and
such the state of the West Street Room. In November the
organization was revamped, making room for Guthrie.
According to its constitution, the affairs of the Group Theatre
were to be administered by an 'Organizer' and two elected
'Intendants' (the Germanism being an evasion of the hier-
archic implications of the title 'Director'). There was also to be
a second elected executive body for each individual production. In practice the two bodies became indistinguishable and
elections insignificant. The actual administration was done by
Greenwood and John Allen; Guthrie and Doone were the
artistic directors; John Moody was stage manager; Isobel
Scaife was treasurer; and Robert Wellington business manager. Wellington had not hitherto been actively involved in the
theatre. His interest in it had been stirred, during his recent
stay in Germany, by the work of Brecht and Kurt Weill. In the
Group Theatre he saw similar possibilities, though he was
scarcely in a position to influence its artistic policy. From time
to time other members held various titles, including that of
propaganda officer. The realities of the organization were that
those who were most willing to work held the executive offices
and that Doone exercised an authority that had nothing to do
with constitutional paraphernalia.

In the West Street Room the Group planned and rehearsed
an 'experimental reading' of *Peer Gynt*. By not committing
themselves to a full-scale production they hoped to be able to
show their acting techniques to better advantage. Guthrie was
to co-direct with Doone and play the Troll King, but he
withdrew to take an engagement elsewhere and Gillian Scaife
stepped in to assist with the direction of the large cast. Medley
designed 'suggestions' of costumes and settings, his first work
in the theatre. Murrill played Grieg's music. Many new

members were in the cast as well as a number of guest actors, of whom Robert Speaight, as Peer, was one. Anmer Hall lent the Westminster Theatre for a Sunday performance, which was given in February 1933. The 'reading' is remembered as one of the best things Doone and the Group Theatre ever did. At the time it was a promise of great things to come and a big boost to the Group Theatre's morale and reputation.

Soon after this, the Group Theatre consolidated its position by taking a lease on 'Rooms' of its own on the third floor of 9 Great Newport Street, next to the Arts Theatre.[34] A few enthusiasts partitioned off an office, built a dressing room cum wardrobe, workbenches and storage cupboards, and decorated the place. The office equipment consisted of Greenwood's typewriter and a circular printing press that he acquired. At the press, he, Medley, Allen and others laboured diligently and ingeniously to turn out 'information'. The Group was always good at making propaganda and, in the early days, their printed ephemera had an air of clever improvisation—one of their best efforts was printed on brown wrapping paper—that testified to the dynamic informality of the enterprise. Most of this home-made printing bore the Group Theatre emblem, designed by Medley, a freely drawn circle balanced on an arrowhead and containing a heart. The heart obviously signified love, the arrow penetration and the emblem may have had more precise, sexual meaning.

In April 1933, the first Group Theatre brochure appeared. It signposted the Group Theatre's PROGRESS since its foundation and listed nearly 200 members, including, among those who were well known then or later: Duncan Grant, Lynton Lamb, Henry Moore, Vanessa Bell, William Coldstream and Victor Pasmore, Anton Dolin, Margaret Craske, Antony Tudor, Flora Robson, Stephen Spender, Havelock Ellis, F. S. Boas, Adrian Stokes and Arthur Elton. Over the course of the next two years, the membership list would be enhanced by such additions as T. S. Eliot, Michel Saint-Denis, John Masefield, Harley Granville-Barker, Clifford Bax, Nevill Coghill, Harold Nicolson and Geoffrey Grigson.[35]

Certain patterns of recruitment were obvious. The Westminster group proselytized their fellow actors; Medley carried the word into Bloomsbury; and Doone got dancers to join. Relatives and friends were signed up to give a guinea to a good cause on a quite personal basis. Singers, dancers and actors, both professional and amateur, joined what looked like a promising venture in itself and one that might lead to other openings. Havelock Ellis was an interesting special case in being the Group Theatre's only link with the Workers' Theatre Movement, though it was probably his enthusiasm for dance rather than for Socialism that brought him in.

Homosexuality clearly had some bearing on recruitment though many members were quite unaware of this factor and would have been very surprised at the suggestion that it had any influence on the work of the Group. In fact, homosexuality was both one of the reasons for artistic collaboration and an important, though inhibited, theme in the plays of Auden and Isherwood. Others, as well as they, probably fused (and confused) homosexual love, artistic collaboration and Communism. But whereas the homosexual aspect of the plays received almost no public attention, their Leftist tendencies, and those of the Group Theatre, were often exaggerated. Some members were, or became, Communists or strong sympathizers for at least brief periods and may have harboured ambitions—even followed instructions—to make the Group Theatre an instrument of Communist persuasion but the Group Theatre did not define itself politically. It was probably even less of a Communist cell than a homosexual fraternity—whatever the ambitions of some of its members—though these sexual and political orientations of influential personalities in the Group necessarily contributed to its complex collective character.

The Group Theatre's only means of gathering support was by an expansion of its membership and it went about this with mixed motives. It wanted artistic collaborators and 'participating spectators' and it wanted subscriptions. Prospective members were enticed with the promise that they would not be mere 'passengers' and not a few joined with the intention of laying hands on the ropes. By 1934, the Group Theatre numbered some 250 members, a not unimpressive count considering that it was not a club or society guaranteeing a certain number of performances—or any at all. But expansion of the membership tended to obscure what little definition the proto-ensemble had attained. Moreover, as far as the active membership was concerned, the Group was being pulled in two directions at once.

Both Doone and Guthrie insisted on the necessity of teaching actors to sing and dance, but the Group Theatre also attracted singers and dancers who were not actors. So its attention was divided between attempts on the one hand to devise *composite productions* in which singers, actors and dancers had distinctive roles and, on the other, to integrate the arts through *individual performances*. The great, and largely incompatible, examples that lay behind the Group's efforts in these directions were those of Diaghilev and Copeau.

After *Peer Gynt*, the Group's next experiment was in the Copeau vein, with a production of Henry Medwall's *Fulgens and Lucrece*. The text of this Tudor interlude was a modern rediscovery and the Group Theatre's production was to be the first for 400 years. It was of great interest not only for this reason but as a play that would test the Group's professed dedication to simplicity and directness of presentation.

Medwall's play is in the form of a debate between a wealthy suitor of noble blood and a poor one of noble mind. Lucrece and her father choose the right man, without being unrealistic about the pecuniary and eugenic advantages of the rejected suitor. The theatrical debate is enlivened by the two 'Intruders' who come out of the audience, are pressed into service by the suitors and mimic their masters' wooing in a gross manner. These Intruder roles (which Auden and, probably, Eliot were to imitate) afforded an ample opportunity for inventive clowning, which Desmond Walter-Ellis and Ormerod Greenwood exploited to the full. The Group Theatre's production was further embellished with songs of the period, reset by

Murrill, and with the interpolation of a mumming dance of 'Death, the Fool and the Hobby Horse', choreographed by Doone.

Fulgens was something of a revelation to the actors and their audiences at the Westminster and Everyman Theatres, in the Great Hall of King's College, London, (where it was played in the round) and elsewhere. The play presupposed a very intimate relationship between players and spectators, physical and vocal virtuosity in the acting, and direct address. In fact, the Group had found in *Fulgens* an English ancestry for the very qualities they admired in the work of the Quinze and its playwright, André Obey.

After a series of performances of *Fulgens*, in the summer of 1933, the Group took its 'Diaghilevian' tack with a composite production: *The Group Theatre in Songs, Dances and a Play*. For this, Guthrie directed a chorus of fifteen singers in a suite of folk songs and Doone choreographed a set of dances to be performed by himself and two former members of Anna Pavlova's company.[36] The dances were modernist in character, especially 'Witch Dance', which Mary Skeaping danced to the beat of Doone's tambour in the manner of Mary Wigman. The songs and dances, together with a short play by Clifford Bax, made up the programme that the Group tried out in July in Suffolk. Later in the month they presented a similar bill for a week at the Croydon Repertory Theatre, where the Bax play was replaced by the medieval romance, *Lancelot of Denmark*, and Doone's dance from *Fulgens* appeared on the programme as 'The Dance of Death'. For the Croydon bill, too, Auden wrote a piece of 'continuity' linking *Lancelot* and the second half of the programme.

Crude as it is, this first piece written by Auden for the Group bears its author's stamp. Some of the actors in the play come on to the stage in the new guise of themselves, on their way home. They act a micro-drama of sexual rivalry at cross purposes in which two actresses, who have already made assignations with fellows in the audience, are courted by two actors. The 'Prompter' comes on to the stage and cuts the knot. The actors cannot leave since they are wanted for the later items on the bill. The audience is also urged to stay since,

> *Tyrone Guthrie who is tall and thin*
> *Married and living in Lincoln's Inn*
> *Has arranged some songs for you to hear*
> *Of Johnny tarrying at the Fair*
> *Of Herod and his cock that crew*
> *Or if your choice is dancing, then for you*
> *Rupert Doone with his odd-shaped skull*
> *Will dance as a chinaman. It won't be dull. . . .*
> *Shout if you like for we shall not be pained*
> *Perhaps we look it but we're not refined.*[37]

Whether it was more in the manner of village mumming or sophomoric introversion, Auden's little piece emphasized the non-illusionistic character of the performance and the communality of players and audience.

The printed programme for the Croydon performance did double duty as a recruiting pamphlet in which, *inter alia*, the Group Theatre declared its intention of forming 'on a co-operative basis a PERMANENT, SELF-SUFFICIENT COMPANY supported by a sympathetic audience and a training school for young members'. A list of over fifty plays under consideration for the next season abundantly confirmed the assertion that the Group Theatre would be 'neither archaeological nor avant-garde' in its choice of plays, the titles being apparently an inclusive compilation issuing from some democratic moot. In fact, the Group Theatre produced none of the plays mentioned. The list contrasted in this and most other respects with the one, beginning with *The Agamemnon* and ending with Brecht, that Auden drew up for Doone shortly afterwards.[38]

After the week in Croydon, the Group Theatre decamped to Suffolk where it entertained local audiences with a similar bill. Auden visited them there. He was a rather remote marvel for most of the actors, though one of the local newspapers did divine his function in the Group Theatre well enough to credit

him with the authorship of *Fulgens and Lucrece*! Not being, as
yet, a Group Theatre playwright, the visit helped Auden to
become one by providing him with *materia dramatica*.
Stephen Spender thought that Auden's 'secret fantasy of the
poet was Cocteau's image in *Orphée* of Death as the surgeon
with white coat and rubber gloves'.[39] That Auden did, indeed,
envision some such figure moving in the midst of the Group
Theatre would shortly be seen.

Back in the Group Theatre Rooms, classes were continued
and, in November, *Fulgens* was put into rehearsal again for a
performance at Nugent Monck's Maddermarket Theatre in
Norwich, where it was very warmly received. In November,
too, *The Dance of Death* was published.

The Group Theatre had begun as an actors' co-operative
dedicated to the formation of an ensemble. Having taken the
first step, the founders had quickly embraced the co-ordinate
aims of collaboration between actors and other artists; the
establishment of a school; and the operation of a theatre
centre. They wanted to create a theatrical community in
which an ambience of experimentation and discussion would
be the context for production and training. The acquisition of
the Rooms, the classes and talks given there, and the convivial
occasions were all in pursuit of this comprehensive ideal.

As to the productions, *The Provok'd Wife* and *The Man
Who Ate the Popomack* were effusions motivated by the
compulsion to *act*; the 'experimental reading' of *Peer Gynt*
was an exploration of ensemble style but using 'visiting'
actors; *Fulgens and Lucrece* was expressly intended as an
exercise in acting, song and dance for the ensemble that the
core members hoped to become; while *The Group Theatre in
Songs, Dances and a Play* was conceived as a way of using the
talents of an active membership that included a group of
singers and some dancers. These productions were eclectic
probings rather than a well-defined series of experiments but
they did serve as a focus for training and prepared the
Group—and Auden too—for *The Dance of Death*. The

production of this piece was decisive. Based on what the Group had become, it led them further away from the ideal of a small acting ensemble and brought them, willy-nilly, into an artistic and political avant-garde.

3
W. H. Auden and *The Dance of Death*

Au fond Mr Auden n'est pas du tout persuadé que
Karl Marx . . . puisses régénérer notre société
bourgeoise: il est trop pessimiste pour y croire.[1]
LOUIS BONNEROT, 1934

L'art n'est pas un jeu gratuite, c'est une activité
offensive.[2]

LURÇAT

Drama was Auden's element. As schoolboy and schoolmaster
he found it a way of satisfying his predilection for rituals, play
and display: as poet he was always ready to adapt his craft to
the theatre though his ambitions as a playwright did not
outlast the thirties and his later contributions to the theatre
were the relatively modest ones of a librettist. At the outset of
his career he seemed set fair to become a dramatist of the first
rank; one, it might be, with an attendant acting company.
That this great promise was not fulfilled is part of the story of
the Group Theatre.

Undoubtedly the existence of the Group gave Auden a
further, strong motive for playwriting but he had been
experimenting with dramatic form—sometimes in collaboration with Isherwood—for several years before the Group
Theatre was founded. He was stimulated by T. S. Eliot's acute
interest in dramatic poetry but, unlike Eliot, he did not have to
break the spell of Elizabethan and Jacobean drama before he
could develop as a playwright. He found his models in
theatrical territory less frequented by English poets: in
medieval plays and mumming, melodrama and charades. And

he also kept a sharp eye on the experiments of contemporary poets at home and abroad.

Auden's first published play, or 'charade' as he called it, was *Paid on Both Sides*. It was a strikingly original piece but it did not come altogether out of the blue. Its immediate precursors were plays by such poets as Lascelles Abercrombie, John Masefield, Wilfrid Gibson, and Gordon Bottomley. Following John Millington Synge's example, these Georgians attempted to rediscover in England a rooted language and life on which poetry and drama might draw. They favoured remote rural settings in which some brutal or passionate action takes place among folk whose dialects still reflected the power of the elements, the seasons and rudimentary passions. Bottomley's *The Riding to Lithend* and Gibson's *Kestrel's Edge*, with their respectively Norse and North Country settings and their dramatizations of feuding people, are especially pertinent to *Paid on Both Sides*. Auden may well have arrived at a point of departure for playwriting by subjecting the organic, neo-romanticism of the Georgians to a modernizing process of irony, harsh juxtaposition, thematic overlayering and verbal discordance.

The basic situation of *Paid on Both Sides* is a feud between two North Country families. There is no exposition or elaboration: death is immediately followed by birth, friend-ship by parting, tribal enmity by private love in an action reduced to the bare bones. Dramatic clichés are renovated by the superimposition of the congruent but distinct codes of the Norse sagas, the Officers' Training Corps and the rugger club. The poetry spoken by the Chorus (dressed in rugger gear in an early version) and by some other characters is as compressed as the action. There are some lyrics that could be set to music, and a dance.

In the published version, Auden added to his earlier draft characters from the mummers' play: Father Christmas, the Doctor and his Boy. They cut clean across the existing style and action, thoroughly repudiating any illusionist intention and making its mood more playful. The mumming also engages the audience, which is assigned the role of a wedding party.

Paid on Both Sides was a shrewd experiment in the synthesis and adaptation of traditional and recent forms, the popular and the esoteric: an attempt to unite the folk and the coterie as the implied audience. Auden hoped to have the charade performed at the house of some friends but they balked at the idea, saying, apparently, that 'the village won't stand it'.[3] So the audience remained for a while merely implied. Eliot, however, thought it 'a brilliant piece of work' and published it in the *Criterion*.[4]

Shortly after completing *Paid on Both Sides*, in 1929, Auden asked himself in his journal, 'Do I want poetry in a play, or is Cocteau right: "There is a poetry of the theatre, but not in it"?' His answer was both. 'A play', he asserted, 'is poetry of action. The dialogue should be correspondingly a simplification.' On the other hand, though, poetry should be retained for its own sake, since 'poetry after all should be recited not read'.[5] Auden's resolution of these contradictory claims, in the play he was then writing, was to hive off the poetry 'as interlude'. He was feeling his way, in fact, to the kind of juxtapositional structures that Yeats had adopted in his *Plays for Dancers* and Brecht in his use of lyrics to counterpoint rudimentary parabolic action. Obey would take the method to its greatest extreme in *Le Viol de Lucrèce*, in which the speakers are completely separated from the mimed stage action to give both verbal and gestural 'poetries' their due.

Auden felt the influence of Yeats and Cocteau at the outset of his playwriting career and registered that of Brecht and Obey very soon afterwards. In 1934, in a review of a book on poetic drama, he remarked that 'the influence . . . of the continental writers like Cocteau, Obey and Bert Brecht' had been slight in England.[6] So it had. Its first significant manifestation was in his own work, which was governed by the principle that these poets held in common: that a real poetry of the theatre would necessarily be founded on primary collaboration between poet and performers. 'I don't want any characters, any ideas in my play, but stage-life, something which is no imitation but a new thing,' said Auden.[7] Only by working in the theatre and exploiting *its* poetry could that 'stage-life' be created. Like Yeats, Cocteau, Brecht and Obey, Auden needed a complete theatrical apparatus to serve his poetic turn and his fairy godmother could hardly have given him a nicer gift than the Group Theatre. Auspiciously enough, the gift came through Robert Medley who, when they were at school together, had first brought Auden to recognize his poetic vocation.[8]

After *Paid on Both Sides*, Auden turned his hand to at least three more plays, or versions of plays, before his association with the Group Theatre began. *The Reformatory*, mentioned in the journal notes, was inspired by Peter Martin Lampel's *Revolte im Erziehungshaus*, an indictment of harsh and ineffectual institutional discipline. Auden burlesqued Lampel's theme, which was part of the material that he and Isherwood salvaged from *The Reformatory* in *The Enemies of a Bishop; or, Die When I Say When: A Morality in Four Acts*. In this complex farce, two escapees from a reformatory, one of them in female disguise, are hotly wooed by two gentlemen admirers of different sexual inclinations.[9] Had Auden thought well enough of the play to want a production he could have offered *Enemies* to Doone in 1932, but he did not.

In the autumn of 1930, Auden completed another play, *The Fronny*, now lost.[10] Apparently it was about the search for a lost Englishman by one Alan Norman, who was to show up again, still engaged on such a quest, as the hero of *The Dog Beneath the Skin*. In another part of *The Fronny* the eponymous hero makes his will in a Berlin night-club as Death would in the final scene of *The Dance of Death*.

Common features of these early experiments were the use of poetry as 'interlude'—or the interpolation of poems—and elaborate plots. Auden would continue in this vein in *The Chase* (for which, in 1934, *Enemies* was cannibalized) and, with Isherwood, in *the Dog Beneath the Skin* (which likewise consumed *The Chase*), *The Ascent of F6* and *On the Frontier*.

The first work he wrote for performance by the Group, however, belonged to a different gentre altogether. Far from having an elaborate plot, *The Dance of Death* had none, and poetry was almost entirely excluded in favour of dance, doggerel and song.

The idiosyncrasy of this piece is partly attributable to the circumstances of its composition, which were explained by Doone in this way:

> I had asked Auden if he would write me a ballet to choreograph and perform in, on the theme of Orpheus' descent into the Underworld. At the same time I suggested he might write a play on the theme of *la danse macabre*, the late medieval poem, which he had brought me to read.
>
> The result of my suggestions was that Auden combined the two themes, with his own conceptions added, and presented me several months later with what I think can best be described as a political ballet-charade, with music. . . .[11]

The ballet scenario that Doone asked for in July 1932 was obviously intended as a successor to *The Enchanted Grove*, and had nothing to do with the Group Theatre, for which the play was wanted. Not surprisingly, given Auden's low opinion of ballet, the work he actually composed was for the Group Theatre, though it also satisfied Doone's needs as a dancer-choreographer. One of the consequences of this fusion of the two proposals was that Doone's efforts were channelled away from classical ballet and into the dramatic theatre. This may have been Auden's intention. He was certainly out to be practically effective in such ways with *The Dance of Death*.

Auden made a start on the 'Orpheus stuff' and enjoyed it as a 'holiday task' until he took up a teaching appointment at the Downs School in September 1932. Then, the work on the scenario came to a halt: 'I've written a thing but frankly it's no use,' he told Doone.[12] The boys at the Downs School got Orpheus in the shape of Cocteau's play, adapted and directed by Auden, and what Doone eventually received was a rich theatrical stew in which dance, choral movement, symbolism, mumming, revue and agitprop were all ingredients.

By December 1932, Auden had written something resembling *The Dance of Death* and he discussed his text with Isherwood over the Christmas holidays, in Berlin. In March, he warned Doone that the performance would need all the actors in the Group Theatre 'and a choir too'. A composer would also be required but Doone was not to worry about that since Auden (who had Michael Tippett in mind) had found one.[13] A draft was near completion in the spring of 1933 and in August the work was sent to Eliot for publication and to Doone and Medley. By this time, Auden had incorporated a burlesque of the Group's 'Summer Study' session in merrie Suffolk and had worked in a diagnosis of the peculiar behaviour of Doone and his followers.

Doone and Medley were mightily surprised at the egg Auden laid in the Group Theatre's nest, but by November, when *The Dance of Death* was published, they had enthusiastically begun to brood over it. Relishing the prospect of performing the first work written specially for the Group Theatre, they were quite untroubled by any thought that the Group's artistic or political innocence might have been violated.

The Dance of Death had just gone into rehearsal when Hedli Anderson first encountered the Group. She had lately returned from Germany, where she had been training to be an opera singer until she recognized that she would never realize that ambition. Now she was looking for some other way to develop a career as a singer. At first view, she was dismayed by the amateurishness of the Group but deeply impressed by the work it had in hand. In Germany, she had been just 'a girl studying opera and living in a bedsitter', but she had seen enough of the effects of the social upheaval going on about her to know how serious it was, and enough of Fascism to recognize its menace.[14] Back in England, she was shocked by the prevailing political complacency. *The Dance of Death* was exceptional in this respect and since its appeal to her political conscience was coupled with the opportunity to get started in the theatre, she took a chance on the Group's amateurishness and accepted Doone's invitation to join the production. She was to become one of the principal performers of the Group—cast by Auden and Benjamin Britten as the Lotte Lenya to their Brecht and Weill.

The amateurishness of the Group was partly an emanation from *The Dance of Death* itself and inextricable from the political awareness that Hedli Anderson approved. The production called for the kind of mobilization that went into the making of pageants and such communal celebrations, its ludic spirit embracing a whole (though hypothetical) community. It was up to the Group Theatre to realize Auden's Marxist hypothesis of an advance party of the doomed middle class celebrating and perhaps accelerating its own imminent destruction.

Whether Auden was acquainted with the German agitprop groups or the British ones that took them as a model, he was obviously familiar with the style, elements of which he commandeered. Even in aspiration, though, *The Dance of Death* was not an attempt at workers' theatre proper but a newer phenomenon: an adaptation for a middle-class audience and partly professional company of agitprop techniques. With its political message couched in blatantly didactic terms, its use of a chorus in a collective role, strict choreography on a bare stage, doggerel verse and simple words, caricature and revue structure, *The Dance of Death* was the first attempt to forge a link between 'bourgeois' and workers' theatre in England.

Auden's depiction of the historically inevitable death of the middle class was unabashedly by, of and for the middle class, and there was deep consistency in his assumption that a middle-class audience would be entertained by the spectacle, since he assumed that its fatal disorder was its death wish. The reviewer who thought that Auden was 'consciously trying to write poetry for the ideal proletarian' and supposed that 'a technique . . . so simplified that it required the help of the stage, with song and dance' must have been adopted in order to reach the simple workers was decidedly off the mark.[15] He would have been nearer to it if he had accused Auden of artfully picking the proletarian pocket in order to bring the English theatre into new country aesthetically, as well as politically.[16]

At a time when literary Marxism was an unfamiliar feature on the landscape, its middle-class variety was hard to comprehend. *The Times Literary Supplement*, having an inkling of what was going on, was irritated by the cheek of it:

> We find Mr Auden in the attitude of one desiring revolution . . . he is a gamin jeering at the tumbril. . . . Those on stage are the outmoded who, like the damned in a foundering ship, are occupied with trying to escape and being frustrated: a situation which is supposed to delight us, which we are expected to enjoy without pity—this is the fundamental and rather adolescent flaw.[17]

'Tumbril' and 'damnation' suggest some unwilling assent to Auden's (or Marx's) prophecy, but the reviewer did not quite see that Auden was himself in the cart and, with merry irony, inviting his fellow passengers to join the dance.

From its different viewpoint, the *Socialist Review* was also rather dissatisfied with Auden's attitude. Seeing that it was 'good that Auden should be on our side', and 'waving the red flag', it had to admit his Marxism 'seemed to misfire'.[18] And a severer comrade, diagnosing the ideological weakness more precisely, objected that 'the death of capitalism is not accompanied and promoted by any conscious and accelerating pressure. Its theoretic deficiency is that of the intellectualistic, deterministic approach.'[19] Far from simply promoting the revolution, Auden presented the emergence of a new proletarian order ambivalently and since the Marxist prognosis was offered in anything but a serious manner, a Communist might well have suspected that Communism was being made a game of; as, rather in the manner of the games played with

Christianity in the medieval cycle plays, it was. With its air of detachment, Auden's political ballet-charade adumbrated some happy, far-off, post-revolutionary period in which the passions of yesterday's struggle would long since have been distilled into myth and play.

There were other ways in which *The Dance of Death* was quite unlike the workers' theatre that influenced it. The allusions that the overt simplicity of language and form slyly concealed were decidedly highbrow. For the cognoscenti, Auden offered a subtext rich in personal and literary reference and he displayed his virtuosity in yoking together such diverse phenomena as epilepsy and shamanism; *fin de siècle* poetico-spiritual despair and aeroplane flying; Gerard Manley Hopkins and Fascism; D. H. Lawrence's Rananim and the folk-dance movement; Karl Marx and Father Christmas and thus, by extension, the archetypal symbolism of the death and birth of the year with the thesis of the *Communist Manifesto*. Yet far from being an intellectual rag-bag, the work was thematically unified and stylistically coherent.

The Dance of Death was also distinct from workers' theatre in making use of the techniques of symbolist theatre and ballet. Auden was following Cocteau's track in combining these 'high' forms with 'low' ones. The 'backstage' motif, the music-hall turns, the shipwreck theme and the use of a megaphone are some of the unconsidered trifles that Auden picked up from *Parade*, Cocteau's *ballet réaliste* with words, presented by Diaghilev in 1917. The 'cult of athleticism' in *The Dance of Death* echoes another Cocteau creation, *Le Train bleu*, an *opérette dansée* as Diaghilev called it. This satire of Riviera escapism and the sporting life was designed to exploit Anton Dolin's skills as an acrobatic dancer. It was presented in Paris and London in 1924, its novelty evoking such headlines as BATHING BEACH BALLET and DANCING GOLFER WITH PLUS FOURS AND A PIPE.[20] As in *The Dance of Death*, Terpsichorean beach exercises were performed by dancers in bathing suits, and Kodaks and the flight of an aeroplane underlined the utter contemporaneity of the piece that drew artistic images from ephemeral fashions. Auden's treatment of escapism was less purely aesthetic. Whereas Cocteau had attempted to wrest the techniques of circus, music-hall and revue from the possession of the vulgar to give them new theatrical functions, Auden, going further, made them ideologically significant.

As politically tendentious choreography, *The Dance of Death* also had something in common with the most impressive political ballet of the thirties, Kurt Jooss's *The Green Table*.[21] In this dance of death, which reached London in 1933, the grotesquely masked statesmen of Versailles tortuously gesticulated their negotiations and the live-bodied soldiers went to their destruction. Jooss's mordant choreography was etched on the minds of many who saw it, including Doone and Medley, and it may well have influenced the Group Theatre production of *Sweeney Agonistes* as well as *The Dance of Death*. In contrast with *The Green Table*, though, Auden's *danse macabre* was a parochial and playful one.

Another of the contemporaries whose work influenced Auden was Bertolt Brecht. While Tyrone Guthrie, in 1932, looked back to Nigel Playfair's 1920 revival of *The Beggar's Opera* as the starting point of a reintegration of music and drama, Auden looked towards Brecht's caustic adaptation of it. For the most part, humour mollifies satire in *The Dance of Death* in an un-Brechtian way but the last scene, with its song of the thieves, pimps and prostitutes, recalls *Die Dreigroschenoper*. Auden uses Berlin rather as Brecht used London as the setting for a seamy underworld that betrays the hollowness of the social system. Murrill's music was bland; had it been otherwise the scene would have been very Brechtian indeed.

Closer to *The Dance of Death* in terms of genre was the minor Brecht–Weill collaboration *Die sieben Todsünden der Kleinbürger*, which was performed in London (under the title *Anna, Anna*) in 1933, with Lotte Lenya as one of the Annas.[22] In this ballet with words Brecht transposed the medieval allegory of the seven deadly sins into contemporary anti-capitalist terms. In these works, Auden and Brecht were

mining similar theatrical ore but *Anna, Anna* had none of the
festive spirit of Auden's ballet-charade.

The festiveness of the *The Dance of Death*, immediately
clear in the theatre, was hard for *readers* to comprehend. As
one critic reflected,

> The very fact that many people, reading the text in
> advance, found it incomplete and unsatisfactory simply
> underlined the point that it was expressly intended as part
> of a whole which should include dancing, music and
> grouping; and when these other elements were added, the
> success of the words for their particular function in the
> whole was realized.[23]

Auden insisted that *The Dance of Death* was meant 'for acting
not reading' and depended 'on the music and dancing to give it
body' but he allowed it to be published without even scene
divisions, let alone any more detailed indications of the
theatrical effects he wanted.[24] But for the essential effect there
was no need of a stage direction: it was that the performance
itself should be a real act, with the actors of the Group dying
the death of their class as they played it. As in the cycle plays
the enactment of the death of God is both mere play and real
celebration so with the middle class in *The Dance of Death*.

One of Auden's frequent reminders about where his
audience and the performers are, and what they are up to,
comes in Death's last will and testament:

> *And last he would like to congratulate*
> *The actors, orchestra and authors tonight*
> *Upon this performance and soon as it is done*
> *May engagements be offered them by everyone.*[25] [p. 35]

The wish could hardly have been closer to the desires of the
participants but we note that this is *Death*'s wish, just as the
transmission of power from the bourgeoisie to the proletariat
is *Death*'s bequest. Death presides over this performance as
over all the spectators' and actors' doings.

The voice part in Herbert Murrill's setting for the first number of Auden's
The Dance of Death

Auden was using Marxist dogma as an intellectual scaffolding but the result was less Communist propaganda (though that is what it looked like to its first audiences) than an ethically timeless—even religious—*memento mori*. It is analogous to Sir Thomas More's meditation on the theme of the dance of death pictured in St Paul's:

> Not the very apparition of a ghost itself is half so grisly as the deep-conceived fantasy of death in his nature by the lively imagination graven in thine own heart. For there seest thou not one plain grievous sight of the bare bones hanging by the sinews, but thou seest (if thou fantasy thine own death, for so art thou by this counsel advised), thou seest, I say, thyself. . . .[26]

In such a manner Auden made the actors hold up the glass to themselves and to the audience. T. S. Eliot, as one of those present, responded enthusiastically —at first—and some of the enthusiasm he felt for *The Dance of Death* may be attributed to his recognition of a spiritual lamb in Marxist clothing, an example of the celebratory reality that he thought vital for the regeneration of the theatre.

Celebrating the longings and fears of his time and class, Auden focused particularly on the Group's own yearnings for renewal and its particular dance of death. He did so by designing a mask for the Group Theatre so like its face as to be more a revelation than a disguise. The Group did not know exactly what Auden was up to but they knew how to do what he wanted because that was what they had been doing. Like the Chorus on the stage, they were middle-class folk intent on revitalizing their dust; given to arduous training, choral singing and dancing, and co-operation; idealists who sought a communal art but accepted an artistic dictator; who dreamed of an artistic country colony and took refuge from perplexity in physical accomplishment; who looked for new life in the theatre but harboured nostalgia for the mumming and melodrama of 'simpler' times, and were fascinated by cabaret and other manifestations of contemporary cultural 'decadence'. Auden himself, needless to say, was one of the members most strongly swayed by these impulses. His self-image was projected as clearly in the figure of the Announcer as Doone's was in that of Death the Dancer. In *The Orators*, Auden had exhibited a few of his friends as part of the fantasy but in *The Dance of Death* the Group Theatre as a whole was imaginatively deployed. If there was a risk that this theatrical verism would lead to a self-indulgent display, the risk was offset by the conviviality and the possible therapeutic value of a performance that was, in itself, what it represented.

As an exercise in mass participation, *The Dance of Death* was scarcely conducive to the development of a highly trained ensemble, but in other ways it was precisely in keeping with the Group Theatre's aims. As an 'epic' construction with a strongly sequential choreographic, scenic and verbal montage, but without benefit of plot, it required the contributions of composer, choreographer and director to bring the conception to life. The burden of the thematic development was carried by the Announcer's words and the lyrics conveyed the changing sentiments of the collective, choral protagonist, but the affective power of the performance had to come mostly from the dancing and the music.

As intended, Doone choreographed and danced the role of Death. For the other main collaborator, Doone persuaded Auden to accept the Group Theatre's own composer, Herbert Murrill, who played and directed, as well as wrote, the music.[27] Murrill's composition consisted almost entirely of parodies of popular forms: a lively foxtrot, a soupy waltz, a sea shanty spliced with Elgarian patriotic strains, the old school song, and so on, which brought out the gusto and humour in Auden's writing rather than its darker side. As to the stage design, Medley made costumes and such properties as flags and parasols the chief means of visual expression, emphasizing the actors' gestures and leaving the stage clear for choral movement. A key symbol, the sun mask worn by Death, was designed and modelled by Henry Moore.[28] The task of rehearsing the Chorus fell initially to Doone. Later, Tyrone

Guthrie was called in to help and without him *The Dance of Death* might never have reached the stage. Guthrie was in his element directing a large company in an intricate sequence of movement and song, though quite out of it as far as the political theme was concerned.

Anmer Hall lent the Westminster Theatre for two Sundays. It was a generous but insidious arrangement that got the Group Theatre's new departure off on the wrong foot. Sunday performances were a way of getting a hearing for new or neglected plays without going to great expense but *The Dance of Death* was not a play and to be appreciated at all it had to have much more than a *hearing*. Yet to mount a full production, such as this was, for only two performances was poor economy in every way; not least in minimizing the opportunity for the Group to develop their technique through performance. Sunday performances were the Group Theatre's compromise between a run in a commercial theatre, for which they lacked the backing, and the use of some humbler playing space. Professional productions outside the regular play-houses were unusual and the Group Theatre was deeply averse to compromising its professional aspirations; even though its own experience had already indicated that the use of alternative playing spaces could be artistically as well as economically advantageous.

In its vacillating way, the Group Theatre was a forerunner of 'alternative' professional theatre and might have gone much further along those lines if it had not hobbled itself with its Sundays at the Westminster habit; and if it had put more emphasis on the development of a company, less on a professional setting.

In the two private performances at the Westminster, *The Dance of Death*, which has a playing time of about an hour and a half, was preceded by *The Deluge* from the Chester cycle. This juxtaposition brought out the strong thematic parallels between the two works and helped to make Auden's stylistic intentions clear. The audience was further prepared for *The Dance of Death* by the inclusion in the printed programme of an elaborate synopsis that brought out the precise symmetry of the work; dividing it into three sections, called 'Utopias', each comprising two precisely balanced scenes. In the synopsis the significance of the structure of the theatrical montage is made very clear. From it, from the prompt book, from photographs and recollections of the actors it is possible to reconstruct, to a degree, *The Dance of Death* in the flesh: a very different quantity from its ghostly, printed form.

Fanfare. A spotlight defines a space in front of the curtain and a tall figure steps into it. On his white boiler suit two arrows are painted, pointing towards the crotch: the modern equivalent of a codpiece. In a mumming this character would be the Presenter coming in first to 'make room'. Here he is the Announcer, equipped with a megaphone. He introduces the theme and behind the curtain the Chorus sighs its reponses:

ANNOUNCER: We present to you this evening a picture of the decline of a class.
CHORUS: Middle class.
ANNOUNCER: Of how its members dream of a new life.
CHORUS: We dream of a new life.
ANNOUNCER: But secretly desire the old, for there is death inside them. We show you that death as a dancer.
CHORUS: Death for us.   [p. 7]

Twenty of the dying are revealed as the first scene, described in the synopsis as 'The present day cult of athleticism', opens. Removing their wraps they display smart bathing suits (courtesy of Jantzen). They are very lively and quite attractive but their exposed bodies are not entirely beautiful. There is no mistaking the Westminster for the Windmill: this is a different class of performers altogether. Two groups on the stage weave in and out of each other, dancing their exercises and singing 'Gents from Norway / Ladies from Sweden' to the rhythm of a foxtrot. Four of the most accomplished singers (Hedli Anderson is one of them) are grouped round the piano and carry much of the song from there:

Strip off your shirt
Kick off your shoes
It won't hurt
To leave behind those office blues
Here on the beach
You're out of reach
Of sad news, bad news. . . .   [p. 8]

The opening number ends with a little acrobatic display by one
of the actresses. The performers are detectably having fun.

   Death enters as a 'vital young man' and the Chorus greets
him effusively. A Medwall-like Intruder, planted in the stalls,
calls out, 'E's a bit of orlright, ain't 'e, Bill?' It was a line that
called for close scrutiny of 'Mr Auden's attitude in the matter
of "class" ', said Dr F. R. Leavis, reasonably enough.[29] No
illusion is intended. This is not supposed to be a worker who
has somehow strayed into the Westminster—on the contrary,
the caricature assumes that author, players and audience share
an amused detachment from the working class.

   Death's entrance acts as a sexual stimulus to the Chorus of
bathers who pair off for a song-and-dance routine. The song,
'You were a great Cunarder, I / Was only a fishing smack. . .',
appears to be just a smack at Coward, or perhaps a straight
imitation. The couples waltz off stage to plunge into the sea (of
life). As they depart, Death, assisted by his Nurses, makes off
with their wraps. He returns wearing the mask of 'Sun God,
creator and destroyer' and dances the death of the sun, ending
prostrate on the floor. Standing over this crumpled form the
Announcer speaks a poem:

Do not be mistaken for a moment about this stranger,
The lives of many here are already in danger.
He looks on the just and the unjust as he has always done.
Some of you think he loves you. He is leading you on.
                                                    [p. 12]

This is from one of three passages of poetic commentary that
stand out from the surrounding lyrics as the voice of the
omniscient, authorial observer.

The Bathers return, 'stiff and mechanical from the cold'. Their wraps are gone and the sun is down. So much for sun worship, trust in love, the body and Nature. The first scene has ended and the transition to the next is made by means of a pantomimic exchange between the same Intruder in the audience and her Daughter in the Chorus. The Intruder accuses Death of stealing the clothes and he vainly tries to silence her with his drum. The Bathers turn on him. They want to make the sun (meaning time) stand still but in trying to catch him they only make him run. At last he is cornered and they signify their victory with the Communist salute, but at this moment the 'Theatre Manager', a German Jew (played by the refugee Stefan Schnabel), arrives and sends a couple of 'Stage-hands' for a hamper of clothes. Much better than the ones stolen by Death, these turn out to be costumes from an old musical revue. Completely distracted from their revolution, the Chorus seizes on the costumes with delight. The new scene has begun.

Its title is 'Flashback to pre-war arrogance and prosperity', but this is not quite consistent with what the audience is told from the stage. According to the dialogue, the costumes are from *The Lady of the Guard*, a revue presented in 1916 'in aid of the wounded'. In character and function the scene is strongly reminiscent of a Workers' Theatre Movement sketch by Tom Thomas called *Their Theatre and Ours*, which contains 'burlesque inset scenes of the capitalist theatre and films'.[30] Auden's inset scene is a double-edged satire. The patriotic fervour aroused by the Great War is feminized and the nostalgia for the wartime years is made dangerous by allusions to the next war as well as the last one. The artificiality of show business nicely balances the nature worship of the first scene, exhibiting the confusion and volatility of the Chorus. The slapstick and *coups de théâtre* grate against the seriousness of the allusions, and the characterization of the Jew is alarmingly ambivalent. Decked out in the costumes from the old show, the Chorus recalls its hit song, 'Soldiers of the King of Kings', sung by . . . and here she is emerging from

the hamper to sing the song once more . . . Miss Annabelle
Eve! The Manager asks the conductor if the musicians can
accompany her. Murrill says they can and strikes up a rousing
march:

> *They are ever stepping onward*
> *They are eager with the hope of youth. . . .*

As in the year of the Somme, the entertainment industry —
managed by a German Jew, we note—does its bit to preserve
the status quo. But the fun within the fun is interrupted by one
of the politically alert members of the Chorus:

> *One moment, sir, the Kellogg Pact*
> *Has outlawed war. . . .*

Members of the audience, that is the six performers planted as
'a chorus of Communists at the back' of the stalls, join in the
demonstration:[31]

> *One, two, three, four,*
> *The last war was a bosses' war,*
> *Five, six, seven, eight*
> *Rise and make a workers' state.* [pp. 15–16]

One of the Nurses produces a red flag and the Announcer
directs the Chorus's reactivated anger against Death. The
Manager, who is also in danger, promises Death double salary
if he can quell the Chorus. Their exchange marks the end of the
scene and of the first 'Utopia'.

The second 'Utopia' presents 'Death as a Demagogue', the
first scene of which is 'Fascism the revolution suited to English
conditions to abolish class'. In making an English analogy to
Hitler's accession to power in 1933, Auden was stretching
probability to the utmost. By the time the scene was played,
however, actual events had made it a warrantable admonition.
In fact, the climactic and brutal Olympia meeting of 15,000
British Fascists lay only a few months ahead. On stage, the
revolution is represented by Death's hypnotic exploitation of
the Chorus's subliminal sexual impulses. He induces the

transformation from Communism to Fascism, which the Announcer articulates, speaking in the style of sinister, cultivated reasonableness that Eliot was to adopt for the Knights in *Murder in the Cathedral*:

> Comrades, I absolutely agree with you. We must have a revolution. But wait a moment. All this talk about class war won't get us anywhere. The circumstances here are quite different from Russia. Russia has no middle class. . . .

Under the spell of the dance and the Announcer's rhetoric, the Chorus begins to sway, backwards and forwards, arms loosely raised:

> Our first duty is to keep the race pure, and not let these dirty foreigners come in and take our jobs. Down with the dictatorship of international Capital. Away with their filthy books which corrupt our innocent sons and daughters. English justice, English morals, England for the English.   [p. 17]

The xenophobia of the Chorus takes the form of a Salvationist meeting in which the traditional rousing hymn and the individual witness are, for the occasion, combined. Greenwood steps forward and sings:

> *I was a farmer during the war*
> *I sold my bacon at two and four,*
> *If you keep out Denmark, I can do it once more—*
> *I'll follow thee.*   [p. 18]

He is followed by a prostitute, an ex-Black-and-Tan and an unemployed derelict. All are ready to follow Death, who so rouses their masculinity that their arms jerk up in the Fascist salute. After this pseudo-erection, detumescence comes with an assault on the Manager, directed by Death and the Announcer. In a ghoulish mime, hands are plunged into the body of the 'dirty Jew' and withdrawn with sucking noises.

Thus purged, the Chorus re-forms as a shipshape Fascist

state. The outside members make the bows of the vessel, with hands placed together as for diving; the shoulders of two more make a bridge for Captain Death. As the ship ploughs the waves, Elgarian strains celebrating good order and racial purity are spliced with a sea shanty. But a storm blows up, the ship rolls and founders, the members of Chorus become the drowning, all spinning on the spot, some sinking to their knees and gradually to the floor. In a burlesque of Hopkins's 'The Wreck of the Deutschland', the victims appeal to the Announcer, to God and, finally, to 'Mother, Mother, Mother!' So much for reliance on gods, heroes—and mothers! The scene has ended . . . but Doone is still whirling round. The Chorus rises and crowds round him. Doone falls. Prompter, pianist, 'Stage-hands' and all come on to the stage.

As in the first 'Utopia', the transition between scenes is a passage of intrusions from the stalls. A Doctor found in the house diagnoses an epileptic fit and orders Doone to bed. Since the performance cannot proceed without him, it will have to be stopped, much to the general dismay. This, of course, cannot be allowed to happen. Another Intruder, Sir Edward, climbs on to the stage. An important figure in the medical establishment, he does not want to disappoint his even more important companion in the audience—and neither, after a short conversation with Sir Edward, does the first Doctor. After all, there is not only the audience to consider but the Group Theatre, which badly needs the collection due to be taken at the end of the performance. (The actual take was about £60.) To oblige all the parties, the Doctor fixes Doone up with an injection. This Doctor is a less benign figure than his prototype in the mummers' play, who brings the dead back to life with a bottle of alicumpane. In the political allegory he is a reminder that the present enactment of the death of a class is a function of that class.

The Doctor's ministration, gratefully received, is accompanied by an injunction:

But mind. There's to be no excitement of any kind—no politics, for instance, something quite peaceful, something, shall we say, about the country or home life.

[p. 23]

And so we move into the second scene of the second 'Utopia', 'Escape from machine civilization (country colony)'. Rustication has little to do with 'Death as Demagogue' but a lot to do with the Group Theatre and D. H. Lawrence's Rananim. In their 'Summer Study' sessions the Group sang and danced in the open air, sometimes wore masks to free themselves from inhibition and did maypole dances round a flagstaff. Now, masks and maypole, folk dance and folk song stand revealed as a hidden desire for a Lawrentian 'will of the blood' and a return to 'primal integrity'. Death finds a flaw in the set-up, however, and the Announcer voices it for him:

It's about the girls. Man must be the leader whom women must obey.   [p. 24]

From the audience, the feminist cause is urged with middling success. Some of the girls get to stay on as scenery—a bird, a tree, a cow: roles with which the company was quite familiar. The rest of the girls get to join the men in a song-and-dance sequence. It begins on a contemporary note:

Are you living in the city
Where the traffic won't stop. . . .   [p. 25]

and glides into a country dance with a lyric written by Auden during a rehearsal.[32] But *Blutbruderschaft* cloys, and the dance breaks up in boredom and dissatisfaction. Some new spiritual adventure is required:

For the Eternal Word
Has no habitation
In beast or bird
In sea or stone
Nor in the circumstances
Of country dances. . . .   [p. 27]

So ends the second 'Utopia', and to introduce the third, the Intruders in the audience become the spectators and betters at a grand sporting event.

Auden's elaborate description of the third 'Utopia' goes, in part:

> DEATH AS PILOT TO THE HEART OF REALITY
> Disillusioned the crowd ask for a pilot to the 'very heart of reality'. Death presents himself. But he collapses through the inanition of a class. Disintegration is complete where they attempt, in the night-club, simply to satisfy their individual sensuous desires. The Dancer appears among them in the last stages of senility. He accepts his dissolution and makes his will. . . .

This 'Utopia' follows the now established pattern in having one scene that links the past with the present and one linking the present with the future. Here, the first scene alludes to the 1890s and to 1927. The spiritual high-flying of the Catholic, decadent poet, Lionel Johnson, is coupled to the flight of Charles Lindbergh, remarkable for a 'loneliness . . . that fires the imagination'.[33]

The Chorus stands perplexed:

> *Now who will be our master? Who will be the one*
> *To teach us how to fly from the alone to the Alone?*
> [p. 28]

The allusion is not (primarily) to Greta Garbo's often expressed desire for solitude but to 'Mystic and Cavalier'.[34] Lionel Johnson's words in that poem are 'Lonely to the lone I go' and Auden handsomely acknowledges their author by placing him in a corner of the canvas. Box of the BBC picks him out to the crowd for us:

> Away to the right a member of the Green Cheese Society is making a spirited speech. David Johnstone, the six-year-old marvel, is thrilling a portion of the monster audience by the instantaneous conversion of monster

logarithms into improper fractions. There are a lot of
distinguished people here.   [p. 30]

The transmogrification of Johnson's conjuration of Evil
('improper fractions') out of Beauty, his intellectual precocity
and arrested sexual development, his membership of the
Rhymers' Club (which used to meet at the Cheshire Cheese)
and his fall off a bar stool to his death (in Ezra Pound's
heightened version) is too richly recondite to be very
functional on the stage, though it must have been a
delightful fillip for the literati. But the theatrical conceit of
the flyer is a master stroke. Helmeted like an airman and
rubbed down like a horse (which makes him a kind of
Pegasus) Death is led round the enclosure. Intruders stake a
wife, a house, a grouse moor and other valuables on his
daring and skill. The commentators-on-the-spot are lovingly
created caricatures of BBC employees. Box, with the microphone, and Cox, with the field-glasses, are (appropriately
in the Catholic context) old Ampleforthians. Their commentary on the event that the audience sees for itself is a
theatrical *tour de force*. Death's spectacular, spotlit flight
ends, needless to say, in disaster. He, like Johnson and
Lindbergh, is 'one of those that fall'.

The general significance of the scene is brilliantly clear,
though its more particular satire of a special form of
decadence is rather obscure; but T. S. Eliot would not have
missed the relevance to himself of the allegory of spiritual
refinement destroying itself in its flight from corruption.

The Manager, reintroducing himself to the audience, sets
the final scene. Having become the proprietor of the 'Alma
Mater', he hangs up its shingle on the proscenium—Brecht-style, as befits the Berlin location. The club
caters to the nostalgia as well as the sensual vices of its
clientele, whose nationality is detectable from their
elementary German, conveniently translated back for us:

> *How goes it then?*
> *It goes me well.*

Comst thou with?
Self-understandingly I come.   [p. 32]

They are in a sad pursuit of compensation of various kinds.
One wants a mother substitute; another a substitute for a dead
dog; another the special delectation of sex without desire.
Death, dying, is wheeled in to make his will. To the chords of
'Casey Jones' the Announcer chants Death's bequest of all
England's estates, raw materials, industry and money, 'all the
power and the glory of his kingdom . . . to work their will
among the working class'. Alternating with the Announcer's
chanted words, the Chorus sings, to the tune of the ballad, a
history of Western civilization that brings us up to the
transformation of the peasantry into the proletariat, by the
bourgeoisie:

They invited them into a squalid town
They put them in factories and did them down
Then they ruined each other for they didn't know how
They were making the conditions that are killing them now.
                                        [p. 35]

The 'Alma Mater Song' that follows, set by Murrill as the
quintessential school song, is a spirited Betjemanic paean to
the status quo, sung by prostitutes, thieves and blackmailers:

Hail the strange electric writing
Alma Mater on the door
Like a secret sign inviting
All the rich to meet the poor
Alma Mater, ave salve
Floreas in secula.   [p. 35]

But their complacency is short-lived. There are shots offstage.
It is not a police raid, but the beginning of the revolution,
farcically represented by the entrance of 'Mr Karl Marx' with
a couple of his friends. The arrival of the Father Christmas of
the thirties signifies the end. The social and economic saviour
gives Death the *coup de grâce*. Draped in the Union Jack,

Death the Dancer is Hamlet-like borne off, to the strains of Chopin's *Funeral March*.

The Dance of Death was the best beginning made in the theatre by an English poet for many years. Verbal poetry, it is true, was little in evidence, but neither, on the other hand, was there any Shakespearean pastiche. More positively, Auden's handling of a poetry *of* the theatre and his synthesis of many theatrical forms was both remarkable in itself and fraught with promise. Two major factors complicated the reception of the work: the relation in it between literature and the theatre; and that between aesthetic and political radicalism.

Doubtless the Group Theatre and its audience were in some manner politicized by *The Dance of Death*, having been implicated in an event that had the air of fellow-travelling, if not of professed Communism. The performance made the Group Theatre appear politically *engagé* and this new look was welcome to it since it proclaimed a keen sense of contemporary awareness, at least. Whether the art of the theatre was being exploited for political purposes or Communism was being taken for a theatrical ride was by no means certain. Most of the actors and 'participating spectators' would themselves have found it difficult to say where play ended and political commitment began, if the question had held any interest for them. It was something that really mattered only to those who admired the dramaturgy but had no sympathy at all for the politics; to Tyrone Guthrie, for example, and T. S. Eliot.

As for literature, Auden caused some consternation by wringing its neck so ruthlessly in order to hang a theatrical millstone round his own. At a time when advanced literary opinion insisted that Shakespeare's plays were dramatic poems, literary critics were inclined to see the theatre as poetically irrelevant at best. Gavin Ewart thought that,

> The Group Theatre is perhaps to blame for the demands it makes on its members; the words seem certainly to be

'words for music' rather than words existing in their own right. But good opera is not good literature.[35]

Whether *The Dance of Death*, not being 'good literature', had any merit as opera or anything else, he did not offer to say. Another reviewer in the same corner was sure that 'satire in jazz-lyrics' was unlikely to have the 'force or seriousness' of a poem, and that *The Dance of Death* would not 'perturb the audience much more than Mr Coward's back-patting mockery'.[36] Coward and Cochran were the favourite critical sticks in the hands of the book reviewers who took note of Auden's theatrical ambitions, but most ignored the theatre or pleaded ignorance of it—without, of course, limiting the force of their judgements thereby.

One of the exceptions was Louis Bonnerot whose approach was quite distinct from that of any of his English confrères:

> L'emploi de choeurs, à l'antique, rapelle Aristophane mais l'importance des rôles du metteur en scène et du compère indique clairment que nous avons à faire à une sorte de revue-ballet. C'est donc à la scène ... qu'il faudrait la voir pour apprécier son mouvement, l'animation créée par les commentaires et interruptions de l'auditoire qui participe ainsi directement à la représentation, le pittoresque, souvent un peu facile, des tableaux et la cocasserie des répliques.[37]

Criticism of the two private performances was sparse but what there was differed utterly from most of the reviews of the book. The *New English Weekly* emphasized the theatrical richness of the performance:

> To have verbal dexterity, poetic quality, metrical resourcefulness allied to a studied and significant movement on a stage was a pleasure made almost uncritical by its rarity.[38]

The reviewer, A. D. Hawkins, did manage to be pointedly critical but affirmed his solidarity with an audience that 'rose to demonstrate that something had at last HAPPENED on a London stage'. The *New Statesman* saw the happening as the possible beginning of a theatrical revival:

> The impression that it made was distinctly one of being present at the laying of the foundation of a new dramatic art. But nothing is wholly new and it was interesting to discover that Mr Auden's technique has something in common with a much older technique, that of the mystery or pre-Elizabethan morality play. *The Dance of Death* has absolutely nothing in common with the degenerate theatre of the present age. For one thing it is a return to reality and mystery.[39]

The reviewer himself had not, of course, discovered the connection between *The Dance of Death* and early English drama; that was one of the statements implicit in the performance of *The Deluge*, though by no means the only one.

'Noahs', moaned Hugh MacDiarmid in his 'A Prayer for a Second Flood', 'are o'numerous nowadays', and there were grounds for the complaint. As a biblical analogue to modern catastrophes, the Flood was a familiar trope. D. H. Lawrence, Shaw, and Yeats were some of the many writers who had used it in this way. Brecht had taken the theme for a radio play.[40] Cecil Day-Lewis used it for a play intended for the Group Theatre. Most pertinently, Obey's *Noé* had recently been seen in London.

As a medieval play with great contemporary resonance, *The Deluge* made an excellent foil to Auden's morality, highlighting the theme of judgement and destruction and tuning the audience to the style. Although the text was not significantly altered, the contemporary relevance of the medieval play was emphasized by calling the Noahs and their children the 'Unemployed Family' and by giving the Good Gossopes names that sound as though they might have come from a Happy Families pack custom-designed by Auden for Communist nurslings: 'Mrs Empire Builder', 'Mr Capital Profiteer', 'Miss

Old Lily', 'Tory Statesman Esq.', and 'The Reverend Googles'. The most memorable features of a production that is not well remembered were the initial sweep of the cast through the stalls and the building of the ark in mime, with actors mimicking the construction noises. *The Deluge* was not accounted a great success but it obviously served its turn as a curtain-raiser to the second half of the bill.

When *The Dance of Death* was revived in 1935 to open the first Group Theatre Season, it was given with a different companion piece: *Sweeney Agonistes*. By this time, Eliot's *The Rock* had been performed—not by the Group Theatre—and had been critically coupled with *The Dance of Death* as the second swallow of a new theatrical summer; the Group Theatre had earned much praise with a studio production of *Sweeney*; and Auden and Eliot had been heralded as the founders of a 'new school' of poet-playwrights. But though they had begun to work in the theatre at about the same time and were learning very quickly from each other, part of what they learned was that they were not in the same school at all. *The Dance of Death* had much more in common with *The Deluge* than with *Sweeney*.

4

T. S. Eliot and *Sweeney Agonistes*

Forget your groups.[1]
T. S. ELIOT, 1934

T. S. Eliot had every reason to pay close attention to the performance of *The Dance of Death* in February 1934. He was responsible for its publication, convinced of Auden's brilliant promise as a poet-dramatist and he had recently become practically involved in the theatre himself.

In the previous year, Eliot's appetite for the stage had been whetted by the production, five years after its publication, of his *Sweeney Agonistes*. This was during his visit to America, when Hallie Flanagan had presented the work in her Vassar College Experimental Theatre, as part of a *mélange* called *Now I Know Love*. Eliot had written a concluding passage for the performance, which he attended, and had given his advice on the staging.[2] With Hallie Flanagan, he had found himself following in young Auden's wake, theatrically speaking, for Hallie Flanagan had produced *Paid on Both Sides* two years earlier, in 1931.[3]

Sweeney Agonistes, subtitled 'Fragments of an Aristophanic Melodrama', was the residue of an abandoned attempt to make a modern equivalent to the ritual from which Attic comedy had sprung. In a preliminary sketch, Eliot had outlined a structure consisting of: a *Prologue* in which Doris and Dusty would appear (as in the first of the published fragments); a *Parados* in which Wauchope, Horsfall, Klipstein, Krumpacker, Swartz, Snow and, eventually, Sweeney would arrive; an *Agon* in which Sweeney would deliver a monologue (somewhat in the manner of the second of the published fragments, it may be supposed); a *Parabasis* which would include the chorus 'The Terrors of the Night' (which appears in the published fragments); a *Scene* in which Mrs Porter would debate with Sweeney and be murdered, and there would be interruptions by an Old Clothes Man, a Dustman, a Tenant from below and Pereira; a second *Parabasis* which would include theological and political matter; an invocation to the muse in a *Chorikon*; a second *Scene* which would have Sweeney scrambling eggs, a distribution of eggs and the return (resurrection, presumably) of Mrs Porter; and an *Exodus*.

Eliot estimated that the whole work would comprise some 1,600 lines, of which the published fragments represent about a fifth. In these fragments the fundamental structure is not apparent though; as will be seen, Eliot appears to have reverted to it—or to something like it—later.[4] What can be seen in them is an influence from Yeats's *Plays for Dancers*; *Sweeney Agonistes* being the grotesque, modernist counterpart to Yeats's mythical actions. It was as though Eliot, as well as going back to the Attic model, had also subjected the romanticism of Yeatsian drama to a process of transformation similar to Pound's 'modernization' of a few of Yeats's lyrics.[5] But the Sweeney fragments were scarcely a play, and before Hallie Flanagan staged them they looked more like an academic exercise by an accomplished poet than the prentice work of a new dramatist; an impression that seemed to be confirmed by the fact that Eliot's intense interest in drama had had no other practical issue. In 1934, however, he began to tackle the theatre in earnest.

E. Martin Browne, well known for his work in religious drama, had undertaken to mount a show as part of a campaign to raise funds for church restoration. At first, he had in mind a pageant that would incorporate historical sermons and make use of a chorus, and he persuaded Eliot 'to provide the words' for the latter. But when Browne discovered that the performance was to be given at Sadler's Wells, he abandoned the idea of a pageant as inappropriate for such a setting. For a long time, he cast about, rather desperately, for another kind of scenario that would allow for historical perspectives yet evade the 'toils of chronology'. At the end of November 1933, after several discussions with Eliot, Browne found his model:

> At that time, producers like Charles Cochran and André Charlot were making a success with a type of revue which, instead of being a collection of separate 'numbers', had a thread of plot. Might it not be possible to weave a thread out of the building of a contemporary church . . . and to use scenes from the past as illustrations to the builders of the way in which the Church had tackled, and therefore could still tackle, its problems?[6]

Browne hit on the model of the Cochran-type revue some three weeks after the publication of *The Dance of Death* and, since he was regularly consulting Eliot, it is inconceivable that Auden's experiment in the *métier* escaped his attention and most likely that Auden, rather than Cochran, was —however unconsciously—his immediate source of inspiration. In any case, Eliot's contribution to the newly conceived scenario, which eventually became *The Rock*, was strongly affected by *The Dance of Death*.

In *The Rock*, the main action is the construction of a church by a crew of Cockney labourers. By theatrical licence, episodes from the history of Christianity are interspersed with the contemporary scenes. Eliot's assignment was to write prose dialogue for 'scenes of the usual pageant pattern' and verse choruses.[7] He was immersed in this work when he attended the first performance of *The Dance of Death*. At this time, too (that is, several months before he received the commission for the Canterbury Festival that resulted in *Murder in the Cathedral*), Eliot decided to begin a new play of his own, and he gave Doone reason to hope that the Group Theatre might produce it. Eliot conceived the new play, as well as his part of *The Rock*, with the impression of *The Dance of Death* still very fresh in his mind.

At first, Eliot was enthusiastic about the Group Theatre's production of the Auden piece. It was 'extremely well done', he reported to Hallie Flanagan.[8] She arrived in England in time to attend the second performance, and her criticisms of it elicited from Eliot the admission that

> on retrospect *The Dance of Death* was rather a mess. Perhaps Doone spent his time in trying to arrange choreography for people who couldn't dance—when I saw the bathers I thought there was something to be said for the ordinary musical comedy chorus after all—and so the verbal part got rather neglected. Certainly it was impossible to hear what they said.[9]

Actually, they had very little to *say* at all but the Group, not surprisingly, had not overcome the difficulties inherent in the mixture of music, dance and words. Moreover, they had fallen between two stools in attempting to combine a *Bewegung-schor*—the 'lay' chorus advocated by Laban —with professional dancers and singers. Nevertheless, the response of the audience indicated that the Group had achieved at least a fair measure of success. Eliot's second thoughts probably came less from the quality of the performance than from a clearer sense of what was uncongenial to him in Auden's form in itself. It was a form that, ironically enough, incorporated some of the radical suggestions that Eliot himself had made.

In the twenties and up to about the time he began to work in the theatre, Eliot's ideal theatre poet was one who would have 'a part to play in society as worthy as that of the music-hall comedian', who could give 'expression to the life of an audience, in raising it to a kind of art'.[10] He insisted on the actuality of the performance in itself:

> The play, like a religious service, should be a stimulant to make life more tolerable and augment our ability to live; it should stimulate partly by the action of vocal rhythms on what, in our ignorance, we call the nervous system.[11]

Auden had embraced this conception of drama as celebration and, as Eliot had suggested, looked to the popular theatre for models. He also found the complement to Eliot's concern with 'vocal rhythms' in Cocteau's corresponding emphasis on the visual rhythms of line and body. Most significantly, Auden had found in workers' theatre a socio-political context that might be adapted to such theatrical experimentation.

As Eliot imitated and parodied *The Dance of Death* in *The Rock*, he self-consciously diverged from Auden's experiment, finding that some of his own earlier suggestions for a more sensuously vital theatre were not, after all, conducive to the effects he wanted. After an uncertain moment (in which probably he contemplated a new version of *Sweeney Agonistes*) he began to fashion a dramaturgy in which, over the course of his development as a playwright, stage movement, gesture and music would become less and less important. He praised Martin Shaw's music for *The Rock* but this part of the conception was Browne's, not Eliot's. In *Murder in the Cathedral* liturgical music was essential but the chorus physically immobile. In the later plays even musicality in the verse tended to be strained out and stage movement was strictly circumscribed by setting and situation—hence, partly, Eliot's difficulties with the visualization and disposition of the Eumenides in *The Family Reunion*.

This progressive curtailment of the sensuousness of the theatre was unexpected in one who had been so preoccupied with its ritual origins and had a high regard for the music-hall. It was partly, no doubt, a matter of temperament, of a certain disaffection with the human body; and, with respect to the use of the chorus—the element that dominated Eliot's attention in the thirties—there was the powerful consideration that *how* the chorus was used, quite apart from anything it might say, carried strong ideological connotations, of which he became acutely aware.

In his new 'Cochranesque' scenario for *The Rock*, Martin Browne had ended the first part with an air raid scene, but Eliot 'had certain qualms about any suggestions of the late war' and looked about for 'some other appropriate catas-

trophe'.[12] Whereas Auden could play on the Great War nerve
to good Marxist effect, it was harder, in 1934, to put that
cataclysm in a convincing Christian perspective. Eliot found
more up-to-date and, for a Church of England audience, less
contentious material nearer at hand in the temptations of
Communism, Fascism and unmoderated capitalism. Out of
these foils to Christianity, he made the only scene in *The Rock*
for which he was wholly responsible. This scene, wrote
Browne,

> proves how acute his dramatic sense already was. It
> makes use of the methods of the German Expressionists
> of the twenties, reminding one of some of the earlier plays
> of Auden and Isherwood who were influenced by them.[13]

But Eliot's acuteness was actually a matter of adapting
Auden's experiment and any reminiscence of Expressionism
that does not derive from Auden is indiscernible.

Eliot's ophidian Plutocrat, bearing a golden calf, is a close
equivalent of Auden's Theatre Manager with his hamper of
nostalgia, though Eliot's workers resist the temptation of
materialism. The Redshirts and the Blackshirts portrayed by
Eliot are likewise ineffectual but in other respects they strongly
resemble Auden's Chorus in its Communist and Fascist
phases. As in *The Dance of Death*, Eliot uses choric
formations, facile rhymes and broad caricature for his satiric
effects. But whereas Auden had contrasted Communists and
Fascists choreographically as well as verbally, Eliot's two
groups are indistinguishable physically though sharply contrasted verbally. The brief Red revolution in *The Dance of
Death* is a spontaneous free-for-all and the Fascist takeover
highly regimented. Eliot, by contrast, calls for 'military
formation' for both parties, which, in the case of the Redshirts,
obviously contradicts their words. As in the very name
'Redshirts', they are choreographically the Tweedledees to the
Fascist Tweedledums. Prosodically, however, Eliot's parties
are distinct. His Blackshirts chant monotonously regular
verse:

We're law-keeping fellows who make our own laws—
And we welcome SUBSCRIPTIONS IN AID OF THE CAUSE!

The verse of the Redshirts draws even more attention to
itself:

Our verse
is free
as the wind on the steppes
as love in the heart of the factory worker
thousands and thousands of steppes
millions and millions of workers
                              all working
                                 all loving. . . .[14]

The association of politics with choreography and prosody,
burlesque though it is, indicates Eliot's sensitivity to the
ideological implications of the form in itself. So, much more
seriously, does his use of two distinct kinds of chorus. The
Audenesque choruses of Redshirts and Blackshirts in *The
Rock* are mere straw men while the *real* chorus is the vehicle
of Eliot's poetry.

When Derek Verschoyle described *The Rock* as a 'contribution to English dramatic literature', Eliot scrupulously
repudiated the evaluation. *The Rock*, he said, embodied no
such pretensions: in his contribution to it, his 'only seriously
dramatic aim was to show that there is a possible *rôle* for the
Chorus'.[15] The Eliot who, in 1934, found no connection
between the form of revue and dramatic literature was
obviously on a different tack from the Eliot of a decade
earlier, who had observed that 'our problem should be to
take a form of entertainment, and subject it to the process
which would leave it a form of art'. Even in 1920, though, he
had added a caution:

I am aware that this is a dangerous suggestion to make.
For every person who is likely to consider it seriously
there are a dozen toymakers who would leap to tickle
aesthetic society into one more art debauch.[16]

In 1934, the danger lay in a different quarter: there were serious artists bent on transmuting forms of entertainment not into aesthetic toys but into propaganda. The use of the chorus crystallized the issue.

What Eliot did *not* have in mind as a possible function of the chorus was the inculcation of revolutionary, mass sentiment, as proposed by the contributor to *New Theatre*, who proclaimed that

> mass dance, or choric dance, as well as the folk dance, can be put to revolutionary uses ... set simple and clear patterns of group movement into a form that presents our revolutionary ideas movingly and meaningfully. The dancer learns to move communally, to express with others a simple class-conscious idea.[17]

To ensure against ideological error, the author suggested that there should be a committee 'to see that the leader thoroughly understands the theme'. In artistic as in other activities, communality needed strong direction!

For Socialists, choral singing was a hallowed tradition (on which, in 1925, the National Executive of the Labour Party had put its imprimatur by sponsoring a Choral Union) and choral song, speech and movement became characteristic features of Workers' Theatre Movement productions. The chorus implied two kinds of unity that reflected each other: artistic integration and the corporate identity of its members.

As burlesques of the Auden–WTM kind of chorus, Eliot's Redshirts and Blackshirts in *The Rock* are the counterfeits that give negative definition to the real thing, which is a chorus that does not represent groups, does not sing, dance or even move much but speaks as the abstract voice of the *individual* against group behaviour:

There is no help in parties, none in interests,
There is no help in those whose souls are choked and swaddled
In the old winding sheets of place and power
Or the new winding sheets of mass-made thought.

O world! forget your glories and your quarrels,
Forget your groups and your misplaced ambitions,
We speak to you as individual men;
As individuals alone with GOD.
Alone with GOD, you first learn brotherhood with men.[18]

The chorus, said Eliot, 'were speaking *for me*, not uttering words that represented any supposed character of their own'.[19] In the dramatic context, this authorial voice was also 'the Voice of the Church in God'. The use of a number of voices speaking in unison was a way of making an emphatic, authoritative and impersonal, yet dramatic, statement. His stationary chorus, dressed to look like stone carvings and speaking poetry, had much more to do with liturgical usage than with Greek tragedy and nothing to do with either Cochran's or Auden's dancer-singers. In his true choruses, Eliot was trying to transcend world and flesh; Auden, in his, to animate the body politic. Eliot's poetry *in* the theatre was dedicated to the sacred: Auden's poetry *of* the theatre celebrated the profane; or so it appeared.

Although Eliot's ideas about the theatre were diverging from those of Auden, and though Auden and the Group were loosely considered to be Communist sympathizers, Eliot joined the Group Theatre in 1934 and remained a consistent, though cautious, supporter. He agreed to Doone's proposal for a production of *Sweeney Agonistes* in Cambridge in May 1934 and tried to help with the arrangements.[20] In the event the Cambridge plan fell through and *Sweeney Agonistes* was presented in the Group Theatre Rooms later in the year. That was an important event for Eliot, one of the instances in which his association with Doone and the Group Theatre substantially affected his development as a playwright.

Eliot and Doone remained in contact for many years. On Doone's side there was deep admiration for Eliot's poetry and on Eliot's an appreciation of Doone's artistic conviction and instinct, from which he profited. When Eliot showed him an early draft of *Murder in the Cathedral*, Doone made a suggestion of fundamental importance to the structure of the play.[21] Even more significantly Doone's production of *Sweeney Agonistes* anticipated Eliot's theme in *The Family Reunion*. The missing element in their association was the new play that Doone hoped for in 1934. Sixteen years later he was still hoping for it. But the moment had been and gone in the first phase of Eliot's career as a practising playwright when, for a time, he did, apparently, intend to write a play suitable for production by the Group.

In February 1934 Eliot was planning 'something new of the same kind' as *Sweeney Agonistes*, on which he intended to make a start after finishing *The Rock*.[22] In July he still had it in mind but shortly thereafter he accepted the commission for the Canterbury Festival and this assumed priority. At this point, Eliot put aside the 'something . . . of the same kind' as *Sweeney Agonistes*. It has often been regretted that Eliot did not pursue the *Sweeney Agonistes* experiment but it appears that he may, in fact, have done so and that *The Superior Landlord* was the result.

The Superior Landlord is the complete scenario for a Sweeney play. It was not written before the published fragments—though this has been assumed.[23] In the scenario, Eliot sketched an entirely new version of the earlier work. As in the published fragments, the action of the scenario takes place in the flat rented by Pereira and occupied by Dusty and Doris. In the course of it, various 'Intruders' (as Eliot, apparently following Auden and Medwall, calls them) interrupt the bottle party going on in the flat. One of these Intruders is Pereira himself, who turns nasty and threatens the girls with eviction. He is defeated in argument by Sweeney, who accuses him of subletting the flat illegally (or using it for immoral purposes) and reveals that he in turn is *Pereira*'s landlord—the 'superior landlord' of the title.

Sweeney, Dusty and Doris are expecting the arrival of Mrs Porter, who eventually arrives singing (like the Announcer and Chorus in *The Dance of Death*) a modified version of 'Casey Jones':

And the neighbours knew by the shrieks and the groans
That the man at the throttle was Casey Jones.[24]

At the climax of a stichomythic quarrel, Mrs Porter is killed by
Sweeney; probably not for the first time, since he shows no
surprise at her later resurrection.

The scenario ends with a hymeneal procession led by
Sweeney and Mrs Porter. This allegorical reunion of body and
soul is accompanied by Mendelssohn's 'Wedding March', a
seemingly deliberate allusion to the end of *The Dance of
Death*, where the same music is used for the entrance of Karl
Marx. *The Superior Landlord* might be described as an
attempt to find a theatrical form answering *The Dance of
Death* in which to express spiritual desolation and renewal.

At one point, Eliot made his whole play into the dream of
one of the Intruders, 'the Tenant Downstairs', but he thought
better of this idea. He also deleted in the scenario an interlude
between the parts that would have been an appropriate piece
for the Group Theatre:

> INTERLUDE. As the Chorus ends a Viennese wal[t]z is
> heard beginning very softly. The actors assume fixed
> positions, and the stage becomes dimmer and the scene
> melts away. The music becomes louder. A bright sky blue
> drop scene descends, and two dancers (male and female)
> drift across in a ballet, in period-costumes. Ballet last[s]
> only about 3 minutes. After they have left the stage a
> diseuse (hidden) recites a passage of poetry which will be
> in complete contrast to the verse of the play. The whole
> scene is completely in contrast in setting and mood to the
> play itself, but melts into it at beginning and end. The
> scene rises on
>   Part II

The beginning of this second part is distinctly reminiscent of
the Group Theatre production of the fragments:

> The party has been going on for some time, many empty
> bottles, remains of food on plates. The end of the

> Interlude music overlaps the gramophone of the party.
> The men are sitting about stolidly, while Doris and Dusty
> are wal[t]zing together like two automatic dolls. As the
> record ends and the girls return to their seats . . .

As for why Eliot should have abandoned *The Superior
Landlord* the reasons would not be far to seek. The piece was
too Audenesque and Group Theatre-ish and a less promising
basis for new work than the play that (probably) had
overtaken it, *Murder in the Cathedral*. Particularly after the
abandonment of the plans for a Poets' Theatre which, as will
be seen, brought Eliot into close collaboration with the Group
Theatre and under some pressure to produce new work
quickly, he would have had no compelling motive to do more
with Sweeney.

Whether it was *The Superior Landlord* or some other work
that Eliot (before he embarked on *Murder in the Cathedral*)
had in mind, it included a chorus, and he was admonitory
about the efforts the Group Theatre would have to make if
they were to perform it to his satisfaction:

> If I write the play I have in mind, it would require a
> chorus, and my recent experience warns me that choruses
> need long and arduous training.[25]

Doone correctly drew the inference that Eliot doubted the
Group Theatre's ability to produce an adequate verse-
speaking chorus and he also discovered that Auden now
shared Eliot's particular concern:

> I am getting on with the play and am completely recasting
> it in a way that will make it more suitable for the Group
> Theatre. My only difficult demand is a verse-speaking
> chorus which I think you will be able to provide. I gather
> Miss Fogerty's lot in *The Rock* were very good.[26]

What Auden had gathered was by common consent the case.
Trained by Elsie Fogerty and Gwynneth Thurburn, the chorus
gave the outstanding performance in *The Rock*; one that

contrasted sharply with the performances of the amateur players in the individual roles. In his new play, *The Chase*, Auden was using a chorus somewhat in the manner of *The Rock* or of Thomas Hardy's *The Dynasts*, with the function of making a commentary on the action rather than embodying it as in *The Dance of Death*. Auden's and Eliot's warnings and Elsie Fogerty's example were not lost on Doone, who began to emphasize training in verse speaking in the Group.

Eliot's misgivings about the Group Theatre were allayed by the production of *Sweeney Agonistes* in the Group Theatre Rooms in November 1934. It was billed as the first of a series of 'revues' and two performances were announced. They met with such an enthusiastic response that a third and, in intention, 'final' performance was given in December. On this occasion Yeats was present, and so was Brecht. The latter told Doone that *Sweeney* was 'the best thing he had seen for a long time and by far the best thing in London' and he offered the Group a play.[27] Desmond MacCarthy also attended the December performance and, by making it the subject of a broadcast, put 9 Great Newport Street on the theatrical map. Nothing loath to meet the demand from the beau monde for tickets, the Group put on more performances in January and February. These did good service in making the Group known and in helping to create a following for Eliot the dramatist.

Eliot himself was 'very pleasantly surprised by Doone's skill in presentation in these circumstances, and the general level of intelligence' shown in the production.[28] But the circumstances were scarcely a hindrance. In the Rooms, Doone was able to exploit the Group's slender material resources to best advantage with a text well suited to the place, the players and himself. Eliot's fragments were utterly contemporary in feeling and their very fragmentariness—which Doone emphasized by a series of blackouts—gave the effect of a preconceived Expressionist montage. It may even have been a consequence of Doone's production that Eliot thereafter left the fragments to stand by themselves and made no further attempt to incorporate them in a fuller work.

In his production, Doone thoroughly subordinated the minor characters to make Sweeney the central figure in a *danse macabre*, and he added a violent conclusion—suggested by Eliot's poem 'Sweeney Erect'—that rounded out the action. John Moody, as Sweeney, gave a spine-chilling performance; the small cast, drawn from the Group, was finely orchestrated; and in the enforced intimacy of the Rooms, the audience was deeply and very deliberately implicated in the action.

Desmond MacCarthy's review was a great help in arousing the expectations of the spectators who found their way to this 'underground' theatre at the top of the stairs:

> I had a rather out of the way experience as a playgoer the other night. I had received a notice from some players of whom I had not heard before. They called themselves 'The Group Theatre', and the circular announced that I should be able to see at No. 9 Great Newport Street the performance of an unfinished play by Mr T. S. Eliot. . . . I found myself in an L-shaped room on the third floor, round which chairs had been arranged . . . leaving an empty space in the middle. . . .[29]

MacCarthy went on to give a vivid sketch of the 'grisly impressiveness' of the presentation in the empty space. His impressions can be amplified from other records to give some idea of what the performance was like.[30]

The playing space is set as a seedy bedsitter with no definite boundary between it and the audience. The furniture is rudimentary: a gate-leg table, two upright chairs, a small red carpet, a sideboard and, ominously, a black-covered divan. The sideboard doubles as a bar and dressing-table. There is a preliminary blackout and the pink-gelled light comes up on two young women seated at the table. Wearing half-masks which give them a plump-cheeked 'resemblance to a common kind of prettiness', they appear to be from 'the class of rather humble prostitutes'. (These masks, made by Robert Medley, revealed 'the hidden terrors behind the normal everyday expression'.[31] said Auden.) Dusty is smoking and eating chocolates. Doris, wearing a dressing-gown with feathery trimmings, goes to titivate at the sideboard. They exchange the desultory lines about Pereira. Dusty, answering the telephone, makes Doris's excuses to Pereira—'She's got her feet in mustard and water'—as Doris pours drinks.

The girls turn to fortunetelling. The closeness of the audience requires that the right cards be preset. The two of spades signifies a coffin—for herself, Doris supposes. She flops on to the black divan which would serve her, equally compliant unto copulation or unto death, as couch or bier. The mood of foreboding and ennui is dissipated by the arrival of Wauchope, Horsfall, Krumpacker and Klipstein. Their masks have heavily masculine, aggressive features. Klipstein (played by Desmond Walter-Ellis, the Group's chief comedian) accompanies their songs on the accordion. According to Doone's programme note, they are portraying the 'empty . . . heartiness' of a decadent society, 'immoral but never immoral enough'.[32] There are drinks all round, a clinking of glasses, a little sexual groping and dancing to the gramophone. The first fragment ends with Wauchope and Dusty collapsing, in drunken laughter, on the floor. Blackout. In the dark the gramophone plays on and somebody groans.

The lights go up on Sweeney facing Doris across the table. The other characters sit apart, detached from the action as a 'commentating chorus'. They are to be understood as, in Doone's words, the 'Eumenides or Bogies of Sweeney's persecution'. They sing Eliot's song, set by William Alwyn, as a dreamy South Seas background to Sweeney's confrontation with Doris, and they speak the final chorus, which Eliot wrote to the rhythm of a street drill, into tumblers that distort the sound—'When you're alone in the middle of the night. . . .'

Sweeney does not wear a mask and Doris has removed hers. Nothing like the retired pugilist that Eliot imagined Sweeney to be, Moody wears pinstripe trousers and black jacket. Steel spectacles complete the image of a sinister solicitor's clerk. MacCarthy described the ambiguity in the playing of the scene:

If you want to suggest in terms of actuality retribution for some sordid crime, could it be better done than this? Sweeney is speaking. You must imagine a man under a lamp sitting at a table . . . speaking the lines . . . with unemphatic horror, speaking out of himself, out of his inner terror. He is addressing the girl opposite him, but he is also addressing us: it is half a sinister soliloquy, half a confession—or perhaps a threat to her;

> *I knew a man once did a girl in*
> *Any man might do a girl in*
> *Any man has to, needs to, wants to,*
> *Once in a lifetime, do a girl in. . . .*

Sweeney suits the deed to the word when, at the end of the play, he begins to pursue Doris round the table, a cut-throat razor in his hand. The audience hears a police whistle, a scream from Doris, a knocking at the door . . . then blackout. If this has been Sweeney's nightmare, in which all the characters except his victim are projections from his mind, the audience has experienced it too.

Nevill Coghill was powerfully impressed by the 'exquisite blend of violence and restraint' in the performance but perplexed by what it meant:

> The cool, rich, level voice of Mr Doone . . . saying 'Let Mr Sweeney continue with his story,' sent a shiver down my back. He offered an almost entirely different interpretation of the play to that I had worked out. As he presented it it was a study in the psychology of a Crippen; he made it seem we were all Crippens at heart. . . . I went away overwhelmed and bewildered, yet reassured of the greatness of the play in this admirable production.[33]

Coghill later asked Eliot if Doone's production coincided with the authorial intention. If Sweeney in the Group Theatre Rooms seemed to 'justify the ways of Crippen to woman' that must be what the work meant, Eliot allowed, even though that was not what *he* had meant at all. But though Eliot was at pains to point out on a number of occasions that Doone's *Sweeney* was 'entirely alien' to his original conception, his high opinion of the production was not at all diminished by this difference. What he had actually meant was not discernible, or at least not producible, from the fragments as they stood. 'In order to be produced at all, in fact, with any effect, the fragments have to be interpreted differently from my original meaning,' he said later.[34] That meaning probably included, as *The Superior Landlord* did, an intimation of the transcendence of mortal life and death.

If Eliot's meaning—as opposed to that of his work—did not emerge from the Group's production of *Sweeney*, that production did help to elicit his meaning in *Murder in the Cathedral*. Just as Doone had subordinated the minor characters in *Sweeney Agonistes*, so he suggested that what Eliot had conceived as objective, historically based characters in a draft of *Murder in the Cathedral* should become projections from Thomas's own consciousness. Adopting the suggestion, Eliot made them into the Tempters. Eliot was even more fundamentally indebted to Doone, it appears. Taking a hint from Eliot's epigraph to *Sweeney*, Doone presented the protagonist as 'a modern Orestes', which is what the main character of Eliot's next play, *The Family Reunion*, would be. Eliot and Doone obviously understood each other very well.[35]

5
Ends and Means: The Group Theatre
1934–5

Only a cause can give the bond, the common
assumptions between author and audience which the
serious dramatist needs.[1]

T. S. ELIOT, 1934

Pull out your purse, then, pay or we perish
Act on the instant, your onus is ours
You shall not hunger at the harvest your efforts yield.[2]

W. H. AUDEN, 1935

The production of *The Dance of Death* not only encouraged
Auden to go on working with the Group Theatre but was an
incentive to other theatre-minded poets. So, at the beginning
of 1934, the Group's prospects for new plays were excellent:
Auden promised one, Stephen Spender another, and there was
reason to suppose that Eliot might let the Group produce the
play that he had in mind. It was questionable, though, whether
the Group could develop into an acting ensemble capable of
collaborating fruitfully with the poets. Auden had half
succeeded in moulding the Group Theatre into a theatrical
commonwealth of participants but the last thing its leaders
wanted was to continue in the manner of a semi-amateur
society, even if such a precarious position could be maintained.

Since the Group wanted poets for playwrights, composers
for musicians and painters for designers, the fact that Murrill,
Medley and Auden had artistic vocations outside the theatre
accorded well with the Diaghilevian premise of combining,

not subordinating, the arts. These three also had jobs as teachers and, though teaching was not utterly incompatible with artistic production, they were all under strain. Herbert Murrill, as performer as well as composer, spent an immense amount of unpaid time and energy on the Group Theatre; Robert Medley exhausted himself pursuing three occupations at once; and Auden would eventually rebel against being, economically speaking, an amateur playwright. Still, the crying need in 1934 was not to improve the conditions under which these artists were working; it was to find the actors the wherewithal to live, that is to say, to achieve a professional status for the Group.

At the beginning of 1934 it looked as though the Group Theatre would become, of necessity, an amateur society in which only those with a regular income from some outside source could afford to be active, in so far as their paid work allowed them to be so; or an organization like the Stage Society, bringing like-minded professionals together on special occasions. It was in a desperate attempt to steer between this Scylla and Charybdis and form a professional ensemble that the Group made a general appeal for financial support over and above membership subscriptions.

Tyrone Guthrie, speaking from the stage after the second performance of *The Dance of Death*, opened the campaign. The Group Theatre was asking for money to enable Doone, Auden, a designer (presumably Medley), a composer (probably Murrill) and twenty actors to retire 'to a house in Suffolk for intensive training; under contract to give the Group Theatre in exchange for board and lodging their whole time for six months'. Auden was to write a new play and adapt others. While they were in Suffolk, the Group would perform frequently for local people. When they returned to London they would stage Auden's work, the play promised by Spender and perhaps another by an unnamed playwright (probably Eliot, possibly MacNeice). The estimated cost of the scheme was £500, of which the Group Theatre had £100 in hand and the promise of as much again.[3]

The low financial estimate and the severity of the terms for the prospective company attested to the idealism of the authors of the appeal and betrayed their ingenuousness. Their annual fortnights of 'Summer Study' in Suffolk had been practical and enjoyable busmen's holdiays but the proposed retreat was an ill-considered imitation of the Compagnie des Quinze. It must have been obvious that the sum sought would scarcely pay for their keep; that there was no provision for the cost of the productions that were eventually to be mounted; and that to attempt to form an ensemble, rehearse several new plays and be a light unto East Anglia, all at once, was a fuzzy plan, to say the least. Coming as it did immediately after Auden's satire, the idea of a country colony must have provoked a certain amount of amusement at the Group's expense. In a more serious vein, Eliot warned them of the dangers inherent in collective rustication. He also agreed, however, to vouch for the Group Theatre's bona fides, as did Lilian Baylis, E. McKnight Kauffer, Charles Laughton and— the man who knew most about the difficulties involved — Michel Saint-Denis.[4]

The appeal failed to raise the requisite £300 and, in any case, there was some doubt whether as many as twenty sufficiently talented and dedicated actors could be found. The Group would have done better to set about acquiring a hall in London—which was what Saint-Denis actually did when, with the failure of the Group Theatre to become an equivalent of his Quinze, the field was left open for him to test his theatrical principles in England.

While the Group was trying to fund a period of training in Suffolk, Saint-Denis and the Quinze were struggling to survive in a country house in Beaumanoir in Burgundy. Two members of the company there, Marius Goring and Vera Poliakoff, were also members of the Group Theatre. Both had played in *The Dance of Death* before joining Saint-Denis in France. A few months after the Group Theatre launched its appeal, Goring was attempting to raise funds in England to support the French ensemble. These efforts were unsuccessful; but

when Saint-Denis decided to move to England, £5,000—of
which a considerable portion came from Tyrone Guthrie —
was quickly raised to found the London Theatre Studio under
his direction.

Saint-Denis's first priority was a theatre school:

> The kind of actor I wanted was not to be found ready
> made. Training and experiment seemed to me more
> important than the quick gathering together of a
> company without meaning or unity.[5]

He held fast to this principle but he was not—as has been
claimed—the first director in England to extend 'the ideas of
Diaghilev and Cecchetti . . . to the training of actors'.[6] In this
respect, as in other ways, Rupert Doone and the Group
Theatre had prepared the ground for him.

In Marius Goring's statement of them, the overall aims of
the London Theatre Studio were almost identical with those of
the Group Theatre. They were:

> To produce a homogeneous group of people working in
> the theatre—a troupe that can work by itself and for
> itself; with writers, musicians, mechanics trained to
> support it. As well as being a school, it will be a dramatic
> centre and will attract to itself many people who are
> already in the theatre.[7]

The acting troupe, as distinct from playwrights, musicians,
etc., had a clear priority in the London Theatre School and, in
this way, its emphasis was different from that of the Group
Theatre. And though Saint-Denis 'experimented a great deal
with the relationship between music, the spoken word, and
choral expression', he insisted that his 'chief practical purpose
was wholly and above all to serve interpretation'. This
attitude, adopted as he said 'to avoid conceit and extravagance', contrasted with Doone's insistence on an essentially
creative role, beyond interpretation, for the performer.

It was not merely an accident of fortune that the London
Theatre Studio and the Group Theatre succeeded and failed in

complementary ways. The Group Theatre established neither company nor school, and no considerable actors emerged from it, though some played for it; but it did produce new plays and it anticipated styles of presentation that came into the English theatre decades later by other routes. It was also the point of entry into the theatre for a clutch of notable artists of whom several would gravitate towards opera. The London Theatre Studio, on the other hand, produced no new drama and did not form a company but it had a considerable influence on acting style.

Despite the coincidence of major aims, the Group's admiration for Saint-Denis and good will on all sides, nobody even considered a merger between the London Theatre School and the Group Theatre. Saint-Denis did direct a play for the Group Theatre's 1935–6 Westminster Theatre season but this arrangement was not intended to lead to full collaboration. Apart from the impossibility of dividing the leadership of any combined effort between two such personalities as Doone and Saint-Denis, the Group Theatre's growing preoccupation with new plays and its willingness to put on politically tendentious ones was a divergence from its original objectives. And, partly under the influence of Auden and his political aesthetic, the Group's feeling for the 'low' forms of cabaret, revue, music-hall and melodrama had developed in a way that was decidedly, if not deliberately, incompatible with Saint-Denis's 'poetic realism'.

Early in 1934, while the Group Theatre was still looking for donations for itself, it gave performances for other charities. One, in April at the Westminster, in aid of the Kingsley Hall University Settlement, was a revival of *Lancelot of Denmark*, presented with Doone's (not to be confused with Auden's) 'Dance of Death', a mumming dance.[8] Another was a performance of *Fulgens and Lucrece* given in June in the grounds of Fulham Palace.[9] A few days later, the Group Theatre took the same production to Worcester College, Oxford. There, the warmth of the reception was partly based on the misunderstanding that the performers were a theatrical wing of the Oxford Group, an impression that the theme of the play—not inconsistent with Buchmanite doctrine—may have confirmed.

In August 1934, after the failure of its fund-raising campaign, the Group Theatre departed for the now customary fortnight in Suffolk. On this occasion they were based at Summerhill School and toured the locality with *East Lynne*, a play that gave them the opportunity to practise the kind of melodramatic roles that Auden was writing into his new play. After their return they rewarded themselves by turning some of the juicier material into revue sketches for one of their Midnight Cabarets. Classes and readings were also resumed in the autumn, and a series of talks begun that went on through the winter. Among the speakers in the Rooms were: Tyrone Guthrie, John Wilmot MP, Nevill Coghill, Alistair Cooke, Geoffrey Whitworth, W. J. Turner, Oliver Elton, Kurt Jooss, Herbert Read and T. S. Eliot, who took 'The Use of a Chorus for a Modern Theatre' as his topic. Read spoke about 'Contemporary Form and Contemporary Content' and Guthrie about 'Naturalism'.[10] The membership was told that Auden's new play (*The Chase*) had been put at the disposal of the Group. Privately, though, Doone considered that *The Chase* was not ready to go into rehearsal and so *Sweeney Agonistes* became the main production effort. At this time, too, Doone brought the Group (without consulting its members) into a consortium that planned to start a new Poet's Theatre.

One of the instigators of this venture was Ashley Dukes. The author of *The Man with a Load of Mischief* and other plays, the translator who had done most to introduce German Expressionism into England, a critic and a connoisseur, Dukes was also the owner of the tiny Mercury Theatre at Notting Hill that his wife, Marie Rambert, used as her ballet studio. Doone had danced there for Rambert and had been the choreographer for Dukes's first dramatic production there in 1933.[11] Now Dukes offered to back a season of plays by poets to be performed by the Group Theatre at the Mercury.

The original suggestion may have come from W. B. Yeats, who, in any case, energetically promoted it. What Yeats wanted was a theatre based in London where his own work would be performed alongside that of the radicals, Eliot and Auden. He 'chose' the Group he said, because they could sing and dance and were 'adepts in concerted movement'.[12] And as well as an artistic motive he had the personal one of advancing the career of his mistress, the actress Margot Collis.

In October, Yeats began to organize with his old energy, plotting with Doone and securing Eliot's active co-operation. Earlier in the month he and Dukes had attended a theatre congress in Rome at which Yeats spoke of the founding of the Abbey Theatre and Dukes about the importance of the little theatre movement in England.[13] In Rome, Dukes prophesied the emergence of English equivalents of Eugene O'Neill and the Provincetown Players.

Dukes further prepared the ground for the new Poets' Theatre in one of his regular articles in *Theatre Arts Monthly*. Asserting that *The Dance of Death* and *The Rock* 'must be considered as primitives of a new school', he continued:

> When in a few years' time the new school is in full productivity, the primitives will be played again with better chances in performance as well as appreciation. For the present nearly everything in the technique of presentation is against them—which means everything from the first architecture of the playhouse to the last actor's gesture.[14]

The last actor was, of course, a member of the Group Theatre, which in Dukes's view was not a vital constituent of the new school. He approved of the collaboration of playwright and company but what he had in mind was 'a small regular company' of his own.[15]

At its most expansive, the Poets' Theatre season at the Mercury was to comprise *The Dance of Death* and *Sweeney Agonistes* in a double bill, three plays by Yeats (including his new *A Full Moon in March*), Auden's *The Chase* and Eliot's

Murder in the Cathedral (which was to be presented by the Group at the Mercury prior to the Canterbury performance). But, after several months of negotiation, these plans were wrecked by the suspicions, muddles and jealousies of the collaborators, among whom only Eliot seems to have acted really constructively.

Dukes mischievously played on Yeats's fears that the Group Theatre, being 'Communist' and out of sympathy with his romanticism, might undermine his plays in production. Warily, Yeats insisted that Guthrie should be the director of his work, even though he had earlier found Doone's ideas for *A Full Moon in March* very exciting.[16] Doone himself soon became lukewarm to a scheme of which he was not, by any means, in control.

The complexity of the misunderstandings was such that the real artistic differences scarcely surfaced. Eliot was chiefly concerned with getting actors who could speak verse; Yeats with the combination of music, choric movement and poetry and with presenting a contrast between his and the younger poets' styles; Dukes's ambition was to be midwife to a new, non-political poetic drama. Yeats had the authority to reconcile the artistic claims of poets, musicians, designers and directors but much of the time he was out of London, trying to keep abreast of events by post.[17]

While the planning for the Poets' Theatre was going on, *Sweeney Agonistes* opened the Group's 'revue series' in the Rooms. Several cabaret entertainments followed but no more plays were presented in the Group's own space. This was not for lack of suitable material, for Auden's *Paid on Both Sides* and Yeats's chamber plays were at hand. Eliot, in fact, urged a Group Theatre production of one of Yeats's plays but his suggestion was not taken up. That Yeats himself would have been interested seems to be indicated by his last plays, in which the influence of the 'satiric' style of Auden and Eliot is evident and which imply some such playing space as the Group Theatre Rooms. As he pointed out in 1934 (in a book that he sent to Doone), he had already written plays that 'should suit

Cellars and Garrets' of Communists or Republicans.[18] In such places—as opposed to some aristocratic drawing room—the Prologue to *The Death of Cuchulain* might 'spit three times' without violating decorum. In the Group Theatre Rooms, Yeats would have defied the new 'vile age' on its own ground.[19]

Had the 'revue series' in the Rooms continued as it began, it might have served to develop the Group as an avant-garde company working outside the professional theatre. But that was not what they wanted. What they were looking for was an opportunity to work in a thoroughly professional setting; and in the summer of 1935 they got their wish.

Ormerod Greenwood, acting as 'buffer and interpreter' for Doone, successfully negotiated an arrangement whereby Anmer Hall agreed to back and 'present' the Group Theatre in a six-month season at the Westminster Theatre. Hall agreed also to make various improvements in the theatre, including the construction of an apron stage, but he was not so obliging as to give the Group a completely free hand. He, Gillian Scaife and Doone assumed the artistic direction of the season, while Greenwood, Moody, Medley and Murrill took the key artistic and administrative positions.

In June, Doone made his first suggestions for plays: John Skelton's *Magnificence*, Marlowe's *Edward II*, Sheridan's *The School for Scandal*, Ibsen's *Peer Gynt*, Ernst Toller's *No More Peace!*, *The Dance of Death* and *Sweeney Agonistes* in a double bill, and *The Dog Beneath the Skin* (as *The Chase* had now become). It was an ambitious and considered list, with a thematic focus on political and individual integrity. Auden's hand in it was obvious. He was reading Skelton at the time and thought highly (then, but not later) of the Tudor poet's dramatic treatment of the corruption of a ruler swayed by bad counsellors and his redemption by good ones.[20] *Edward II* had not been recently revived in England, but the fact that the German adaptation of the play by Brecht and Lion Feucht-wanger had made a great impression some years earlier may have been in Auden's mind, and its treatment of interwoven homosexual and political motivations was doubtless of interest to him.[21] Marlowe's theme amplified Skelton's, and Toller's *No More Peace*! which also has to do with a dispossessed ruler, was congruent with both.[22]

The Skelton, Marlowe and Toller proposals were not accepted: the rest passed into the announced programme. *Peer Gynt* followed naturally from the Group Theatre's earlier success with the 'experimental reading' of the play and, moreover, its theme and episodic structure stood to illuminate *The Dog Beneath the Skin*. It was to be given in a new translation made specially for the Group by the Communist poet, Randall Swingler. The remaining play from Doone's list, *The School for Scandal*, was a favourite within the Group, several of whom had played minor roles in Harcourt Williams's 1933 production.

Greenwood tried to get Shaw's newest play, *The Simpleton of the Unexpected Isles*, which had recently been staged at the Malvern Festival. Shaw said he would keep the Group Theatre in mind, but nothing came of the idea.[28] Doone tried to persuade Cocteau to collaborate in a production of his *Infernal Machine* or, failing that, let the Group Theatre make use of the text and the costumes from Jouvet's recent production. Jouvet refused to lend the costumes and Cocteau pleaded lack of funds, presumably because Doone had overlooked the matter of a fee.[24]

Doone's idea was that each production should run for two and a half weeks, with a new one opening every third week. There was nothing very surprising in repertory production at this rate—at the Festival Theatre, Guthrie and Hall had exceeded it—except it was altogether inconsistent with the Group Theatre's professed aims.

In August 1935, the *Sunday Times* announced that the Group Theatre was to be 'given a fair chance to get on its feet' and 'make a real attempt to establish an art theatre in London'. As a preliminary it was 'rehearsing in Suffolk rather on the lines of the famous Vieux Colombier company'.[25] At the same time, the Group Theatre opened a subscription campaign. In taking its 'biggest step forward', it wanted 1,000 subscribers to the season of 'nine or more modern and classical plays', including, now, *Timon of Athens* and, one of Gillian Scaife's favourites, *A Month in the Country*. Since the dates of the performances were indefinite, subscriptions were sold as books of nine tickets which could be exchanged for reservations to any performance.[26]

One of the ways in which the Group Theatre was ahead of its time was in its acute grasp of the utility of well-managed propaganda, but at the Westminster Theatre in 1935–6 it exceeded itself. The promotion of the season was peremptory, naïve and confusing, but one thing was made crystal clear: the Group Theatre's intention of forming 'a company trained in common'. In the course of the season, it became obvious that the Group Theatre had auctioned off its aims and ideals even as it was proclaiming them and it was lashed for its insincerity by such former supporters as Geoffrey Grigson and Michael Sayers. Privately, and from a distance, Edward Gordon Craig was equally scornful.

Early in 1935, Greenwood, who had been in sporadic contact with him for five years, solicited Craig's interest in the Group Theatre, apparently without effect.[27] Just before the Group Theatre opened its season, however, Craig—who was perhaps stirred by the attempts of Saint-Denis at the London Theatre Studio and John Gielgud at the New Theatre, as well as that of the Group, to form permanent companies—made a *pronunciamento* in *The Times*:

> It is, I suppose, quite well understood that you can only have a great theatre in any land if you have one building, one organization, one group, and one purpose, and the public of one mind. There can be no such thing as a great theatre if some of the actors are to be found playing in one playhouse today and going to play in another next month . . . and some dramatists coming in and out at odd times.[28]

An editorial in the same issue pointedly, and ominously for the Group, identified the main hindrance to theatrical excellence as the two-week repertory system. This Craig would have taken to be elementary. Nevertheless, Greenwood saw the glimmer of an opportunity to capture Craig for the Group Theatre's repertory season and offered to put at his 'disposal the Westminster Theatre and the Group Theatre organization and personnel'.[29] Craig was sufficiently intrigued to want to know what this meant. The Group Theatre wanted his help but was it prepared to help *him*? Did it have the money and people to realize *his* plan? Was it, in short, prepared to be *his* theatre? He had, he intimated, 'something of worth to give a company . . . in a theatre of my very own' but nothing on any other terms.[30]

The best offer Greenwood could make was 'a production in the Group Theatre season, on a very modest scale and in a manner which would involve compromise, but which would give some opportunity of testing the possibilities of co-operation'. He felt obliged to qualify even this modest bid with the confession of his doubts that Craig and Doone would be able to work in harmony, though he assured the master that Doone was anxious to do so.[31] Surprisingly, this did not put an end to the correspondence, which continued well into the season. It was not until mid-November that the hope and fear of Craig's descent finally receded: 'What I wanted to learn', said Craig, 'was whether the Group Theatre had an idea and a plan to carry it out with; and I can see neither. . . .'[32]

As assessed by Greenwood, the Group Theatre's strength when it embarked on the Westminster Theatre season was about 300, of whom one third were actors, 'mostly beginners, one or two already good, several promising, the rest hopelessly bad'. There were 'thirty or so writers . . . not all writing plays and a handful of painters, some with little experience in designing scenery or costumes'. Finally there was a 'tiny core' who supplied 'the motive power of the whole'.[33] Greenwood's misgivings about the Group were shared by Doone (who, in due course, would number Greenwood himself among the superfluous members) and this lack of solidarity was largely the result of the indefiniteness about the meaning of membership. Ideally all the members were participants, not

merely the supporters of a 'tiny core': in practice, participation, even for the aspirant performers among the membership,
meant merely paying a subscription.

The members of the 'tiny core' decided that a 'rough and
ready repertory company' drawn mostly from the membership
of the Group would be 'worse than useless'. It was also clear
that other directors besides Doone would be needed. The
twofold solution adopted by Hall and the Group's leaders was
to invite several directors each to select a play and cast it,
without being under any obligation to use members of the
Group. In this way a full, though partly nominal, Group
Theatre season could be presented, in which the Group
Theatre proper would appear 'at intervals'.[34]

By the end of July, Anmer Hall had signed up two of the
outside directors for the season: Nugent Monck, of the
Maddermarket Theatre, Norwich, who had had some
previous contact with the Group Theatre and much sympathy
with its aims; and John Wyse, who had neither. A third
director, appointed later, was John Fernald, well known for
his work with amateurs and with large casts. The last to be
appointed was Michel Saint-Denis, who had just directed his
first production in English; a translation of Obey's *Noé* with
John Gielgud in the title role.

Tyrone Guthrie was one of the directors named but his
contribution to the season was limited to the co-direction of
the revival of *The Dance of Death*. He and Doone might have
realized something like Guthrie's plan for a permanent
company working under two directors but Guthrie had other
priorities. Greenwood, who had persuaded him to join the
Group Theatre in the first place, was one of those most put out
by Guthrie's lack of commitment. Unlike Doone, Guthrie
always knew what he wanted from a production, was
considerate of others and capable of getting the best out of
them, Greenwood thought,

—BUT lacks most of what Doone has; a real integrity,
depth, sure judgement, and creative originality. . . . He

thinks he can serve the Group Theatre and Saint-Denis on the one hand and still make his West End/Broadway productions on the other.[35]

It would have been difficult to find a member of the Group Theatre who would not have gone 'commercial' given a good opportunity and, indeed, the Group Theatre was busily compromising itself in just that way. Greenwood was right, though, about the conflict in Guthrie between artistic ideals and the lure of the West End, as Guthrie himself later acknowledged.[36]

Apart from his ambition, there were other reasons for Guthrie to detach himself from the Group Theatre. One was his support of the London Theatre Studio, which was more precisely dedicated to the aims that he endorsed. Another was that it had become clearer that the Group Theatre was Doone's fiefdom. By his own account, Guthrie, at this time, was filled with 'missionary zeal' and, like many a lesser light, 'had the ambition—very secret and in no way practical; perhaps daydream is a more accurate description—to have a theatre of my own'.[37] Had Guthrie been pushier, had more conviction about the Group Theatre or felt more need of it, he could easily have taken a dominant role, but not without diminishing Doone's, whose ambition was no secret and no daydream.

Nor was the loosening of Guthrie's ties with the Group Theatre an entirely one-sided affair. In 1934, Auden intended to dedicate *The Chase* to him, doubtless in recognition of his contribution to *The Dance of Death*, but *The Chase* remained unpublished and its successor, *The Dog Beneath the Skin*, bore a very different, possibly unintentional, message to Guthrie. It was earmarked for production 'by the Group Theatre under the direction of Mr Doone'. This nicely ambivalent notice on the flyleaf not only appointed Doone the director of the play but also helped to establish the idea that the Group was Doone's private troupe.

In putting *The Dog Beneath the Skin* outside Guthrie's

bailiwick, Auden and Isherwood defined his position *vis-à-vis* the Group Theatre. Being a 'sucker for jokes and horseplay and for Great Moments, however corny', Guthrie would have relished the style of the new play; being also 'vehemently averse to political and social propaganda' (though he tried to be 'unprejudiced') he would have found its ideological tendency uncongenial.[38] Auden and Isherwood must have been aware of Guthrie's apolitical attitude, which was no secret; also, perhaps, of his fear that Auden would ruin the Group Theatre, in attempting to politicize it. Whatever his motives, or those of Auden and Isherwood, after the 1935 production of *The Dance of Death* Guthrie slipped anchor and took no further part in the Group's activities.

In 1934, the Group Theatre had been trying to finance six months of intensive training. In 1935, with no such preliminary, it began six months of intensive production—a theatrical gamble that made it look more like an impudent rival to the Old Vic than anything else. Greenwood explained the compromise to Craig:

> We appealed last year for a few hundred pounds to enable us to take a farmhouse, and train a company of young actors so that we should be fit to give plays when the time came. But everyone thought we were lunatics. When however we ask to put on a season of plays in London without any preparation or knowledge, we can find the necessary money and support without difficulty. Now who are the real lunatics? But what were we to do: we had to accept this offer or fade away from sheer starvation. So here we are, doing our best in a compromise way and hoping to prove at least that we are fit to have charge of things, so that at the end of six months here we may be able to impose our own ideas more fully.[39]

If Doone, Greenwood and the 'tiny core' underrated the Group, it was partly because they were desperately trying to steer clear of the whirlpool of amateurism, partly out of deference to Hall's prudence; but there was also an element of sheer opportunism and betrayal. It is impossible to suppose that the Group's aims would have been brought closer to realization even if the 'First Group Theatre Season' had achieved the kind of success its leaders sought. In the event, the season was an expensive failure and the productions in which the Group had departed furthest from its ostensible aims fared worst.

The Dog Beneath the Skin was a success, however. Like *The Dance of Death*, it forced the Group to use its own resources to the utmost. The production of *Dogskin* had demonstrated how mistaken the Group Theatre had been to undertake a repertory schedule that it could not sustain, since the Auden–Isherwood play ran much longer than its scheduled two and a half weeks. When the Group turned to the kind of work it professedly wanted to do, there was an enthusiastic audience ready for it; or, at least, for its new playwrights.

6
The First Group Theatre Season, 1935–6

I like the Group Season . . . like the way
members of the cast dart off the stage from time to
time and skirmish around the audience waving razors
or daggers or scimitars . . . and make their
appearances, like Gargantua, out of your left ear.[1]

E C. LARGE, JANUARY 1936

When *Sweeney Agonistes* and *The Dance of Death* opened the season at the Westminster Theatre on 1 October 1935, many actors were in roles they had played before and they had had sufficient rehearsal time in the theatre. Auden had been on hand, revising his text to meet the needs of performance, and Guthrie had come in to conduct some late rehearsals to very good effect.[2] The cast of *The Dance of Death* was smaller than for the private performances in 1934 and it now included a stronger contingent of dancers. If the Group was ready, for once, to face its audience, the theatre critics were ready for the Group. Derek Verschoyle, a consistent antagonist, put a shot across its bows from the *Spectator*:

> The Group Theatre, which after three years of incubation has now emerged to challenge and reform the theatrical world with these two brief charades . . . appears to be the latest recruit to the intellectual brigades now so demonstratively and fashionably engaged in the flight from reason.

He condemned the performers' 'acrobatic posturing' and 'tedious dancing', Auden's primitive, 'comic strip' style and, most emphatically, the 'crude inconsistency' of his attitudes to Fascist and Communist violence.[3] In all these particulars,

Verschoyle was echoing Ivor Brown, who was also doing his best to put the Communistic nuisance down:

> The Group Theatre might surely have arrived with some rather less tattered luggage than a creed of masks instead of faces, of acrobatics instead of acting, and of the 'liquidation' of a decadent bourgeoisie by the Up-and-Coming Saints in Scarlet. All these notions have been knocking around the Germanic and Muscovite theatres for years, and have been discredited because they are either dreary or nonsensical. This business, for example, about the inanition and moribundity of the bourgeoisie seems to me flatly contradictory to social fact.[4]

Brown demonstrated the vigour of the British bourgeoisie at some vituperative length but he missed the evidence, that *Punch* adduced, of the contradiction between the 'exuberant high spirits' of the youthful middle-class company and their representation of the supposed senescence of their class.[5] Brown did, however, concede some vitality to the performance:

> The Group Theatre seems to admire the methods of the corporate state: it specializes in mass movement and individual acting is scarce. The choruses and combined movements had been carefully rehearsed and were well done, and there were elements of good revue sketches in the burlesque of sun-bathers and Maypole-dancers. Only it was the kind of thing that Mr Charlot and Mr Cochran do so much better—and without all this pretence about the Dead Bourgeoisie and the Noble, Vital Proletarians.

The Group's theatrical style was both politically tainted *and* similar to Cochran's; or, to put it another way, Auden and the Group Theatre had found a way of imbuing a popular theatrical style with a new kind of meaning. Not that Brown and Verschoyle were inclined to attribute much originality to the production; or any to the authorial credo printed in the programme.

Auden's statement would come as no surprise to those who were 'aware of theatrical events in German and Parisian cellars during the past decade,' said Verschoyle: Auden was merely 'trotting out the most jaded nags from the Left Wing stable' by way of dramatic theory, said Brown:

> His pronouncement . . . about the art of drama is a re-hash of all that the Little Theatre Highbrows and Moscow 'fans' have been saying for fifteen years.

If we take the Muscophiles as the Workers' Theatre Movement and the Highbrows as Copeau, Cocteau and Eliot, then Brown was not far off the mark, though he ignored the interest and novelty of such a conjunction; and had he pursued his analysis further he might have recognized that Auden's red nags had seen earlier service in the cause of Christian theatre.

As spectators and performers were one body in the plays of Corpus Christi, so Auden now saw them as joint participants in an immanent *temporal* reality:

> DRAMA BEGAN AS THE ACT OF A WHOLE COMMUNITY. IDEALLY THERE WOULD BE NO SPECTATORS. IN PRACTICE EVERY MEMBER OF THE AUDIENCE SHOULD FEEL LIKE AN UNDERSTUDY.
>
> DRAMA IS ESSENTIALLY AN ART OF THE BODY. THE BASIS OF ALL ACTING IS ACROBATICS, DANCING, AND ALL FORMS OF PHYSICAL SKILL. THE MUSIC HALL, THE CHRISTMAS PANTOMIME, AND THE COUNTRY HOUSE CHARADE ARE THE MOST LIVING DRAMA OF TO-DAY. . . .
>
> THE SUBJECT OF DRAMA IS THE COMMONLY KNOWN, THE UNIVERSALLY FAMILIAR STORIES OF THE SOCIETY OR GENERATION IN WHICH IT IS WRITTEN. . . .
>
> DRAMATIC CHARACTERS ARE SIMPLIFIED, EASILY RECOGNIZABLE AND OVER LIFE-SIZE.
>
> DRAMATIC SPEECH SHOULD HAVE THE SAME COMPRESSED, SIGNIFICANT, AND UNDOCUMENTARY CHARACTER AS DRAMATIC MOVEMENT.
>
> DRAMA IN FACT DEALS WITH THE GENERAL AND UNIVERSAL. . . .[6]

One who found and approved a correspondence between Auden's propositions and the Group's attempt to demonstrate them was Michael Sayers. Under the headline 'Theatre at Last!', his review nicely counterbalanced Brown's:

> Here is theatre springing from the rhythms and idiom of your own life, the only life you know, with its slang and jazz heightened into poetry, your own fevers and languors made tragic, pathetic, comic, so that the action seems familiar, and at the same time disturbing, almost an exposure of your thoughts, a satire of your secrets.[7]

Sayers was hardly less concerned with the response of the rest of the audience than with the performance.

> The middle class element loathed it. Much preferable in its opinion, to be the Peeping Tom who pays for the privilege of prying through the fourth wall. . . . It is against this attitude that the Group Theatre has to fight.

Since the audience was middle class to a man, Sayers must have been referring to those whose unregenerate middle-class attitude was demonstrated by their reaction to the performance! As to the critics on the other side, 'nothing since the advent of Ibsen', said Sayers, had 'so successfully exposed [their] wretched incompetence. . . .'

Sayers would change his tune about the Group Theatre before the end of the season; and, already, the most eagerly welcoming reviewer of the 1934 performance had lost patience:

> It always seems unwise to shoot down one's own army, and for that reason criticism of the Group Theatre has tended to be propaganda for the laudable aims of the Group Theatre. . . . If it can be agreed that what is involved in the Group Theatre is of more importance than anything else in the English theatre, we might then look with sharper eyes at the present production. I concede that the chorus work . . . is greatly improved but did not

Mr Sayers have an uneasy feeling that the Westminster
Theatre was pervaded by . . . a *stench* of artiness. . . ?[8]

He was hard on the chief performer, too:

> Mr Doone's dancing was bad. The sooner someone says
> so the better for everyone, including Mr Doone. His
> movements were prim, constricted and pompous. He
> seemed to patronize even his own limbs. One felt
> infinitely obleeged every time he condescended to twiddle
> his fingers.

Approval of the Group's aims but not its performance
would become common enough but, for the most part, the
critical dispute that marked the opening of the Group Theatre
Season was clear cut. It was founded on real hopes and fears
not only for the English theatre but for English society. If the
applause, remonstrances and alerts were louder than they had
been in 1934, it was not only because very few critics had been
present at the earlier performances but because the need to
make up one's mind about which side one was going to be on
was now more urgent. It was no longer possible to suppose
that the theatre was a politically neutral territory. The Group
had made this clear and if they had only managed to keep the
controversy going they might all have been made men.

Whatever else it may have been, the first performance of the
season was energetic and confident: one that might 'prove
epoch-making', *Drama* thought.[9] And *The Times*, fastidiously
discriminating between the meaning of *The Dance of Death*
and its theatrical method, allowed that the production had
merit:

> Do these choruses parading in front of a simple
> backcloth, those performers scattered about the audi-
> torium, the jazz orchestra, the dancer representing Death
> and the Announcer speaking for Death through a
> megaphone, all striving to combine realistic incident and
> fantastic illusion, express their meaning in good dramatic
> terms? On the whole we think they do. In performance

this piece has a lucidity which it lacks in print, and the general amusingness of the stage movement, the emphasis of the jazz band, and the singing and dancing are aids, not hindrances, to the assimilation of the author's ideas.[10]

Since the writer strongly deplored the ideas, the unuttered but ineluctable conclusion was that, on stage, this was a particularly insidious piece of political theatre. Auden had found in Communism unsuspected theatrical possibilities and even Louis MacNeice was impressed by the discovery. Poetic dramatists, he thought, had to recover a certain *naïveté* if their writing was going to be effective and they might 'even do it by becoming Communists. . . .'[11]

The Dance of Death overshadowed *Sweeney Agonistes* on this occasion, and many reviewers were either silent about Eliot's 'curtain-raiser' or dismissive. The effects that had proved chilling in the Group Theatre Rooms looked meretricious on the stage of the Westminister Theatre. A. V. Cookman was typical in finding it 'a not very lucid fragment presented with the tricks of Expressionism' but his prophecy 'that Mr Eliot would be infinitely more at ease renovating a traditional form' was unique.[12] Eliot, who was frequently present at the performances, may have been coming to that conclusion himself.

The Auden–Eliot double bill did moderately good business for its scheduled two-week run, after which *Timon of Athens* was put into rehearsal. Meanwhile the season was carried on in the name of the Group Theatre with Rudolf Besier's *Lady Patricia*. Adversaries of the Group were utterly routed by this sudden manoeuvre; and so were its supporters. 'The spectacle of a foolish husband and more foolish wife indulging in an obviously unreal passion with a girl and a boy . . . won't bear very close inspection,' had been *The Times*'s unexceptionable comment in 1911, when *Lady Patricia* was new.[13] Then, the most fetching thing about this drawing-room comedy, archly set in a tree house, had been Mrs Patrick Campbell in the lead; now, it was Phyllis Neilson-Terry. The director, John Wyse, offered a further justification: asked to produce a comedy of manners, he had chosen the play, he said, because 'pre-war days are remarkably remote, and in certain lights their leisured elegance becomes attractive and—I dare say—enviable'.[14] Working in the uncertain light of the Group Theatre, Wyse did his best to extinguish it.

The *Daily Telegraph* was full of delighted appreciation for the 'outward charm' of *Lady Patricia*: so delighted, indeed, that it reviewed the play twice. The second reviewer was forcibly reminded by this 'daring experiment'

> that it is possible brilliantly to scarify a type, lampoon and render laughable a class, make targets of sentimentality, and ridicule without any need for drifting into animus, bad temper or vulgarity.[15]

Mr Auden take note! But it was too soon by several years for Auden to be much interested in advice from such a quarter.

Harold Hobson guessed that the Group's intention in reviving a not-very-old play apparently 'for its antiquarian interest' must be 'deliberate parody . . . doubly removed from life', but this interpretation was too subtle.[16] All the Group Theatre had done was to lend its name to precisely the kind of stuff it despised: a bit of West End flummery with an imported star, staged with the tinsel and trappings that audiences still liked.

Offstage, the Group Theatre was frantically trying to sell subscriptions on the strength of its two first productions, but *Lady Patricia* had revealed all. Prospective member-subscribers were told that for the 'present there will not be a permanent company for this can only be formed by long search and special training'.[17] What *Lady Patricia* had to do with the search defied public explanation: privately, it was written off as a sop to Anmer Hall. Within the Group Theatre there was dissension; about it, confusion. And the subscribers were not forthcoming for the next two openings that could be announced: Jean Giono's *Sowers of the Hills*, directed by Michel Saint-Denis, and *Timon of Athens* directed by Nugent Monck.

Giono's play makes a symbolic link between a peasant's disastrously greedy exploitation of his land and his sexuality. It had been presented in London twice before; in an English version and, in French, by the Compagnie des Quinze, for whom it had been written.[18] The English production, by Esmé Percy, was said to have lost the poetry of Giono's original, so a main interest of the revival at the Westminster lay in the hope that, under Saint-Denis's direction, in a revised translation and with Sarah Allgood heading the cast, Giono's poetic realism —often compared with Synge's—might be brought home, even in English. From the Group Theatre's point of view the most important thing about the production was that it was the work of a director the Group admired and emulated. It also gave Medley, as designer, the opportunity to learn from Saint-Denis's meticulous stagecraft.

Saint-Denis's direction, in which no attempt was made to find an English equivalent to the 'flavour of Provence', was respectfully received. The acting of D. A. Clarke-Smith, Marius Goring and Sarah Allgood was praised. Few faults were found with the staging, apart from the essential one that the language and symbolism seemed to have nothing much to do with each other.[19] A certain sense of the inconsequentiality of the production derived, perhaps, from its coincidence with the General Election campaign. It certainly had no obvious bearing on the Group's declared ambition to be a 'social force'.

Had Saint-Denis achieved a resounding success with *Sowers*, the Group Theatre might have been eclipsed. Instead it merely looked like a rather muddled imitation of the Quinze that the arrival of Saint-Denis himself, and the founding of the London Theatre Studio, made superfluous. As announced in the programme for *Sowers*, the London Theatre Studio was another version of the Group Theatre idea: it was to be 'the basis of a permanent company, trained to act together' and associated with 'artists, musicians, authors. . . .' The inference that the active members of the Group Theatre would do well to throw in their lot with the Saint-Denis venture was obvious; as, indeed, John Allen and Oliver Reynolds soon demonstrated when they left the Group for the London Theatre Studio.

Members of the Group were regularly seen as English 'disciples of the Compagnie des Quinze' and Doone tried to remove the label. Inaccurately, he asserted that the Group Theatre had been founded in ignorance of the methods of the Quinze and that none of its members had worked with Saint-Denis. He acknowledged the broad similarity of aims but insisted that the 'tone and character' of the Group's work was 'entirely unlike the lyrical mood of the Compagnie des Quinze'.[20] This was true, but the difficulty was to make the distinction quite clear. Auden's manifesto in the *Dance of Death* programme went some way to making it, and so did a similar one by Doone. But their effect was muffled. They were merely two of a series of statements that appeared in the programmes for the season under the common heading, 'I Want the Theatre to be. . . .'[21]

Doone's contribution to this forum was an avowal of the Group's dedication to artistic collaboration, to which he now added that

> SOCIETY MUST BE CHANGED IF WE WANT A LIVING THEATRE. THE THEATRE SHOULD SUGGEST CHANGES.[22]

Doone was true to himself in advancing the condition of the *theatre* as a reason for *social* change, but for him to think of the theatre as in any way a political instrument was a shift in attitude, one that was general, in differing degrees of intensity, within the Group.

Doone's stylistic approach to the social objective was through an amalgam of realism and fantasy, an attempt to give theatrical expression to the interpenetration of mental and objective events. (As in Edward Upward's *Journey to the Border* objective reality became indistinguishable from nightmare, in Picasso's *Guernica* the nightmarish reality of war would be depicted, and in Day-Lewis's 'Newsreel' the connection between dream and horrific actuality would be made.) Given the tendency of the theatre to convey external more emphatically than psychic reality, such devices as masks and conventionalized movement were used to express the fantastic, mental aspect. Doone's 'method' was not simply derived from German Expressionism but concocted by himself in a pragmatic way and his conception of 'fantastic realism' became the Group's most distinctive stylistic feature, one for which its playwrights, and Eliot also, were indebted to him.

With *Timon*, the fourth production, directed by Nugent Monck, the Group Theatre proper surfaced again and so did its desire to be a 'social force'.[23] One of the members who felt most keenly about this was the composer for the production, the 22-year-old Benjamin Britten, recently recruited by Auden. *Timon* was Britten's first music for the theatre. That he began with this particular play and started to write for Left Theatre very shortly afterwards was an indication of the political attitude he brought with him.

Timon had not been one of the plays originally proposed but was an afterthought—obviously a politically inspired one. As the embodiment of 'an ideology . . . relevant to the present', the play had a 'logical place' in its season, the programme claimed.[24] It was 'Shakespeare's comment on a world which was then beginning, and is now at an end'—another version, that is to say, of the dance of the death of capitalism. Doubtless the audience was supposed to see in Timon's retreat from his personal gold standard an analogy with the abandonment of the gold standard by Britain.[25] Marx's admiration for Shakespeare's depiction of 'the real nature of money' as the 'visible deity' working 'the transformation of all human and natural properties into their contraries' was not mentioned, though it was probably in the mind of whoever suggested the play. Whether this was Monck or some other member of the Group Theatre, the choice—unlike those of *Patricia*, *Sowers* and *The Impresario from Smyrna*—was attributed to the Group Theatre collectively.

For his Timon, Monck had wanted Donald Wolfit (who had declared himself willing), but it was Ernest Milton who actually took the role. Harcourt Williams was cast—ill cast, by all accounts—as Apemantus and Torin Thatcher played Alcibiades. Most of the other roles were taken by members of the Group Theatre and since the elaborate staging of Timon's feast, with choreography by Doone and music by Britten, was a dominant feature of the production, it was recognizably a Group Theatre effort.

Timon has often proved disappointing on the stage and this revival was no exception. Ernest Milton gave some magnificent performances, it is said, but the first night was not one of them. On this critical occasion he apparently flagged disastrously in the second part of the play and became unintelligible. 'The production deserved a better Timon,' said one reviewer and others agreed that Milton was inadequate.[26] After the erratic leading actor, it was the sick author who came in for most of the flack. The *New Statesman* thought that the play itself had 'little more than a curiosity value'; Ivor Brown that it had been written when Shakespeare was on, or over, the verge of madness.[27]

Nugent Monck had been directing Shakespeare for over ten years at the Maddermarket Theatre, Norwich, but this was his first attempt in London to work in the 'Elizabethan tradition of a formal stage and swiftly played scenes, using the full stage and the half-stage alternately'.[28] His stage direction was well received, though there were objections to actors spilling into the auditorium. The permanent setting, designed by Medley with a view to the uninterrupted flow of the action, was a wide, raised platform surmounted by delicate arches and with steps to the downstage area. It was considered, not surprisingly, too delicate, fussy and undynamic for the matter of the play.[29] Britten's music, though powerful, was certainly not the making of the production as Purcell's had once been. Those who saw fit to remark on it did so with distaste, notably Agate:

> Timon bids the sun 'draw from the earth rotten humidity', and Mr Benjamin Britten bids a concatenation of bassoon, oboe and clarinet . . . echo this feat.[30]

The score included a funeral march and the music for a ballet

danced at Timon's feast. Performed chiefly by Doone and
Renata Kuh, the ballet was too reminiscent of the Playfair
Beggar's Opera for Ivor Brown's taste. Agate, predictably,
described it as a piece of 'stylized junk'. Most reviewers passed
over it in silence.

The production of *Timon* brought together a promising
configuration of talents but, somehow, the right chemistry was
lacking. 'The Group Theatre', said Brown, 'must pull itself
together'. At this stage of the season a friendly critic might
have said as much.

A play about a group of squabbling artistes came next:
Goldoni's *The Impresario from Smyrna*. The English version
was by Clifford Bax, a member of the Group Theatre, and it
was the tongue-in-cheek choice of John Fernald, who directed
it. In *The Impresario* some artistes engage in complicated
machinations to get themselves hired for a company being
assembled, supposedly, by a rich Turk. Eventually they are
told that he has departed in confusion, leaving a gift of 2,000
ducats for distribution among them. The Turkish impresario is
a fiction created by one Count Lasca, the real source of the
ducats, who proposes that the artistes use the windfall to
found a co-operative. Lasca disciplines them with the threat
that, if quarrelling breaks out, he will give all the money to the
best behaved. His final message is:

> I hope you will remain at peace, and all contribute to the
> general interest. That is the difference between a
> communal theatre and one that is run by a manager.
> Under a paymaster, everybody is proud, pushing and
> presumptuous, but when the musicians themselves are
> running the affair they are all contented and willing to
> work their hardest. The impresario from Smyrna is an
> excellent warning to anyone who desires to venture upon
> such a difficult, burdensome, and, for most folk, ruinous
> enterprise.[31]

Morland Graham and Sylvia Coleridge were brought in to
play the important roles of Ali and Lucrezia but most of the

parts were taken by Group Theatre actors, and Murrill composed the music. The run opened two days before Christmas and most of the reviewers found *The Impresario* too trivial even for the holiday season. Whether they stayed for the afterpiece they did not say. It was *A Harlequinade* written by John Allen and acted by some of the more energetic and underemployed members of the Group.

This *jeu d'esprit* had already been staged two weeks earlier, together with a programme of dances, on a single Saturday night at the Westminster Theatre. That event was not part of the official season but took place during an interval of three weeks in which the Group Theatre was becalmed. Not finding enough in the season to occupy them—the old story—some of the Group had got up an entertainment on their own. In Allen's adaptation of *commedia dell'arte* to contemporary political satire, the Capitano was a figurative Mussolini, Cocodrillo was an Emperor Haile Selassie and Isabella, violated by the Capitano, stood for Abyssinia. The satire was heterogeneous, literary and rather tame—especially after censorship. The Lord Chamberlain's Office ruled against the directly rude allusions to Goering, Hitler, Mussolini and Sir Oswald Mosley. Stalin, however, remained an officially permitted target since Britain did not have diplomatic relations with the Soviet Union.

As an attempt to ginger up the Group, *A Harlequinade* was of a piece with another of Allen's contributions to the season—his interpolation into the Leader's speech in *The Dog Beneath the Skin* of a quotation from Mussolini about bombs opening like flowers—a little piece of guerrilla theatre that brought a threat of closure from the Lord Chamberlain. Allen's political conscience soon took him into Left Theatre and from there he went on to become a writer (the main author of *Busmen*) for Unity Theatre. He also became the very energetic and successful organizer of the Left Book Club Theatre Guild. His *artistic* conscience he appeased at the London Theatre Studio, where he was employed as an instructor and writer by Saint-Denis. Allen found a neat set of alternatives to the Group Theatre. For those who remained in it, the search for the right accommodation between politics and art continued—in so far as the requirements for survival permitted.

Half way through its season the Group Theatre was obviously living from hand to mouth. It had staged only two of the nine productions previously announced and had not been able to sustain the schedule of a new opening every three weeks. The 'imported' actors and directors had neither enhanced the Group reputation nor brought good returns at the box office. There was still a chance for recovery with *The Dog Beneath the Skin, Peer Gynt* and *The School for Scandal*, though whether the Group Theatre would be able to produce all of them was becoming very doubtful. Sheridan was the first to go, probably because the Old Vic, inconsiderately enough, staged the play in December and the Group was in no condition to invite comparison.

Geoffrey Grigson made the comparison anyway. Analysing the 'queer case of the Group Theatre', he lashed it for its amateurishness, for being 'technically . . . as distressingly second-rate as the Old Vic' and, most mordantly, for merely 'pretending to have a group feeling and purpose'.[32] At the same time, Barbara Nixon, from her vantage point in Left Theatre, surveyed a theatrical scene in which the best hope, she thought, lay with community theatres that were 'part of the whole society and its life' and in which performers and playwrights could build new (working-class) audiences under the patronage of the trade unions and the Labour Party. In the Group Theatre she detected a contradiction between its overt interest 'exclusively in artistic form' and the Socialist content of the new plays it was presenting.[33]

Barbara Nixon's description would have been contested by the Group, in which there was an intensification of political feeling during the Westminster season. In the course of 1935–6, the international situation was deteriorating fast. Hitler proceeded with conscription; Mussolini began the acquisition of his 'Fascist empire' in Abyssinia, where the use of bombing and poison gas looked like a rehearsal for the European war to come; Germany occupied the Rhineland; and, in mid-1936, the Spanish Civil War began. In Britain, the National Government began to prepare the population for the air raids that would, as everybody supposed, wreak the most appalling destruction in the very first stages of the coming war. It was a time when professed convictions were being tested on the grand scale and—in such instances as the Hoare–Ribbentrop naval agreement and the Hoare–Laval plan for handing over most of Abyssinia—being found utterly hollow. Within the Group Theatre, as in a section of the population at large, there was a Leftward move. Medley, for instance, was barely dissuaded by Doone from joining the Communist Party and John Allen, after a visit to Germany and partly under Medley's influence, began to be more militantly Leftist. Britten was reading Marx.[34] Isherwood and Auden in *Dogskin* had tended as far towards a Communist message as they ever would.

At the beginning of its season, proceeding cautiously, the Group Theatre had declared its desire to be a 'social force'. As the season progressed, and the slither towards the political abyss accelerated, artistic detachment became more otiose and uninteresting. With the 'imported' productions, the Group Theatre had hedged its bets in the wrong direction as far as attracting an audience was concerned. There was much truth in what Barbara Nixon and Geoffrey Grigson said. If the Group Theatre had not vacillated so much between business, politics and art it might have made much more of its great opportunity. Had it managed to reconcile these interests it would have been a wonder to behold. With the production of *The Dog Beneath the Skin* (discussed in the next chapter) it nearly did so, and almost was.

The play had been in rehearsal since early December and, according to the repertory schedule, should have followed about three weeks after *The Impresario from Smyrna*. It did so, but in the form of one of the private Sunday performances that had been promised to members and subscribers. A second

Sunday performance was given a week later, on 19 January, but the regular run did not begin until the end of the month.

'On its merits compared with the average London production,' said Dilys Powell, 'the play should run for five years'.[35] As many months would have suited the Group Theatre very well. Early in the run business was excellent and the audiences enthusiastic. By the end of February, houses were falling off and the last performance was scheduled for 14 March. As the end of the run approached, the box office picked up again but after six weeks it was more than time for the Group Theatre to return to some semblance of its announced repertory programme.

During the run of *Dogskin*, the Group Theatre had been struggling with *Peer Gynt*, which was to follow. Randall Swingler had completed his translation, which was confidently supposed to be better than the one played at the Old Vic in October (and due to reopen in fuller version at Sadler's Wells in May). Medley began work on the design, which was to use a lumber camp as the setting, but he found himself too exhausted to complete it. He had been the major designer of settings, costumes and lighting for the season, had done much of the physical construction, had been called on constantly to give Doone moral support and, for good measure, had been teaching too. He was exhausted.

Doone and the other organizers were also badly frayed, and Anmer Hall had just about reached the limit of the financial loss he was prepared to stand. The best the Group could do was to trot out their old war-horse and finish off the season with a week of *Fulgens and Lucrece*. On 28 March the 'First Group Theatre Season' ended and somebody placed a wreath on the green room door with the message, 'The Group Theatre is dead'.

The obsequies were premature but it was abundantly clear that the Group Theatre had had its big chance and there was very little to show for the £10,000 or so that Anmer Hall had lost on the venture. The Group Theatre had proved its incompetence in management, had exposed its artistic insincerity and had made no headway with the formation of a company.

Michael Sayers, who had championed the Group Theatre so vehemently at the beginning of the season, was correspondingly bitter at its outcome:

> They had control of a well-equipped theatre; there was plenty of talent waiting to get its chance; and still the Group Theatre degenerated into a snobbish, useless clique. Instead of making itself a centre for all the young talent now interested in the theatre, instead of encouraging young players, young playwriters, young producers —it simply went, like any Shaftesbury Avenue shop, after names.[36]

Sayers had not witnessed the whole season and his new attitude was doubtless affected by his recent visits to America and Russia but his attack was not, by any means, unjustified.

Greenwood later reflected that, 'Half the money our backer lost on the season would have kept a student company for two years, and perhaps brought about ... a company with a unified style.'[37] At the time, Anmer Hall became the scapegoat, but there is no knowing how far the Group Theatre had been required to appease him, how far he had provided the cover for a bid for success on compromising terms. What was certain was that the Group had fallen into confusion.

In a very ambivalent way, they had also created a sense of communal theatre, as was observed by a shrewd satirist writing, in the *New English Weekly*, under the name of E. C. Large:

> One goes to the Westminster to enjoy not merely what happens on the stage, but the total spectacle, that of the audience which watches the players, and that of the players ... I incline to the view that of the two masquerading bodies of people—who between them create the 'theatrical situation'—the audience are by far the more interesting and bizarre.[38]

The audiences, he found, varied significantly with the play. *The Dance of Death* 'filled the place with pink jerseys, yellow shirts, soft thin beards and a rumble of abstract words'; to *Lady Patricia*, the ticket-holding intelligentsia, feeling insulted, sent their older relatives, 'mostly from small grocer's shops out Balham way'; *Sowers* attracted 'ladies of title, from as far west of Bloomsbury as Kensington' ... and so on, through to *Dogskin*, for which the audience included 'very respectable people, whose social pretensions were flattered, the Lord knows why, by having daughters who were understudies'.

This same 'E. C. Large' is quoted at the head of this chapter on the way the Group Theatre, going against the Westminster's architectural grain, had tried to live up to Walter Gropius's design for a 'total theatre', which was displayed in the lobby during the season. Like Sayers, he bitterly attacked the duplicity in presenting miscellaneous productions under the Group Theatre label and 'using expensive importations for leading parts', all of whom were 'a distinct flop'.

This satirical account of the Group Theatre, was an inside job. That its author, 'E. C. Large', was singularly well informed may be gathered from his final thrust. Having failed so far 'to meet his obligations as a member of the audience in a total theatre', he was resolved to attend some future production in 'full mountaineering kit and goggles'. Either he had the gift of second sight or excellent sources. Very few people knew, in January 1936, that Auden was planning to write a play about mountain-climbing for the Group. One of the few was Louis MacNeice.[39]

7

The Dog Beneath the Skin

The truth is that those who would write poetic
drama refuse to start from the only place where
they can start, from the dramatic forms actually in
use. These are the variety show, the pantomime,
the musical comedy and revue . . . the thriller,
the drama of ideas, the comedy of manners, and,
standing somewhat eccentrically to these, the
ballet.

Auden made this pronouncement in March 1934, in an
anonymous review.[1] The confidence of its tone was due partly,
perhaps, to the fact that two of his own works had recently
been produced: *Paid on Both Sides* at the Festival Theatre,
Cambridge, and *The Dance of Death* at the Westminster
Theatre. In the first of these, Auden had made use of charade
and in the second of the 'eccentric' form of ballet. For the play
on which he was currently engaged, *The Chase*, he was
exploiting almost all the forms he mentioned but none of them
so thoroughly as one he left out of the list: melodrama.

There are two main elements in the intricate plot of *The
Chase*.[2] One is the search for a missing heir by Alan Norman,
on which he is accompanied by George, who has just escaped
from the local reformatory and is disguised in a dog-skin. This
part of the plot is reminiscent of J. M. Barrie's *The Little White
Bird*, in which a dog takes human form for a day and is
disgusted by what is revealed to him; and it was probably
derived also from *Caesar, the Watch Dog of the Castle; or,
The Sword of my Father*, a melodrama by W. G. T. Moncrieff
(1794–1857), the author of *Tom and Jerry; or, Life in*

London. In *Caesar*, the 'lost heir' is adopted by the family dog, shares his kennel, learns canine behaviour, dresses in a wolf-skin suit, has a humble protectress called Georgette and is eventually and happily discovered in the course of a gala arranged by an uppity general. All of these features have their counterparts in *The Chase*, though the person beneath the skin is not the lost heir, as he is in *Caesar* and as he would be in *The Dog Beneath the Skin*.

The second main element of the plot of *The Chase* has to do with James, George's fellow escapee. Early in the play, the Vicar helps James and George evade their pursuer, Sergeant Bunyan, and in the Vicar's tool shed the two boys find their disguises; the skin for George and female clothing for James. Thus transvested, 'Miss James' remains in the village, where 'she' is hotly wooed by the Governor of the reformatory and invited by him to that institution's concert and prize-giving. Here, 'Miss James', who is covertly distributing revolutionary messages, is discovered sexually and politically. We later hear that James has been killed 'escaping arrest', but not before he has managed to arm the reformatory lads. They remain the flimsy opposition to the General, who seizes power. The reformatory plot was derived from Peter Martin Lampel's fierce protest against social and sexual repression in Germany, *Revolte im Erziehungshaus*. Auden saw the play in Berlin in 1929, when it caused an uproar. It made less of a stir when it was played in English at the Gate Theatre the following year.[3]

In the final scene of *The Chase* there is a Fascist takeover in the strike-bound village of Pressan Ambo. The General has the good-natured Vicar beaten up for refusing to preach and requires the villagers, represented by the audience, to listen to a recording of the 'Sermon by Armament Manufacturer'.[4] The audience-as-villagers' attention is compelled by a machine-gun trained on the stalls. (This was a theatrical device that Eliot adapted for *Murder in the Cathedral*, in which the audience is verbally threatened by the Knights at the end of the play.) At the end of *The Chase*, three of its four heroes are dead: James has been liquidated; Sir Francis, the lost heir, has died of wounds from police bullets; and Alan Norman is gunned down as he returns (through the stalls) to the village. It is on the fourth hero, George, that the hope in the play rests— on him and on the audience, which is urged to make a different ending.

In its construction, *The Chase* is highly stratified. The choruses (like Hardy's in *The Dynasts*) set the scene, describe the social circumstances and convey a moral point of view. The plot is episodic, more by default than design, and overburdened with story. The audience is frequently implicated in the performance in the manner of *The Dance of Death*—as when the 'Prompter' announces that the actor playing the Vicar has been delayed and the 'performance' is suspended. This provides an opening for the conductor of the orchestra to read out the cast list and so help the audience to disentangle the characters. The text is also studded with in-jokes like the non-functional allusions to Rylands (of Cambridge), Ormerod (Greenwood of the Group Theatre) and various Auden relatives. But, despite its messiness, *The Chase* is a moving allegory of the quest for freedom, integrity and love.

Auden finished *The Chase* in the autumn of 1934 and publication was announced for March, to coincide with the intended production in the Poets' Theatre season at the Mercury. Auden sent copies of the play to Doone and Medley and to Isherwood. Doone was not altogether pleased with it and Isherwood's many suggestions for changes led to its transformation into a new work of which he was the joint author.[5] The new play, into which Isherwood had injected a strongly Brechtian strain, was published in May as *The Dog Beneath the Skin; or, Where is Francis?*.

One of the radical changes made when Auden and Isherwood reworked *The Chase* was the elimination of the reformatory plot. This simplified the narrative at the expense of psychological diagnosis. Revue techniques were substituted for mumming and audience involvement: the school concert cum gymnastic display in *The Chase* was replaced by a different kind of theatre-within-theatre, a sleazy cabaret. Another major change was from an insular to a continental political geography. The heroes now travelled from Pressan Ambo across the Channel and back, passing through Westland (Germany), Ostnia (Austria), Paradise Park (the Riviera) and staying a while at the Hotel Nineveh (in Paris, London or any European capital)—these locations being strung together as the connecting rooms in the European madhouse.

The Chase, like *The Orators* and *The Dance of Death*, is an 'English study'. The miners' strike going on in the background is a specifically English (and Lawrentian) version of the class struggle. Governor Bicknell, the Vicar and Sergeant Bunyan are caricatures of prime English types. Even James, in disguise, is a quintessential English girl, superficially prim but really quite fast; while George and Alan have hearts of oak. The only foreigner in the play is Fritz, one of the reformatory boys, who does a German turn in the concert. In *The Dog Beneath the Skin*, the satire of English mores, instead of being pervasive as in *The Chase*, becomes a more particular judgement on the insularity and culpable simple-mindedness that allows England to follow sheepishly as Europe plunges into disaster.

The Dog Beneath the Skin has a simple, episodic plot. In a quaint, festive ceremony, Alan Norman sets out from Pressan Ambo, as others have before him, in search of the lost heir, Sir Francis Crewe. He is accompanied by the village's stray dog. Alan's reward for success will be personal glory and the hand in marriage of the heir's sister, Miss Iris Crewe, who is not only beautiful but brings a magnificent dowry. This fairy-tale opening gives way to a series of revue-like scenes as Alan and the dog, following meagre clues and accompanied by two knowing journalists, pursue the quest through Europe.

Alan's journey is a political, moral and emotional education. In Ostnia, he experiences the chilling combination of political ruthlessness and aesthetic refinement at court, and the crude commerce of its Red Light District. In neighbouring Westland, lunacy and thuggery prevail. The corruption of international capitalism and its self-gratifying sentimentality are embodied in the financier, Grabstein, whom Alan meets in a Westland train. In Paradise Park, the solipsism of poets, lovers, invalids and athletes is exhibited; in its operating theatre, the superstitious reverence for the mystique of surgery. The false ideals of show business are on display in the Hotel Nineveh and here Alan betrays himself. Forgetting his adored Iris Crewe, he falls for the film star, Lou Vipond, a 'mechanical bride' so lacking in humanity that she can be represented as a mannequin.

In pursuit of Lou Vipond, Alan runs up enormous bills and is driven to the point of suicide. He is saved by the man who emerges from the dog-skin that has been his disguise for so long and who is none other than the missing heir himself. This recognition scene between Alan and Sir Francis has been well prepared for and is superbly placed. The fidelity of the dog has been an amusing and touching contrast with human behaviour. When it transpires that the bond is not mere animal instinct but intelligent, human love, Alan has found not just the lost heir but a faithful friend and mentor. The personal bond becomes a political one when Sir Francis exposes the rottenness of Pressan to an Alan who now has the eyes to see it.

The episodes that make up Alan's journey constitute an exuberant Bruegelian panorama in which clergy and military, entertainers and doctors, pimps and poets, drug addicts and madmen—all who have a stake in the great capitalist racket—are animated. The caricatures are not all single plane. The portrait of the Führer, for instance, has suggestions of Mussolini and Churchill incorporated in the basically Hitlerian features. As well as alluding to Dolfuss's murderous suppression of the Austrian Socialists and Mrs Dolfuss's 'peace offering' to their families, 'execution day' in Ostnia reflects royal sanctimoniousness nearer home. Some of the allusions are eruditely obscure, like the Byronic 'Conyers Hall' and 'Coghlan's coffin'; some are simply private jokes, like 'Cosy Corner' (an actual homosexual resort in Berlin that Auden and Isherwood visited) and 'Bubi' (Isherwood's boyfriend, whose name was borrowed for Madame Bubbi in the play). 'Mother Hubbard's' was a night-club that flourished in London in the twenties—an allusion that many in the audience would probably have caught. The multilingual, world-disdaining poet up a tree is distinctly Poundian and the fact that he has a Jewish father is doubtless part of the joke. The father, Grabstein, is a clear caricature of the industrialist and Zionist, Lord Melchett, whose biography Auden had reviewed. The Vicar's Curate, caught between the atheist Left and the vicious Right, was thought, plausibly, to resemble T. S. Eliot.[6] But these are mere details in a comprehensive vision of worldly corruption.

The satirical force of the montage is enhanced by the distillation into song of the tenor and mood of the scenes. The cynicism of the two Journalists on the Channel steamer is caught in a smart number that matches its bar-room setting:

> If Chanel gowns have a train this year,
> If Morris cars fit a self-changing gear,
> If Lord Peter Wimsey
> Misses an obvious clue
> If Wallace Beery
> Should act a fairy
> And Chaplin the Wandering Jew:
> The reason is
> Just simply this:
> They're in the racket, too!   [p. 41]

Liturgical chants express the mordant refinement of the Ostnian court and the holy awe surrounding surgery. The Brothel-keepers' song in the *danse macabre* of the Red Light District, calls for a syncopated jazz rhythm:

> When we are dead we shan't thank for flowers,
> We shan't hear the parson preaching for hours,
> We shan't be sorry to be bare white bone
> At last we shan't be hungry and can sleep alone. [p. 64]

The song sung in the train by the sentimental Grabstein invites a blues treatment:

> *Why are they so rude to me*
> *It seems so crude to me*
> *I want to be friendly*
> *But it's no good. . . .*   [p. 88]

For the solipsists of Paradise Park, a waltz is the appropriate measure:

> *When you're in trouble,*
> *When you get the air,*
> *When everything returns your ring*
> *Do not despair, because although*
> *Friends may forsake you*
> *And all skies are dark*
> *You can be gay if you just step this way*
> *Into Paradise Park.*   [p. 93]

Alan's high living in the Hotel Nineveh is evoked by the tempo of a tango:

> *20 cases of champagne*
> *A finest pedigree Great Dane,*
> *Half a dozen Paris frocks*
> *A sable fur, a silver fox,*
> *Bottles of scent and beauty salves,*
> *An MG Midget with overhead valves. . . .*   [p. 138]

The virtuosity and exuberance of *The Dog Beneath the Skin* make it one of the most attractive works ever written for the English theatre; and even more remarkable is the way in which the diverse elements of the piece—lyrics, episodes and choruses—are so cunningly knit together into a unified theme.

Pressan Ambo is very light-heartedly presented at first view. With its Vicar and its Policeman, its Chemist and its General, its dotty old maid and its Boy Scouts, it appears to be a harmonious, innocent world. Fittingly, the lyrics are in the style of W. S. Gilbert. But there is no going back to the early mood at the end of the play. After all that has been seen,

Pressan must be redefined. And this is done in highly didactic prose. Underlying the charmingly eccentric façade Alan now finds the microcosm of a Fascist state. He ends where he began, but aware. As to how much Pressan itself has really changed during Alan's absence and how much his—and the audience's—view of it has merely been clarified is for the audience to decide.

The choruses in *The Dog Beneath the Skin* may be the most effective poetry written for the English stage since the seventeenth century. Many of them were carried over from *The Chase*. One of the uses Auden has for them is to set the scene, often from an oblique angle of approach:

Paddington. King's Cross. Euston. Liverpool Street:
Each hiding behind a gothic hotel its gigantic greenhouse
And the long trains groomed before dawn departing at ten,
Picking their way through slums between the washing and
*   the privies*
To a clear run through open country,
Ignoring alike the cathedral towns in their wide feminine
*   valleys, and the lonely junctions.*
In such a train sit Norman and his dog
Moving backwards through Westland at a mile a minute
And playing hearts with their two friends on an open
*   mackintosh:*
Picture the Pullman car with its deft attendants
And the usual passengers: the spoilt child, the corridor
*   addict. . . .*   [p. 80]

The beginning of this chorus is typical of Auden's 'method' of shifting material from one context to another to make a striking transposition from the familiar to the new. In asking what Paddington, etc., have to do with where Norman is now the audience is lured into making for itself the parabolic connections between its world and the fictional one.

Some of the verse commentaries are didactic extrapolations from the episodes, made with an awe-inspiring directness:

Men will profess devotion to almost anything; to god, to
    Humanity, to Truth, to Beauty: but their first thought on
    meeting is: 'Beware!'
They put their trust in Reason or the Feelings of the Blood, but
    they will not trust a stranger with half-a-crown. . . .

Beware of yourself:
Have you not heard your own heart whisper: 'I am the nicest
    person in this room'?
Asking to be introduced to someone 'real': someone unlike all
    those people over there?

You have wonderful hospitals and a few good schools:
Repent.
The precision of your instruments and the skill of your
    designers is unparalleled:
Unite.
Your knowledge and your power are capable of infinite
    extension:
Act.   [p. 157]

Sections of the choruses, or a whole chorus such as 'Happy the hare at morning . . .', can stand as poems independently of the contexts to which they nevertheless relate. The chorus was a feature of dramatic form that audiences became reaccustomed to in the thirties and that has once again fallen into disuse. Auden's choruses were structurally separate, frequent and long, but far from untheatrical.

Isherwood said that he and Auden were 'much influenced by the *Dreigroschenoper* and [*Aufstieg und Fall der*] *Stadt Mahagonny* of Brecht', when they were writing *The Dog Beneath the Skin* and, he added, 'If the poetic drama has a rebirth in England—and some people think it may—the movement will be largely German in inspiration and origin'.[8] A year or so after *Dogskin* was performed, Brecht returned the compliment by naming Auden, Isherwood and Doone as prospective members of a 'Diderot Society' of theatre people actually engaged in production. The society was to stimulate 'a newer, antimetaphysical and social art' of the theatre.[9] But as it happened, no Diderot Society was formed and it was Eliot, not Brecht, who dominated the attempts to revive poetry on the English stage. Under Eliot's influence, 'poetic drama', as it was so infelicitously called, acquired utterly un-Brechtian connotations and an odour of sanctity. *The Dog Beneath the Skin* remained an isolated instance of the Brechtian influence on English playwrights that would become such a significant factor a quarter of a century later. That the Brechtian graft did not 'take' in the thirties may be attributed partly to the counter-influence of Eliot and partly to the fact that Auden and Isherwood themselves would veer away from Brecht's example shortly after they wrote *The Dog Beneath the Skin*.

There were many small appropriations from Brecht in *Dogskin*. One such, mentioned by Isherwood, comes from the 'Eating' and 'Loving' scenes in *Mahagonny*.[10] Isherwood compounded the exhibition of these related appetites and drove home his satire on 'culinary' entertainment by having one of the patrons of the Hotel Nineveh select a chorus girl for his dinner. The theme and treatment were Brechtian but the hint for 'cannibal stew' probably came from *Sweeney Agonistes*. Another minor borrowing was the ritualistic presentation of the revolver with which the King shoots the Ostnian rebels. A footman presents it on a cushion, much as the late Jim's revolver and other effects are presented in *Mahagonny*.

The structure of the brothel scene in *Dogskin* derived from the hallucination scene in Denis Johnston's *The Old Lady Says 'No!'* (in which the items purveyed by Two Touts include a trip to the Park of Paradise) but its content, manner and viewpoint came from Brecht.[11] Like Begbick's city, the Ostnian Red Light District makes and sells simulacra of all that man desires. There is more emphasis on the basic appetites in *Mahagonny*, more variety in the Ostnian brothels—the names of which appear on placards, Brecht-style—but in both the fundamental source of depravity is a deadly idealism. 'Gentlemen,' says Begbick,

every man carries an image of the ideal in his heart: one
man's voluptuous is another man's skinny. The way this
one can wiggle her hips should make her just about
perfect for you, Joe.[12]

The proprietors in *The Dog Beneath the Skin* are more explicit
about the philosophical underpinning of the flesh trade:

> *Here Plato's halves are at last united.*
> *Whatever you dream of alone in bed,*
> *Come to us and we will make it real instead.* [p. 57]

Alan escapes the toils of the brothels but, like Brecht's Jim, he
eventually has to appeal to 'his' girl for money, only to find, of
course, that their relationship was conditional on his solvency.

There is a more fundamental kind of debt to Brecht in
Isherwood's lunatic scene in *The Dog Beneath the Skin*. In
Mahagonny the inefficacy of escapist daydreams is figured in
the construction of a 'ship' on top of a billiard table, the
characters using materials at hand. Jim, Jenny and Bill enact a
voyage complete with mimic storm but their fantastic ark is no
refuge from the flood of unpaid bills. In *The Dog Beneath the
Skin* the lunatics make an 'acroplane' out of their beds and
take a flight of fancy in it. In both Brecht's and Isherwood's
scenes a mime using non-representational stage properties
conjures up a fantastic stage image, kept scrupulously in the
realm of fantasy. The audience is not itself asked to *imagine* a
ship or plane but only to share in the game of them *being*
imagined. The technique is similar to that called for by Obey in
Noé for the building of the ark, but the effect is totally
different. The Brecht–Isherwood examples are parabolic
juxtapositions. There is no elision between theatre and world
to create a single 'poetic' image, as in Obey. Isherwood
actually cited a non-Brechtian source for his lunatic scene but
it clearly showed that he had absorbed an essential element of
Brecht's aesthetic of the theatre.[13]

In 1936, very few English theatregoers were in any position
to detect the influence of Brecht. Eric Walter White, who was,

was suspicious of it in the way that Auden and Isherwood
themselves became:

> The influence of Brecht and his theories has been
> widespread but often unacknowledged. It is to be clearly
> found, for instance, in W. H. Auden's two poetic plays,
> *The Dance of Death* and *The Dog Beneath the Skin*. If
> any sceptic doubts which is the master and which the
> apprentice hand, he has only to compare the scene in *The
> Dog Beneath the Skin* where Destructive Desmond
> slashes the Rembrandt to pieces with that in Brecht's
> *Badener Lehrstück* where two disinterested clowns try to
> be helpful to a giant clown who is feeling somewhat
> unwell, the only result of their disinterested zeal being
> that they completely dismember him. It is also to be found
> in the pseudo-Communist attitude assumed by many of
> our younger writers. But let them take warning from the
> fact that, during the last few years, the didactic-political
> side of Brecht's talent has tended to get the upper hand,
> his artistic sureness has begun to falter.[14]

Destructive Desmond was not the best example in *Dogskin* of
Brecht's influence. Nearer to the *Lehrstück* manner was
Isherwood's use of a tailor's dummy to represent Lou
Vipond—a rare instance of utter dehumanization for satiric
effect. But White's article, published in *Life and Letters To-
day* in September 1935, makes it virtually certain that Doone
and the Group were well aware of the Brechtian qualities in
Dogskin before they performed the play.

   If the potent example of Brecht influenced the writing of *The
Dog Beneath the Skin*, the emergent style of the work was an
Anglo-German hybrid. *The Dog Beneath the Skin* attempted
to shock its audience by the juxtaposition of a brassy,
Brechtian manner with the humour and melodrama carried
over from *The Chase*. And, thematically, the play is quite un-
Brechtian in seeming to entertain the possibility of an audience
capable of the change of heart that could forestall the need for
political revolution.

While he was working on *The Dog Beneath the Skin*,
European politics impinged sharply on Isherwood's personal
life and he had qualms of conscience about where he stood as
the parties and nations squared off: 'My place is in England
with the Communists. I am a deserter and a potential traitor,'
he confided to his diary and a friend.[15] His situation, in fact,
was very like that of Sir Francis in the play.

In the *Nostos*, for which Isherwood was chiefly responsible, Sir Francis explains how he ran away after quarrelling
with his father over 'the key of the gun-room'. This obviously
has to do with the 'complex of terrors and longings connected with the idea "War"', that obsessed Isherwood and, he
said, his generation. In his canine disguise, Francis has
become a secret, literary and photographic observer:

> I was fascinated and horrified by you all. I thought that
> such obscene, cruel, hypocritical, mean, vulgar creatures
> had never existed before in the history of the planet, and
> that it was my office and doom to record it. . . .
>
> My diary was my greatest friend. I worked away at it,
> like a scientist, polishing, punctuating, searching for the
> exact epithet, devoting months and even years to each
> one of you, noting every gesture, every intonation. I even
> managed to take photographs to illustrate my
> records. . . .   [p. 173]

Francis's return home is as he has often dreamt it:

> I imagined a very dramatic appearance: tearing off my
> disguise and denouncing you all. . . . But the really
> fascinating problem was to decide when to appear, and I
> kept putting it off. . . .   [p. 172]

He puts off his return until events make it inevitable. When
he does arrive home, all the 'old hostility' that he, like
Isherwood at the time, feels for 'the land of the Others',
erupts.[16] If anyone had asked, at the time, 'Where is
Isherwood?', the last act of *Dogskin* would have been some
kind of answer.

The title that the authors first gave the play was the question *Where is Francis?*; to which the answer was partly political. Francis emerges from the skin as a 'unit in the army of the other side' opposing (British) Fascism, which is where the long-absent heir to Marple Hall, Christopher Isherwood, thought he should be. The riddling title *The Dog Beneath the Skin*, which was added at Medley's suggestion, draws attention to the unobserved observer in a different way. Sir Francis is indeed a *dog* from the point of view of the class he has abandoned and betrayed.

The role of Sir Francis is both an uncomfortable one for the actor and exceedingly difficult. Unlike Cocteau's horse in *Orphée*, the dog, *qua* dog, is mute, and when the actor playing the role emerges from the skin to make his very late first appearance as a speaking character he has somehow to engage the audience's sympathy with his delivery of the obviously (but not precisely labelled) Communist tirades. Sir Francis may think he should be a Communist, but the only evidence of his conviction is long-winded protestation. The part seems *meant* to fail in this respect and the authors underlined the character's failure when, for the staged version, they decided to have him shot. By contrast, the emotional resolution that occurs when Francis and Alan find each other is verbally understated. It looks as though politics comes in at the end of the play to mop up the emotional fervour inhibited earlier: Communism standing surrogate to homosexuality. Cyril Connolly, at least, detected the 'authentic rallying cries of homo-communism'.[17]

As became customary with Group Theatre plays, *The Dog Beneath the Skin* appeared in print, and was reviewed, long before the performance took place. The notices were mixed, though mostly favourable. I. M. Parsons thought *The Dog Beneath the Skin* shoddy by comparison with *Murder in the Cathedral* (which had been published and performed a few weeks earlier) and attacked the Destructive Desmond scene as typical of its untruthfulness to life. *Scrutiny*'s reviewer, who also compared the two plays, even-handedly chastised Eliot for being 'cold and academic', Auden and Isherwood for 'a crudity only too common to' the stage. D. G. Bridson described *The Dog Beneath the Skin* as an 'inverted twentieth-century *Faust*'.

Ignoring, as many critics did, Isherwood's joint authorship, Bridson supposed that Auden the Communist was making 'very good fun' of Auden and Communism. An American reader, on the other hand, found the satire unsurpassed for 'sheer disillusionment and horror . . . not pleasant reading, and . . . not meant to be'. Since it was 'Communist propaganda', it was not a good play, though it might, he thought, be 'good theatre'—an interesting distinction.

Montagu Slater—himself a playwright for Left Theatre — did not find *Dogskin* funny, though he admitted that it gave 'morbid neuroses an objective and even amusing life of their own'. The *Times Literary Supplement* had high praise for the theatricality and verbal richness of the play, while John Garrett, in the *Criterion*, commended the 'dramatic instinct and good poetry', delighted in the brilliant funniness of the asylum scene and anticipated the pleasures of the work in performance. For this, however, he would have to wait longer than he, or anyone, thought.[18]

The Dog Beneath the Skin was published in May 1935, shortly after the collapse of the projected Poets' Theatre season in which it would have appeared. A production by the Group Theatre, under Doone's direction and with music by Murrill and masks by Medley was announced for the early autumn. The first, private, performance was actually given on 12 January 1936 and was followed by another the following Sunday. A little over two weeks after the second private performance, the regular run began.[19]

For the Sunday performances, Robert Speaight, who was still playing Becket at the Mercury, was one of the two main choral speakers, and Robert Eddison took four of the important caricature roles. For the run, Speaight and Eddison had to be replaced and other cast changes were made but both casts were drawn mainly from the Group: they had to be, since about thirty actors were required to play the more than a hundred roles.

Between publication and performance, the play underwent major surgery at the hands of Auden—whose final revisions were finished on 8 January—and Doone.[20] Many of the excisions made then and later were deeply resented. Michael Sayers began his review of the performance with the gloomy reflection that 'in order to make *The Dog Beneath the Skin* fit for staging . . . Mr Doone had to omit nearly everything that made it good to read', and he drew the extravagant conclusion that the cutting indicated a failure of dramatic form in the play and in the English theatre generally.[21]

Cyril Connolly was not quite right in asserting that the play had been censored 'almost entirely on religious grounds'. All the satire of religion had, it is true, been eliminated, but as part of a more general purgation. Most ridiculously, the King and Queen of Ostnia underwent a sea change into a Sultan and Sultana. Their Master of Ceremonies became a Grand Vizier and the Archbishop was translated from his Ostnian see to the Grand Eunuchship of an Arabian court. So much for Austria! The Lord Chamberlain's representative, who was present at the first, private, performance passed the emasculated scene for public exhibition but, ten days before the first public performance, George V died and Hall insisted that the episode be cut altogether.[22] The liturgical element in the operating theatre scene was also cut, much to the disappointment of Eliot. MacNeice, who also felt this loss, would later make it good in a play of his own.[23]

Prudery purged the Red Light District. The Grahamgreene-ish refrain of the Boy Tout, 'Come wiv me. Good jig-a-jig,' was shorn and the boy replaced by an ordinary 'Woman of the Quarter'. The whole of the Brothel-keepers' song was cut, along with the remaining allusions to boy prostitution and flagellation. Doone's staging endowed the scene with a macabre intensity but verbally it was no more alarming than a quiet evening in Soho.

The loss of the Vicar's sermon was much lamented.

Auden had inserted this speech into *The Chase* and had
retained it, with less appropriateness, in *Dogskin*. At one
point, Isherwood favoured cutting Sir Francis's long denunciation in favour of the sermon, reasonably supposing that the
audience would not stand for both. Auden and Doone decided
to cut the sermon and keep the denunciation, which was
necessary to the plot, and Auden went on to a wholesale
revision of the last scene.

In the printed text, the return of Alan and Sir Francis
happens to coincide with the first parade of the proto-Fascist
Pressan Lads' Brigade. The official announcement of Iris
Crewe's engagement to the local MP, son of a munitions
manufacturer, is part of the ceremony, which is interrupted by
a bloodthirsty anti-German speech by Mildred Luce. Iris's
betrayal of her conditionally plighted troth to Alan makes it
easier for him to become Francis's political ally.

In the played version, Alan and Francis arrive on the very
day that Iris is going, very reluctantly, to be married. Mildred
Luce tries to stop the wedding:

> *Stop!*
> *O think one moment what you do.*
> *Have you no eyes?*
> *Or have caresses so debauched your judgement*
> *That life seems splendid as a scivvie's dream?*
> *Are you so numbed or naughty you dare think*
> *To order chaos with a common kiss? O look!*
> *Show me one virtue that's not lethal, one vice*
> *That's not contagious as the itch. Look, look, look,*
> *Look at your slaves; the sweaty crowds*
> *That make the beaches stink in summer*
> *Or crawl out daily to their dingy labours. . . .*
> *My sons were lovely and they died for them.*
> *O that the sun would sputter and go out*
> *And all bone crumble in the universal frost*
> *Or that a reef would suddenly rise up*
> *Out of the cold and infinite abyss*

Our aimless cruising to arrest at last
And our ship crammed with all its bestial cargo
Plunge roaring into nothing.[24]

Auden's mock-heroic verse (anticipating Christopher Fry's more general use of the style) introduced an infectiously self-parodic note into the scene, in which the plotting was also very significantly changed.

Francis reveals the source of Mildred's hysteria. She never had any sons but is a spinster whose mother once prevented her from marrying a German officer. Thus provoked, Mildred quite understandably shoots Francis. So the theoretical hardliner dies and Alan is left to act alone on the basis of his new-found knowledge.

Auden's rewriting of the last scene tended to substitute morbid psychology for political conflict. In the collaboration, Isherwood was pulling in the direction of Europe, Brecht and political didacticism; Auden towards England, melodrama and psycho-social diagnosis. In his late revisions, Auden gave the play a final tug in his direction.

A minor change in an earlier episode also modified the political theme. In an amusing and touching scene, one of Alan's predecessors, Chimp Eagle, expires on an operating table, he and Alan singing a Wagnerian duet the while. In the printed text, Chimp, who has been wounded by a police machine-gun in the course of a dock strike, confesses his failure. He has been diverted from the quest for the lost heir by political activism. On the stage he died unrepentant:

Chance made it clear
My work was here
For me the single-handed
Search was ended
But for you I see
It is still necessary
To continue your looking
For what is lacking.[25]

Chimp's total commitment pre-empts the position: in the

160   *Dances of Death*

performed text, the only really good Communist was this dead one.

In the course of rehearsals, Doone cut the Destructive Desmond episode. It was a much criticized decision and one that Isherwood always regarded as a mistake. Destructive Desmond is an artiste in the Hotel Nineveh cabaret. His act consists of destroying priceless objects. Urged on by the spectators and feebly resisted by an Art Expert, whom he cruelly mocks, Desmond goes through an elaborate routine of choosing between an original Rembrandt and a cheap print as the prelude to the frenzied destruction of the Rembrandt. It is a savage and memorable satire on philistinism. Doone rehearsed the episode with Desmond Walter-Ellis, an excellent comedian, as Desmond but they could not fathom its black humour and pathos. Perhaps Eric Walter White's description of it as an inferior imitation of Brecht was an incitement to cut.

Another change made by Doone was to give the part of Lou Vipond to a flesh-and-blood actress instead of using a mannequin. Isherwood's idea was to satirize the egotism in erotic love by having Alan make advances to the dummy, then run behind it to respond to his own amorisms, then back again to deliver more. For a presentday audience, this zany love scene is not at all puzzling but Doone had difficulty with it. He first tried using the Financier's voice for the dummy and, dissatisfied with this effect, cast a beautiful actress in the role. Auden must have approved the change since he added a few words for the actress. The *News of the World* and the *Daily Express* got good pictures out of the change but critics understandably took exception to the real female presence.[26]

One of the most important pre-performance decisions concerned the way in which the choruses were to be spoken. The need for good verse speaking was answered by assigning the verse commentaries to two speakers or 'Witnesses', as they were called, in the manner of Obey's *Le Viol de Lucrèce*. Auden had already used the technique in a limited way in *The Chase*. The Witnesses, a man and a woman, stood one on each side of the stage, wearing evening clothes and domino masks.

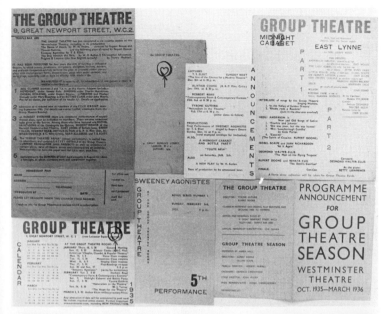

1 *(above)* A Group Theatre collage: much of the publicity material was hand printed in the Great Newport Street rooms

2 *(below)* A 'summer study' session at Summerhill, 1933. Back row from the left: Maurice Orme, Felix Trott, Robert Medley, (unknown), John Allen, Rupert Doone, Richard Wood, Eleanor Garland. Kneeling in front of Trott is Isobel Scaife. Constance Foljambe is in front of Eleanor Garland and Jean Richardson is to her right. Ethel Lewis is second from right in the front row

3 (above) Advance publicity for the 'First Group Theatre Season' of 1935–6

4 (below) 'Strip off your shirt/Kick off your shoes.' Rupert Doone, extreme right, is looking at the camera, Mary Skeaping, in the centre, has her back to it. 'Summer study', 1935

5 *(above)* 'Leave behind those office blues.' Arrival for a 'summer study' in
Suffolk. Left to right: Kathleen Edwardes, Rupert Doone, John Moody,
Biddy Taplow (?), Robert Medley, Ormerod Greenwood.
Seated: Jean Richardson, John Allen

6 *(below)* A respite from the bleak discussions about the Group Theatre's
future that took place at Fawley Bottom Farm, John and Myfanwy Piper's
home, over the August Bank Holiday, 1937

7 *(above)* Rupert Doone and his Spanish Dancers in Nigel Playfair's production of *The Duenna* (R. B. Sheridan), 1924

8 *(below)* On the set of *Lancelot of Denmark* (translated by Peter Geyl), Croydon, 1933, are from the left, Eleanor Garland, John Allen, Rupert Doone, Robert Medley, John Gower Parks, Isobel Scaife, Alan Rolfe, John Moody, and Ormerod Greenwood

desijn for Danne of Death 1934

9 (*above*) Design by Robert Medley for *The Dance of Death* (W. H.
Auden), 1934. The stage had to be left clear for dancing

10 (*below*) Henry Moore's sketch for the mask of the 'sun god, creator and
destroyer', *The Dance of Death*, 1934

11 *(above)* 'My love for these bathers is hopeless and excessive', says the artist in *The Ascent of F6*, 1937. Here is the bathing party from *The Dance of Death*, 1935

12 *(centre) The Dance of Death* reflected bucolic summer study sessions

13 *(below)* The Announcer orchestrates 'an English revolution suited to English conditions' in *The Dance of Death*, 1935

14 *(above)* Sweeney (John Moody) and Doris (Isobel Scaife) in *Sweeney Agonistes* (T. S. Eliot), 1934: Doone 'made it seem we were all Crippens at heart'.

15 *(below)* Dusty (Ruth Wynn Owen) with Doris (Isobel Scaife) fortune-telling. *Sweeney Agonistes*, 1934

16 *(above)* Design sketch by Robert Medley for *Timon of Athens*, 1935.
Ivor Brown called the setting 'miminy-piminy'

17 *(below)* The permanent setting for *Timon of Athens*, 1935. Nugent
Monck wanted a very fast-paced production

18 *(above)* 'They're in the racket too.' From the left, Geoffrey Wincott as the Dog, Henry Rayner as a Journalist, John Moody as Alan Norman, Alan Rolfe as a Bartender, Desmond Walter-Ellis as a Journalist. *The Dog Beneath the Skin* (W. H. Auden and Christopher Isherwood), 1936

19 *(below)* 'Money, money/makes our speech as sweet as honey.' *The Dog Beneath the Skin*, 1936

20 *(above left)* Cartoon from *The Sketch*, 26 February, 1936

21 *(above right)* Ingredients for a cannibal stew: Nineveh girls from *The Dog Beneath the Skin*, 1936

22 *(below)* Thornton Wilder may have recalled this wedding party from *The Dog Beneath the Skin*, 1936, when he visualized the funeral party in *Our Town*, 1938

23 & 24 Production photos of *Fulgens and Lucrece* (Henry Medwall) at the Westminster Theatre, 1936, where some members of the audience sat on the stage

25 *(above left)* Dress designs for Clytemnestra and Agamemnon by Robert Medley. *The Agamemnon* (Translated by Louis MacNiece), 1936

26 *(above right)* The 'stained-glass window' effect aimed at did not work and these masks were abandoned.

27 *(left)* Cassandra (Vivienne Bennett) in *The Agamemnon*, 1936

28 *(above)* In the revival of *The Ascent of F6* at the Old Vic in 1939, Alec Guinness played Ransom, and the climbing gear was authentic

29 *(below)* Design sketch by Robert Medley for *The Ascent of F6* (W. H. Auden and Christopher Isherwood), Mercury Theatre, 1937. The chess-board did not appear in this production

30 *(above left)* Hedli Anderson as the Singer in *The Ascent of* F6, 1937

31 *(above right)* Ransom's quietus on the mountain: William Devlin and
Dorothy Holmes-Gore in *The Ascent of* F6, 1937

32 *(below)* The assault: Gunn (Barry Barnes) and Ransom (William Devlin)
near the summit of F6, 1937

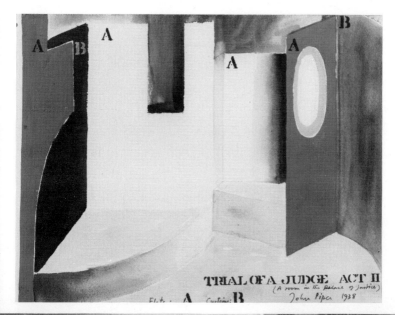

TRIAL OF A JUDGE ACT II
(A room in the palace of Justice)
John Piper 1938
Flats: A Curtains: B

33 *(above)* John Piper's design for *Trial of a Judge* (Stephen Spender), Unity Theatre, 1938. This was Piper's first work for the theatre

34 *(below)* How the design above appeared on the stage. The Judge (Godfrey Kenton) caves in to his wife (Kathleen Boutall) and Hummeldorf (Evan John). *Trial by Judge*, Unity Theatre, 1938

35 The blacks and the reds outside the Palace of Justice. *Trial of a Judge*, Unity Theatre, 1938

Eliot did not enjoy being 'preached at' by them, but others approved the method. Britten thought Speaight's delivery in the private performance 'the best part of the show'.[27]

The more integral choruses were assigned to a group of seven, and Hedli Anderson also had a choric role singing, cabaret-style, into a microphone. 'Seen when the night was silent . . .' and the opening song of the Paradise Park episode were two of her numbers. She also played Madame Bubbi of the Hotel Nineveh, a part that was probably conceived with her in mind.

A choral passage added by Auden specifically for the staged version was in quite a different style from the rest. Designed to introduce the Westland asylum scene, it begins:

> A land ruled by fear may be easily recognized by the behaviour of its frontier officials. Those in whom private terror breeds a love of insult and interference are always with us. But only such a country affords them such a splendid career in the public services. The brutal voices and the fawning, the padlocked, pleasure-hating mouths, the fussy assertive adam's apples, the popping horrified eyes, the furtive rodent noses. Each one dingily afraid of his immediate superior. Picture them now at the frontier between Ostnia and Westland, among the coloured forms in the stuffy little station. The swallows swooping in the dawn over the simmering railway engine. In the background the beautiful ignorant mountains.[28]

The prose, the direct focus on the action, and the implied single speaker distinguish this from the other choruses in the play. There is no reason to suppose, though, that *Dogskin* would have been the better if more of the choruses from *The Chase* had been scrapped and new ones written with the new scenario in mind. On the contrary, the need to connect old and new material elicited Auden's most dazzling intellectual and verbal dexterity and he never wrote better verse for the stage than the choruses for *The Chase* that were carried over into *Dogskin*.

Cyril Connolly suggested that, given the flimsiness of the

text, the only thing to do with the play in performance was to dress it up: 'Handed over to Messrs Cole Porter, Cecil Beaton, and Oliver Messel with a cast of singers and a lavish production something might be made of it,' he said; and Ivor Brown took much the same line.[29] Certain scenes certainly do lend themselves to decorative treatment—the light operatic opening, Paradise Park and the Hotel Nineveh—but the astringency in the play's theme and its verbal richness accorded well with the bare staging it actually received; while the bare staging accorded well with the budget for the production which was about £90.

Kenneth Allott's judgement that it was 'merely thrown on the stage' was an extreme and isolated one.[30] It was probably based largely on the method itself: the improvisatory use of such minimal properties as a set of chairs for the train scene; a rostrum and tables for the Hotel Nineveh; stepladders dressed with a few boughs for the trees up which the Poet and Lovers are found in Paradise Park; flags on various occasions and, at the end of the play, a thicket of black umbrellas carried by the wedding party. This last scene anticipated the well-known stage image of Thornton Wilder's *Our Town* and, if Wilder took a leaf from *Dogskin* it was no more than just recompense for the use Auden, Isherwood and Doone made of his *Pullman Car Hiawatha* for the *Dogskin* train scene.

Dogskin assumed a very large ensemble performing with great virtuosity, the kind of ensemble that did not exist and which could hardly have been assembled from the profession in the normal way, even if the Group Theatre—or Anmer Hall—had had the money. It was a production that drew on the Group's talents for singing, dancing, speaking verse and multi-role playing, and it summoned all their energy and spirit.

Veronica Turleigh's delivery as one of the Witnesses was universally acclaimed but Giles Isham (who, for the public performances, succeeded Robert Speaight) was ill received as the other. John Moody as Alan Norman and Hedli Anderson as the Singer were frequently singled out for praise, and the building of the aeroplane by the Lunatics brought the house down. This and Doone's staging of the Red Light scene were obviously very effective. *Punch* liked the masks worn in several scenes but wanted to know why in the Hotel Nineveh some of the diners were masked, others bare-face.[31] The answer was not shortage of time or money but a deliberate attempt to complement visually the mixture of the fantastic and the commonplace in such surreal dialogue as:

> *Have you read* The Virgin Policeman?
> *Yes we did. We got right to the docks.*
> *There's his new one.*
> *There were lots of children without any socks.*
> *You mean the blue one?*
> *It was divine.*   [p. 124]

Similarly, the denizens of the Red Light District wore grotesque masks that contrasted with Alan's ordinariness, and faces and masks were juxtaposed in the Lunatic scene.

About the songs, the words of which are so enticing, the reviewers, regrettably, had nothing at all to say, though Connolly obviously thought that Cole Porter could have done better. Murrill's music is lost. Britten described it as 'just clever and rather dull jazz'. Britten himself later set one of the songs from the play.[32] In retrospect, it seems that the beginning of the Auden–Britten collaboration was unluckily timed. *Dogskin* included a much richer collection of lyrics than either of the later plays by Auden and Isherwood. Had the performance been endowed with the vitality that Britten's music imparted to *The Ascent of F6* and *On the Frontier*, it would surely have been theatrically explosive.

A little surprisingly, politically Left- and Right-inclining critics were agreed that the new ending was no improvement, though they disagreed in other ways, as might have been expected. A writer in the Fascist paper, *Action*, praised the play for being 'clever and funny', though superficial and, as propaganda, 'pleasantly obscure'. He managed to interpret the Lunatic scene as 'not a parody of Fascism itself, but rather a parody of a startled Social-Democratic notion of Fascism'.[33]

Having shot his critical bolt, he then occupied himself with reviling the Jewish members of the audience.

No doubt there were a good many Jews present, since the *Jewish Chronicle* had asserted in one breathless sentence that the play's

> subject matter, its wildly original form, its crude fury, its fascinating peevishness and its audacious petulance are expressed with such a beautiful sense of literary values, such a sure feeling for the power of the word, whether to express the most vulgar shallowness, the cheapness of minds fed on mass-produced ideas, the heat of thwarted idealism or the queer green enthusiasm of youth, that no person who can think at all independently, or whose feelings have not been stunted, can fail to delight in this orgy of satire.

Kindest of all was the reviewer's opinion that the 'show ought to fill the Westminster for months'.[34]

The *Daily Telegraph* and *Daily Worker* both responded warmly to Doone's production and the *Mail* and *Herald* also praised the all-round excellence of the company. Charles Morgan was of like mind, though he demurred at the play's ideological tendency. Even Derek Verschoyle, having duly castigated the authors for not presenting a 'constructive substitute' to the evils they satirized, was constrained to credit Doone with a 'more balanced production' than the ones he had reviewed so furiously in the past.[35]

With *The Dog Beneath the Skin*, the Group Theatre managed to pull a chestnut or two out of the fire. If, instead of putting themselves on the treadmill of a mixed repertory season, Doone, Greenwood, Hall and the 'tiny core' had had more nerve and sincerity, more confidence in the Group and in *The Dog Beneath the Skin*, they might have established a permanent ensemble at the Westminster Theatre. The actual result was galling; the more so since the modest approach of the rival firm of Dukes and Eliot had proved such a huge success. *Murder in the Cathedral* opened at the Mercury a month after the Westminster season began and was still running strong when the Group Theatre's last production closed. Dukes's managerial expertise in dealing with Eliot's play impressed Auden and Isherwood and the impression made on them by the play itself was even stronger, as would become evident in their next play.

8

The Group Theatre as a 'Collective Theatre', 1936–9

> To the Group Theatre that has performed our plays,
> We leave the proceeds of the Entertainment Tax
> To pay for sets, and actors on week-days.[1]
> AUDEN AND MACNEICE, 1937

After the painful lesson of the Westminster Theatre season, the Group Theatre's priorities were to purge itself of amateurishness and to widen the scope of its operations. The formation of a permanent ensemble ceased to be a serious objective, though it lingered as a domestic piety and was sporadically revived. Classes were resumed but on a different basis. They were now given each evening in two-hour sessions for a fee of 6 shillings (30p) for a six-week term. John Moody taught acting and Rupert Doone concentrated on choral speaking. The dancer Renata Kuh, a refugee from Germany, was responsible for movement and, in a new development, the ballet dancer Mary Skeaping conducted classes in musical comedy. As far as training was concerned the Group Theatre had ceased to be a co-operative and had become an embryonic school, which could be called on to supply, at need, verse-speaking choruses.

As for productions, the Group reverted to the policy of 'occasional' Sunday performances for members. The emphasis was now on types of plays rather than methods of production: on 'contemporary form; documentary plays with social content; and early plays, especially such as have an affinity with modern life'.[2] The category of 'early plays' served as a reminder of *The Deluge* and *Fulgens*, accommodated the prospective production of *The Agamemnon* and indicated that the Group was not to be thought of as merely the thespian retinue of Auden and Isherwood, whatever the appearances to the contrary. The declaration of interest in documentary plays showed that the Group Theatre was attentive to the latest developments in America and recognized that film might have something to give, as well as take from, theatre.

A new problem and incentive for the Group was that, by 1936, it had several rivals. For political theatre there was Unity Theatre Club and Left Theatre; for poetic drama, the Mercury; and for ensemble acting, the London Theatre Studio. Having led—or at least pointed—the way in all these directions, the Group Theatre had less clearly defined aims than its theatrical neighbours. And it was a year or so before it acquired, more by force of circumstance than by choice, a distinctive role in relation to them.

Among the new groups, Unity was the most successful in realizing its aims. A development of the Workers' Theatre Movement, it was dedicated to the consolidation of a united front on the Left. Unlike Left Theatre and the Group Theatre, Unity operated as a club and did not aspire to professional status, though it welcomed, and benefited from, the help of a few professionals; and, unlike the other two organizations, Unity acquired its own theatre, which it managed to keep in more or less continuous operation, and built a regular audience.

The first Unity Theatre, a converted church hall, opened in April 1936, just after the end of the Group Theatre season at the Westminster. One of the plays chosen for the occasion was Clifford Odets's *Waiting for Lefty*, which had been produced a year earlier by the New York Group Theatre. The play's reputation had preceded it to England and the production by Unity was an event of some importance. With its intense portrayal of strikers' solidarity and its radical, participatory form (that brought H. G. Wells to his feet, crying, 'Strike! Strike!'), *Waiting for Lefty* became a model for Leftist theatre.

A review in the *Group Theatre Paper* described Odets as

'among the first to evolve a new drama directly from the ritual of the political platform as, in the middle ages, our present drama was directly evolved from the ritual of the church'.[3] The same might have been said, and with more point, of the author of *The Dance of Death* who, in the more innocent political climate of 1934, had done for the Group what Odets did for Unity in 1936. With *Lefty* Unity immediately became an 'alternative' theatre to be reckoned with; a theatre based on the kind of 'common bond' that Eliot had thought essential to the revival of drama.

Left Theatre, founded in 1934, was also intent on forging such a bond.[4] As a specifically 'Socialist Repertory Theatre', it produced plays that made strong social statements (such as Friedrich Wolf's *Sailors of Cattaro* and an adaptation of Maxim Gorky's *Mother*) and revues. As well as giving Sunday performances in the West End, Left Theatre went in search of audiences to the working-class districts of London, and attempted to engage the support of the trade unions and the Socialist parties for its efforts. Like the Group Theatre, it wanted to establish a permanent, professional company and tried, vainly, to raise the necessary money before reconciling itself to Sunday performances using unpaid performers. Left Theatre's most prominent writer was Montagu Slater, whose *Stay Down Miner* was modelled on *Lefty* as an experiment in a participatory and quasi-documentary form. Britten wrote the music for the play, which was presented for two Sundays at the Westminster Theatre in May 1936, shortly after the end of the Group's season there.

Auden's pronouncement, made in October 1935, that 'the film has deprived drama of any excuse for being documentary' was untimely in that it coincided with the development (of which he obviously knew nothing at the time) of documentary productions in America. Under the auspices of the Federal Theatre Project, the first 'edition' of the *Living Newspaper* series, *Abyssinia*, was collectively created (and officially censored) in January 1936. Other editions, such as *Triple-A, Plowed Under*, followed and were actually staged.

When the film-maker Paul Rotha discovered this theatrical genre in 1937, he was intrigued by the way in which documentary had found different channels in Britain, where it seemed to belong to film, and in America, where it had been adapted, through the use of cinematographic techniques, to the theatre.[5] In Britain, it was to be Unity Theatre that made best use of the *Living Newspaper* model, in 1938, with *Busmen*, a dramatization of the dispute between bus crews and their municipal employers over productivity. *Busmen* was devised and mostly written by a founding and, by then, former member of the Group, John Allen.

In 1936, the Group Theatre's interest in documentary theatre was connected with its new involvement with film. On the theatrical side, Mass-Observation, with its social research based on the reports of an army of volunteers, offered good material, so Stephen Spender went off to Bolton to investigate its possibilities on behalf of the Group; with no practical consequence.[6] The Group Theatre produced no documentary theatre, but there were to be strong traces of the genre in *The Ascent of F6*, *Out of the Picture*, and *On the Frontier*, all of which made use of radio and newspaper bulletins. On the other hand, in *Trial of a Judge*, the one Group Theatre play based on a specific historical incident, Spender was at pains to screen out documentary material.

The expansion of the Group's sphere of interest to take in film went further than a mere declaration and, for a few months, was full of promise. The sprouting of Film Group within the Group Theatre followed quite naturally from the involvement of a few of its members in both media. One such was Jack Beddington, an amateur actor who had joined the Group in 1935. He played a minor role in *Timon* and the major one of Fulgens. Professionally, Beddington was the head of publicity and advertising in Shell-Mex, where he was setting a standard and a style for the patronage of the arts by industrial corporations. He conceived the series of Shell County Guides, edited by John Betjeman; provided commissions for painters; and was responsible for *Contact*, a film

made by Paul Rotha, and later for the formation of the Shell
Film Unit.[7] Auden's scepticism 'about the disinterestedness of
large-scale industry and government departments' involved in
film-making was justified but Beddington himself seems to
have been rather more inclined to use industry to promote film
than vice versa.[8]

In 1936, the fact that films, as Arthur Calder-Marshall
pithily observed, were 'made by the very rich for the very poor'
looked menacing. Documentary film-makers, in particular,
were becoming alarmed at the convoluted deals between
mandarins and financial sharks and correspondingly zealous
to preserve the integrity of their work. The Group Theatre was
an available platform for the documentary gospel. At best it
might even be shaped into a production unit. No doubt
Auden's resignation from the GPO Film Unit early in 1936
was a factor in his attempt to deploy the Group Theatre for
film; and Hallie Flanagan's idea of making a film version of
The Dog Beneath the Skin may have shown him that there was
more common ground than he had supposed between theatre
and cinema.[9] In any event, he persuaded his friend Basil
Wright, already a distinguished film-maker, to head the Group
Theatre's Film Group.

One of the first things Wright did was to correct Auden's
assertion that documentary film was better at dealing with
inanimate objects than with people:

> Auden's plays very rightly take their dramatic start from
> the personal. With film we have essentially to work
> through to the personal from a different starting point—
> the exploitation of the cinema's ability to get around, its
> possession of temporal and geographical elements pecul-
> iar to itself—in fact, to use John Grierson's definition, its
> supreme power of effecting 'the creative interpretation of
> actuality'.[10]

Film Group's slate of instructors in this ultimately personal
art included the most prominent film-makers of the time: John
Grierson, Anthony Asquith, Paul Rotha, Alberto Cavalcanti,

Andrew Buchanan, Ivor Montagu, Stuart Legg and Arthur Elton as well as Wright himself. Between them they were to cover 'Scripting, Camerawork ... Direction, Production, Art-Direction and Set-Construction'. Classes were to be held two evenings a week and, for the first year, the fee was to be 2 guineas. Film Group was not, Wright insisted, a programme for dilettantes. For those with a more casual interest there was to be a separate film society.

Film Group was inaugurated in November 1936, at the Gaumont British private cinema, where a full house saw some films and heard talks by Grierson, Wright and Legg. Unfortunately nothing much happened afterwards—though some classes were given—probably because Wright himself had to put all his energies into the newly founded Realist Film Unit. During the period of preliminary planning, however, some Group Theatre members were working on film in other ways: Auden and Britten continued their cinematographic collaboration with *Negroes* (*God's Chillun*) and with *The Way to the Sea* for Strand Films; and Doone was the dancing figure in Len Lye's brilliant little experiment with colour, *Rainbow Dance*, made to advertise the Post Office Savings Bank.

A noble scheme that came to very little, Film Group reflected the Group Theatre's ambitions to be altogether professional and socially productive on a wide front. These aspirations were also conveyed in the *Group Theatre Paper*, the first number of which appeared in June 1936. Its editor was John Johnson, who had landed himself the assistant editorship of *Life and Letters To-day* when he came down from Cambridge in 1934. He was helped by the poet Randall Swingler (shortly to become literary editor of the *Daily Worker*), whose translation of *Peer Gynt* was still awaiting a Group Theatre production.

The *Group Theatre Paper* was intended to keep members of the Group Theatre abreast of theatrical events 'of special interest, in England or elsewhere'. In fact, 'elsewhere' never got so much as a mention; not even with such immediately relevant items as the American productions of *The Dance of Death*; and there were very few notes on local events. More significantly, the editors were unable to tell the membership much about the Group Theatre's own activities and plans, since there was too little to report. The seven issues of the *Group Theatre Paper*, appearing over as many months, mutely revealed the absence of a definite Group Theatre policy; and the very format of the *Paper*, as it dwindled from printed to mimeographed sheets, reflected diminishing funds and weakening morale. The last number was published in January 1937, just as *The Ascent of F6* went into rehearsal.

The main function of the *Paper* turned out to be exhortation, mainly by Auden, whose own interest in the theatre was, at this time, intense.[11] *The Dog Beneath the Skin* had been successfully staged, and two separate productions of *The Dance of Death* had been given in America. Auden and Isherwood had not yet equalled Eliot's achievement (and earnings) as a playwright but there was a good chance that they might if *The Ascent of F6* received a good production and good management. Before he left for Iceland, in June, Auden urged on the members of the Group in a piece he wrote for the new *Paper*. He dwelt on the value of an experimental theatre consciously attempting to reforge a 'living relation' between social life and the content and structure of art. This 'experiment' was what the membership had to get out and 'sell', he said.[12] The Group Theatre was now 'enriched and hardened with experience'. After four years of experiment, it had 'achieved that co-operation between artists in all fields which alone should be capable of producing the fullest and most up-to-date and most popular art'. Its supporters were encouraged to see the Group Theatre's mission in the broadest terms:

Civilization means nothing unless it is the integration of life, the articulation of a heightened consciousness. Without that consciousness there can be no unity. Without art there can be no consciousness. And without the co-operation of all civilized individuals there can be no art. To support a progressive artistic body is a political and social act of major importance.[13]

The theatre that Auden now envisaged was much less an 'act of the whole community' than a mission to save the community from itself, avoiding both inartistic political commitment and irresponsible aestheticism.

MacNeice similarly proclaimed the need for a 'dialectic' of artistic autonomy and social relevance. He elaborated his views in 'A Dialogue on . . . Tradition and Experiment' that he and Doone delivered in the Rooms:

> Our play must be . . . as objective as a poster or as an Egyptian sphinx . . . clear and definite in its outline, solid and self-contained. Yet on the other hand it must not be self-contained. It must . . . somehow, by attraction, sympathy, magnetism, wireless—any metaphor you can think of—be continuous with, or in gear or harmony with, the life that is diffused in the audience.[14]

MacNeice's translation of *The Agamemnon*, distant from, yet relevant to, contemporary life, achieved this perilous balance. Later Group Theatre plays, however, were more remarkable for their ambivalence than their 'dialectic'.

However serious it may have been in trying to arrive at a position that was morally and artistically tenable, the Group Theatre was not making any real headway in practical matters. In August 1936 some members went off to Summerhill School for what proved to be their last 'summer study', during which they worked on *The Agamemnon*. On their return to London, the forthcoming Group Theatre season was announced: *The Agamemnon, The Ascent of F6* and a new play by MacNeice.[15] The three plays were scheduled for Sunday performances only; and that is how *The Agamemnon* was presented, on 1 and 8 November. It was a striking and much criticized production.

Earlier in the year Auden had spoken of the 'artists within

the company', of the relationships between 'the company and the audience' and of the need to build up an audience for 'the company' to play to.[16] The production of *The Agamemnon* and the plans for *F6* made him face the fact that there was no such company and he changed his analysis of the Group Theatre's most urgent needs.

In the programme for *The Agamemnon*, Auden anticipated criticism of the production in a note headed, 'Are You Dissatisfied With This Performance?' The Group Theatre, said Auden,

> has playwrights who wish to write plays for it, painters who wish to design for it, composers who wish to compose for it. But it suffers under an overwhelming disadvantage. It has too little cash. There are actors who would like to play for it. *IF* they could afford it.[17]

If the performance seemed underrehearsed that was because actors could not afford to *give* enough time for rehearsals. It was implicit, too, that with unpaid professional actors and without the means to rent a theatre, the Group Theatre would be restricted to Sunday performances such as this one.

What the Group Theatre now desperately needed, said Auden, was not more members but one or two substantial donations. It was possible, he said, to

> go a certain way on the membership of a club principle, but only a certain way, and the Group Theatre has gone as far as it can on these lines. . . . We need something more than that. The Group Theatre personnel cannot work any more without money.

It was more of a threat than an appeal and Auden, who was without regular employment at the time, was in earnest about his own need of cash.

Shortly after the first performance of *The Agamemnon*, prospective patrons were invited to a cocktail party at Mrs Geoffrey Whitworth's, where T. S. Eliot spoke on behalf of the Group Theatre. At another such event, James Laver made the pitch.[18] But no successor to Anmer Hall was forthcoming. And since Auden and Isherwood were not prepared to sacrifice their new play as a Sunday offering, they took Eliot's example and let Ashley Dukes produce it at the Mercury.

Dukes had drawn from his success with *Murder in the Cathedral* certain conclusions about the production of new poetic plays. The first requirement was a small enough theatre; the second for the producer 'to go deliberately into the business of playbroking, play distribution and play management'. It was also important that the play not be published before it was performed, and essential for the first producer to control the performing rights for a specified period. One had to remember, said Dukes, that, though poetic dramas were unlikely to be smash hits, 'poets are inexpensive and their copyrights have long lives'. A further desideratum was to forge an Anglo-American connection by which audiences for such work might be developed on both sides of the Atlantic.[19]

Dukes pointed out that the 'Group Theatre, with limited resources making single productions that are too few and far between', had not given *The Agamemnon* an adequate showing, though it had performed 'the same vital function that the Stage Society performed a generation ago'. That the Group Theatre had not adopted up-to-date methods like his own was partly attributable to its contradictory character. It was, said Dukes,

> a director's theatre, which means everything it says about the co-operation of playwrights, actors, painters, dancers and composers, and nevertheless accepts the dictate of a single young artist, Rupert Doone.[20]

A theatre had to be 'the expression of somebody's personal taste', and Doone 'had enough vitality to ensure the survival of his Group Theatre'. The implication, though, was that the poet-playwrights were paying the price for the Group's (and Doone's) survival on the false assumption that they were part of a true co-operative. 'Under the right auspices,' Dukes claimed, *The Dog Beneath the Skin* could still do good business.[21]

Dukes's appreciation of the value of small theatres such as his own was a sound one. At the Mercury, plays had to be squeezed on to the stage with the utmost ingenuity, the audience was cheek by jowl with the players and the box office potential was barely sufficient to cover meagre production costs, but it was possible to keep a new play alive there long enough to build up an audience for it. *Murder in the Cathedral* had an initial run at the Mercury of six months—a very long one for the time. *The Dog Beneath the Skin*, by contrast, ran for as many weeks. But six weeks at the Westminster was the equivalent, in terms of audience capacity, of eight months or so at the Mercury. Had *Dogskin* been put on (as was once planned) at the Mercury, it might have played long enough for the cast to consolidate as an ensemble and done much for the reputations (and bank balances) of its authors.

With *F6*, Auden and Isherwood did not equal the success of *Murder* but Dukes, who used some of his profits from Eliot's play to finance theirs, did well by them.[22] Instead of playing for two Sundays at the Westminster, as Doone had intended, *F6* ran for nearly two months at the Mercury. It was then transferred to the Arts Theatre, Cambridge, for four performances and then back to London to the Little Theatre. Apart from this original production, the play was also presented at the Birmingham Repertory Theatre (where it packed the house and was revived in the next season), at the Maddermarket Theatre and elsewhere in England and America by arrangement with Dukes. Eighteen months after the première, Dukes would justly claim that *The Ascent of F6* 'was and is commercial' and that he had proved it.[23]

In the production of *F6* the Group Theatre was operating 'in association' with Ashley Dukes. This meant that Dukes was responsible for paying a royalty to the authors, for hiring the actors, getting scenery and costumes made, negotiating the transfers to other theatres and managing the performing rights. Artistically *F6* was very much a Group Theatre production in that it was written, directed, designed and with music composed and performed by members. There were also some members in the cast, though it was by no means a Group Theatre company.

As *F6* forged ahead, the Group Theatre bobbed in its backwash. It was only too obvious that if the Group Theatre itself had produced *F6*, it could have covered its costs and, for the length of the run at least, been in control of a company and a theatre. Somehow, it had missed the managerial boat once again. From the earliest days, the Group dreamed of patrons and, in Anmer Hall, it had acquired a generous one. Now, in Dukes, it had been saddled with a producer who showed the Group Theatre how it might have managed things for itself. The conclusion that, with patronage or without, the Group Theatre was incapable of coordinating its artistic aims with its managerial efforts was inescapable.

Lamenting the fact that *The Ascent of F6* had not been created in the matrix of the Group Theatre, and looking back nostalgically to *The Dance of Death* and *Dog Beneath the Skin*, a writer in the last number of the *Group Theatre Paper* touched the sore point:

> The great pity is that playwrights cannot themselves work in the theatre. In the case of the Group Theatre, this is a serious disadvantage both to the playwrights and to the theatre; for many practical and technical difficulties would be overcome and progress made more smooth and rapid. But it is the same old story of economic impossibilities.[24]

It was not altogether an economic story nor the old one. Auden did not attend rehearsals because he was in Spain; and, in its way, the production of *F6* was more intensely collaborative than the earlier ones.

The authors, the composer, the designer and the director worked very closely together; Hedli Anderson's qualities as a performer influenced the theatrical conception and Isherwood spent a good deal of time (though not much effort, he says) in the theatre. But only a small inner group was involved. It was questionable that the Group Theatre organization was necessary to foster the collaboration of a coterie of artist friends. And it was conceivable that 'Rupert Doone and the Group Theatre' had become encumbrances to the playwrights.

In the summer of 1937 dissension within the Group Theatre came to a head at a conference held over the August Bank Holiday weekend to discuss its future. John and Myfanwy Piper were the hosts for the meeting, at their farm near Henley, where a number of the most active members joined in a bitter debate. Auden was thought to be exceedingly overbearing in public and in the 'prefects room' to which he and other principals withdrew for private negotiations. He and Isherwood seemed to be more concerned with the West End success that beckoned them than with the future of the Group. They refused to allow the Group Theatre to control their plays in the way that Dukes now controlled *The Ascent of F6* and were frank about their lack of confidence in Doone.

Doone was in a weak position. Having staked his career on the Group, he no longer had a troupe to lead. He had spurred the playwrights on and had made the opportunities for the productions of *The Dance of Death* and *Dogskin*, but *F6* would have been written without any stimulus from him and had been successfully staged by other directors. The Group Theatre's reason for existence, if it still had one, was to serve the playwrights but it—and Doone—might actually be in their way. What if, as Dukes speculated, *F6* had been offered to John Gielgud for his season at the Queen's Theatre?[25] Surely some such convergence of classical work in the commercial theatre and the work of the new poet-playwrights was bound to occur and without the Group Theatre it might be sooner rather than later.

But if Auden and Isherwood had outgrown the Group Theatre, there were still MacNeice, Spender and other prospective poet-playwrights—Day-Lewis, George Barker and Dylan Thomas, for instance—to consider.[26] MacNeice's *Out of the Picture* was already published and scheduled for a Group Theatre production, and Spender's long-awaited play was nearing completion. They still had a use for some such organization as the Group. And there was also Auden's conception of the Group Theatre as a bulwark of civilization to consider. Had the principles that Auden had so vigorously articulated in the *Group Theatre Paper* become irrelevant?

From a certain viewpoint, the Group itself had become irrelevant: from that of John Allen, now working for the London Theatre School and Unity Theatre. He saw the productions in which he had taken part as merely the manifestations of middle-class neurosis. '*The Dog Beneath the Skin* would mean nothing at all', he wrote, 'to the sort of audiences who go to the Islington Town Hall where *Waiting for Lefty* has an electrifying effect.'[27] However doubtful this proposition, Allen correctly sensed the growing isolation of the Group. At best it was trying to preserve the cultural baby while the dirty social bathwater was ditched. At worst it was so weakly opportunist that, in 1937, while Auden and Isherwood were asserting the need for an unequivocally anti-Fascist stance, the politically very equivocal *F6* was presented in the name of the Group Theatre.

Shortly after the turmoil of August, the Group Theatre addressed itself to a more systematic self-scrutiny. A questionnaire asked whether members were satisfied with the arrangement made with Dukes for the production of *F6*; whether the Group Theatre should attempt to acquire the permanent use of a theatre; attempt to build up a small company of actors; operate collectively in all departments (i.e., including performers) or in one or two only; whether it should become a registered limited company entering into contracts with its members. The old question of where the money was to come from was asked in the new form of how shareholders might be attracted; and the most pertinent question of why, if at all, members at large should be recruited was posed for the first time.[28]

The structure that actually emerged in place of 'Rupert Doone and the Group Theatre' was an artists' alliance run by a commissariat of major collaborators. Doone was the Producer; Spender the Literary Director; Medley and Piper the

Directors in charge of design; and Britten and Brian Easdale
the Musical Directors. John Piper's title looked forward to
his début as a theatre designer with *Trial of a Judge*;
Easdale's recognized his work as the director of Britten's
music for *The Agamemnon* and *The Ascent of F6*. Doone saw
no place for Ormerod Greenwood in the new regime, having
come to the conclusion that his co-founder lacked the
necessary authority. Shortly before a meeting that Greenwood, as Organizer, was about to chair, Doone personally,
unceremoniously and without consultation removed him
from office. So, after five years of dedicated if not always
effective work for the organization that he had largely
created, Greenwood left the Group. It was a ruthless breach
of the trust that obtained, as Greenwood supposed, between
himself and Doone.

There was a flurry of activity in November 1937. Spender
took his new duties seriously and 'in the hope of starting a
really good theatre in London, as an alternative to the
sickening West End stage', looked for supporters and writers.[29] Yet again the intention of forming a 'permanent
theatre' was announced, though this did not necessarily mean
a permanent company or building. *Out of the Picture* went
into rehearsal. The Group Theatre sponsored an exhibition
of Vaslav Nijinsky's drawings which was presented with
flair, attracted a lot of publicity and was a convincing
demonstration of the Group's will to reach out beyond the
playhouse.[30]

From late 1937, also, the Group Theatre took on a more
Leftist appearance (of which the production of *Trial of a
Judge* at Unity Theatre was one, if ambiguous, feature). The
trend may have been partly a response to the contributions of
outsiders who had turned up at the August conference. One
such was Nancy Cunard, who urged positive action in
support of the Spanish Republican cause. Beatrix Lehmann
and Berthold Viertel were also there and their professional
and political orientations—to the West End and the Communist Party—may have carried some weight.

In a propaganda piece written for the *Cambridge Review*, Isherwood explained that the Group Theatre was not 'an exclusive clique, or a private school admitting only converts and devoted disciplines'. It wanted student members 'not only as audience, but as propagandists, as writers, as artistic collaborators'. It was 'in close collaboration with the Left Wing theatre movement' and it aimed at 'a united cultural front, not only in the theatre itself, but in all departments of artistic activity'. Isherwood emphasized the range of the Group Theatre's plans not only for play production but for song and dance recitals and for non-theatrical events such as lectures and exhibitions. He accurately represented the Group Theatre as an artistic collective focused on theatre, but not confined by it. It was a 'Revelation suitcase', he said, 'not Procrustes' bed'.[31]

Over the following months, speakers at the Rooms included Professors Bernal and E. J. Dent, Tom Harrisson (the founder of Mass-Observation), MacNeice, Denis Johnston and Michael Redgrave. In collaboration with Artists' International and Unity Theatre, the Group Theatre sponsored a series of discussions on 'Realism and Superrealism in Art'. Berthold Viertel arranged and directed a theatrical programme consisting of Beatrix Lehmann in Cocteau's monodrama, *The Human Voice* (*La Voix humaine*) and a recital by the *diseuse*, Marianne Oswald. The recital included songs by Jacques Prévert and Joseph Kosma, Bert Brecht and Kurt Weill, and *chansons parlées* by Cocteau, all chosen for their bitterness.[32] This performance was given in July, 1938, for one Sunday at the Westminster.

Later in the year, the Group Theatre arranged an exhibition cum cabaret cum dance 'in aid of the suffering children of Government Spain'. The painters exhibiting included Vanessa Bell, Duncan Grant, Augustus John, Henry Moore and Mark Gertler. For the cabaret, directed by Doone, Hedli Anderson sang and members of the Ballet Club danced. This was one of the bigger 'happenings' (to use an anachronistic but fitting term) staged by the Group Theatre in collaboration with Artists' International.

In the productions at the Westminster, the actors had invaded the auditorium as part of the Group Theatre's effort to make 'total theatre'. After 1937 the Group became even more total. The aims of forming a company, acquiring a theatre and founding a school were not abandoned altogether and after Keynes became an interested supporter Doone tried to enlist his help in realizing them.[33] But as its prospects for a permanent role in the professional theatre dimmed, the Group Theatre began to treat every area of cultural activity as potentially its 'theatre'. Whether in a theatre building or some other setting its principal artists were actors, playing the continuous, often exhausting, real-life roles they devised for themselves.

When Auden and Isherwood put on a dramatic recital for the *Sunday Times* Book Fair it was not billed as an entertainment by the Group Theatre but it was consistent with Isherwood's conception of a group engaged in 'all departments of artistic activity'.[34] In 1938, the departure of Auden and Isherwood for China was a well-publicized performance of which the climax, a party held at Julian Trevelyan's studio, was produced and stage managed by Doone. On this occasion Hedli Anderson sang Auden–Britten songs, as she did 'all over the place'.[35] One of the most dramatic scenes in Spender's *agon* as a member of the Communist Party was staged in the Group Theatre Rooms as a discussion of *Trial of a Judge*, which turned out to be the political trial of the poet. Other 'performances' linked with productions were the speeches given by Spender, Auden and Doone on various opening nights. The amusing one that Auden delivered after *On the Frontier* helped to justify Keynes's refusal to present the play while its authors were away. They were an essential part of the show.[36]

In its last phase the Group Theatre might be described as a cluster of nuclear collaborations. There was the Auden–Isherwood nucleus to which Doone, Britten and Medley might, on occasion, be attached. The Auden–Britten combination was a distinct unit and also part of a trio with Hedli

Anderson. Even productions of plays assumed distinct collaborative formations. For *The Agamemnon* and *Out of the Picture* the basic combination was MacNeice, Britten, Doone and Medley; for *Trial of a Judge*, Spender, Doone and Piper. The Group Theatre as a whole was so loosely structured as to be more an idea than a practical entity: a 'theatre' in the very special sense of an artists' collective serving to promote collaboration and performance.

In constituting themselves a 'theatre', the collaborating artists found relief from isolation, a function for love and friendship, and a system of mutual support. The Group also provided opportunties for showing off and the release of a high, even hysterical, excitement. Isherwood confessed in his diary: 'I am getting ludicrously ambitious. I want to be known, flattered, talked about; to see my name in the papers. And the worst of it is, I can. It's all so cheap and easy'.[37] It might also be claimed that this form of 'theatre' was a gesture of opposition to the big political show which had tanks for props, bombs for effects, and actors who did not go home at the end of the tragedy.

In opposing theatre to Fascism members of the Group took different approaches. Auden and Isherwood were as keen to carry the political offensive (but not too offensively) into the West End as Eliot was to establish a religious beach-head there. Spender had a clear perception of Fascism as essentially opposed to a permanent world of ideas that poetry was witness to. Doone was dedicated to an embodied art which, for him, was more significant than the manipulations of human material by dictators and generals. Britten, Moody, Medley and other members of the Group needed to find a directly humanitarian *use* for their art. MacNeice had an acute understanding of free, serious and artistic play as a means of subverting totalitarianism of all kinds; and so did Auden, who had imbued the Group with this sense of play in its early years, though he himself lost his taste for it as his fame grew.

9
The Ascent of F6

My love for these bathers is hopeless and
excessive.[1]
The Ascent of F6, 1937

By February 1936, Auden had decided that his next play was
to be 'about montaineering', an obviously 'right' choice of
subject for him, as Louis MacNeice remarked, since he had
already made a poetic scenario in which mountain-climbing
was fraught with psychological and political implications.[2] In
one poem he had, indeed, sketched the fable that was now to
be dramatized:

> By landscape reminded once of his mother's figure
> The mountain heights he remembers get bigger. . . .
>
>   this prophet, homing the day is ended,
> Receives odd welcome from the country he so defended:
> The band roars 'Coward, Coward', in his human fever,
> The giantess shuffles nearer, cries 'Deceiver'.[3]

The 'leader / Of doomed companions . . .' found in another
poem anticipated the hero of the new play; and the speaker in
another had a motive for climbing very like that of one of the
characters:

> Fleeing the short-haired mad executives,
> The subtle useless faces round my home,
> Upon the mountains of our fear I climb. . . .[4]

Auden had not only written poems about mountain-climbing but had been written *about* in the same vein. In Day-Lewis's sublimely optimistic *The Magnetic Mountain*, of 1933, 'Wystan, lone flier' is the leader of a group of politico-poetic fellow travellers who are just beginning the ascent that will culminate in an aesthetic and social revolution.[5] Such were the hopes of what Auden had called 'the season of the change of heart'.[6] In keeping with the more pessimistic attitude of 1936, *The Ascent of F6* brought the metaphorical climb to its tragic catastrophe.

From the first it was understood that Auden would write *The Summit*—as the play was then called—with Isherwood; so, immediately after *The Dog Beneath the Skin* closed in mid-March, 1936, he joined his collaborator in Sintra, Portugal, (where Spender had recently been part of the ménage and writing *Trial of a Judge*), and set to work. A complete draft was finished in a month and by September the play was published. It was dedicated to a dedicated mountaineer and brother, John Auden.

In the plot of *F6* the authors evoked hero myths of the late imperial tradition. The story of a British team racing against foreigners recalls Scott's second Antarctic expedition and the fate of Captain Oates. The leader's choice of an unlikely companion for the final assault on the unscaled summit brings Mallory and Irving to mind. It was a yarn fit for a boys' weekly.

F6 is a mountain in Sudoland, a British colony of indeterminate location. (Its coffee beans, sea coast and name suggest Abyssinia, but its monks, Tibet.) Michael Ransom, climber and Renaissance man, thinks he wants to climb the mountain because it is there. His brother, Sir James, the Colonial Secretary, wants him to lead an expedition because the natives have been persuaded that whoever reaches the summit first will rule the region for a thousand years. This is a new superstition that the agents of Ostnia, which disputes Britain's claims to the area, have grafted on to an old one about a guardian demon of the mountain. Ostnia has already dispatched a secret expedition to climb F6 as the play begins.

This is 'prep school atmosphere' with a vengeance but the play has a moral stratosphere too.

'We wanted to contrast mountain-climbing for climbing's sake and mountain-climbing used for political ends,' said Isherwood, but the theme of the play was rather grander than he suggested.[7] In *F6*, the alternative to political manipulation is not merely 'climbing for climbing's sake' but the quest for spiritual salvation. And for this theme the authors were very heavily indebted to Eliot. It was *Murder in the Cathedral* that gave them a starting point and a structure for the dramatization of Michael Ransom's attempt to save himself and redeem others.

Isherwood had been one of the few reviewers who perceived the importance of the connection between contemporary politics and Christianity in Eliot's play, in which he also detected a 'confusion of aims'. Eliot, he argued, was both attracted and repelled by 'the topical aspect of the murder, with its numerous counterparts in present-day Europe'. In the Knights' apologia he had ventured into 'the world of Mr Auden' without knowing how to act there, toying 'with anachronisms, but so gingerly that they merely startle us'.[8]

Isherwood's point was well taken. In *The Rock*, Eliot and Browne had presented Christianity, wishfully, as a *political* alternative to totalitarianism and plutocracy. In *Murder in the Cathedral*, more realistically, the people are left under the firm control of the thuggish Knights, one of whom threatens the audience much in the manner of the General at the end of *The Chase*:

> I suggest that you now disperse quietly to your homes. Please be careful not to loiter in groups at street corners, and do nothing that might provoke any public outbreak.[9]

In terms of the *historical* setting of the play the consolation for political repression is 'another saint in Canterbury' but how this apolitical 'answer' bears on the *contemporary* problems that are alluded to is by no means clear. What, it might be asked, is the *present* expression of the timeless,

spiritual reality that transcends temporal disorders? Faced with
the 'Fascist'—as it unmistakably is—power of the Knights, the
Women and Priests of fifteenth-century Canterbury are vouch-
safed Thomas. But what of the damp-souled housemaids and
carbuncular clerks of the contemporary world of Eliot's
poetry? In what form might spiritual value be made manifest to
them? In *F6*, Auden and Isherwood attempted to face up to the
vision of *The Waste Land*, from which Eliot, in *Murder in the
Cathedral*, had averted his eyes, and looked for contemporary
equivalents for the medieval terms that Eliot had resorted to in
his play. *F6* was, in fact, a riposte to the cunning ambivalences of
Eliot's Christian polity.

F6 begins on an elevated note with Michael Ransom seated
on the summit of Pillar Rock, overlooking Wastdale in the Lake
District. This literal rock is his private church in which he
meditates on a text taken from the poet that Eliot most admired:

> Who was Dante—to whom the Universe was peopled only
> by his aristocratic Italian acquaintances and a few classical
> literary characters, the fruit of an exile's reading—who
> was Dante to speak of Virtue and Knowledge? It was not
> Virtue those lips, which involuntary privation had made so
> bitter, could pray for; it was not Knowledge; it was Power.
> Power to exact for every snub, every headache, every
> unfallen beauty, an absolute revenge. . . .[10]   [p. 14]

The stage direction gives Ransom a pocket Dante, but Eliot's
essays would have done as well. There Ransom would have
found both the quotation to which he refers and Eliot's
endorsement of it.[11] The repudiation of this claim, standing as it
does as prologue to the play, reflects not only on Dante and
Eliot, but also on the motivation of the author of Ransom's
speech. And it is by no means the only occasion on which, in *F6*,
authorial self-mockery is used to exorcize—or perhaps prop-
itiate—the demons of spiritual pride.

In the valley of the living, where Ransom's detachment from
life and his invulnerability to its ordinary temptations give him a
saintly aura, three groups look to him to satisfy their needs: the

political Establishment; his fellow climbers; and the masses. The first of these, Sir James's gang, have much the same use for mountaineering as Hitler had for the 1936 Olympic Games. The second, the climbers, stand in relation to Ransom as Eliot's Priests stand to Thomas à Becket. They try to influence their leader according to their own feebler lights but they also expect him to show the complete moral integrity that they themselves lack. The third group, the masses—rather thinly represented by Mr and Mrs A—seek redemption from a meaningless passivity through vicarious identification with Ransom. This being the modern world, they do not perceive their hero directly, as the Women of Canterbury do, but through the one-way and polluted media of press and radio. Whether Ransom will resist the temptations and manoeuvres of the Establishment, meet the expectations of the climbers and inspire the nameless masses, is the line through the public theme of the play.

Ransom's social role depends on his personal probity and, in contrast with Eliot's protagonist, he succumbs to temptation. Thomas is hypostasized as a saint, but Ransom, in his last moments, is driven back to his natural origin. In place of Eliot's Christian idealism, *F6* offers Freudian 'realism'. The hero fails because he is inescapably a traumatized son of woman. In one version of the ending the dead Ransom becomes mere material for propaganda.

Not only the main theme but also some of the language and versification of *F6* were derived in part from Eliot. Mr and Mrs A come from the same socio-literary class as Eliot's living-dead office clerks, with just a dash of Strube's resilient little man for stiffening. They are seen and see themselves, expressionistically, *sub specie poetatis*:

> *Evening. A slick and unctuous Time*
> *Has sold us yet another shop-soiled day,*
> *Patently rusty, not even in a gaudy box.*   [p. 17]

Here, they echo Eliot's 'Preludes', elsewhere his Women of Canterbury:

I have received singular warnings:
In the eyes of the beggar I have experienced the earthquake
and the simoon.

Sitting in the crowded restaurant, I have overheard the
confabulations of weasels.   [p. 20]

The juxtaposed parodies serve to expose the lack of
connection in Eliot's work between the Pre-Raphaelitish folk
of *Murder in the Cathedral*, for whom salvation can be
imagined, and the much less appetizing working classes of the
poems, who appear unredeemable. If 'history' was Eliot's
refuge from despair, *F6*, with its rigorous contemporaneity,
offered to confront the tragedy of the present. Literary and
remote as it is, Auden's portrayal of the lost masses is less
evasive than Eliot's presentation of the saved ones in *Murder
in the Cathedral*.

As for a contemporay equivalent to Eliot's Becket, an
obvious candidate was Lenin. In 1934, Auden had described
him, in the course of a review of Liddell Hart's biography of
T. E. Lawrence, as one of the two men

> whose lives exemplify most completely what is best and
> significant in our time, our nearest approach to a
> synthesis of feeling and reason, act and thought. . . .[12]

Auden's other great exemplar was T. E. Lawrence himself.

In *The Dog Beneath the Skin* Sir Francis Crewe was a
Lawrence-type hero—an eccentric individualist and rebel —
when he put the dog-skin on, and a severely pragmatic,
doctrinaire Lenin-type by the time he emerged from it. In *F6*,
the authors might have pursued the delineation of a Leninist
hero and made him the modern counterpart to Eliot's saint;
instead they reverted to the Lawrence-type. There was nothing
Leftist about Ransom.

In letting it be known that their hero was based on the late
T. E. Lawrence, the playwrights harnessed to *F6* some of the
avid public curiosity about Lawrence's life and death.

Isherwood told E. M. Forster that Lawrence's name was invoked 'for short-hand descriptive purposes', and that the play was really 'only about Lawrence in so far as the problem of personal ambition versus the contemplative life' was concerned.[13] This was a way of disclaiming any impertinent or crude speculations about the psychology of Forster's friend, but it was scarcely an adequate reason for letting such a powerful genie out of the bottle.

T. E. Lawrence was an eminently suitable prototype for a tragic protagonist. A writer and man of action, famous and enigmatic, proud and self-abasing, of the ruling class and in reaction against it, he was one who 'in his own lifetime gathered about him all the legendary atmosphere of the hero'.[14] His death in 1935 had been the occasion for a kind of secular canonization: 'someone outside [the world's] jurisdiction; someone strangely enfranchised, untamed, untrammelled by conventions, moving independently of the ordinary currents of human action', was how Winston Churchill described him at the unveiling of the Lawrence memorial.[15] In the first edition of *F6*, Mr A, standing in front of the Ransom memorial, expressed a similar sentiment.[16]

Lawrence of Arabia was a contemporary culture hero well able to bear comparison with Thomas of Canterbury and the evocation of Lawrence compensated for the fact that Ransom, as a fictional character in an improbable plot, lacked the solid historical reality of Eliot's hero. It was thoroughly in keeping with the playwrights' conception that, in the 1939 revival of the play, Alec Guinness brushed up on Lawrence as a way of preparing to play Ransom and 'conveyed the ascetic qualities of a modern saint and man of action'.[17]

The use of Lawrence as a model was complicated by the fact that the authors apparently had different views of him. Auden, in 1934, supposed that Lawrence had conquered the temptation to 'blind action', which would have led him 'to enlist in the great Fascist retreat'.[18] With difficulty and resolution, he had transformed himself from the 'Truly Weak Man into the Truly Strong Man'. These terms—so compulsively used by

both Auden and Isherwood—tend to flip, but it is clear that
Auden's 'Lawrence' resisted the desire of the weak to appear
strong and developed a 'truly strong' indifference to seeming
weak, unpatriotic and unsuccessful. And this is the kind of
man—so unlike her husband and her elder son—that Mrs
Ransom has attempted to make of her son Michael:

> He cannot live an hour without applause.
> No one can say that I have stinted it.
> But you, you were to be the truly strong
> Who must be kept from all that could infect
> Or weaken; it was for you I steeled my love
> Deliberately and hid it.   [p. 47]

This maternal rigour is not quite what it seems, since, like
Thomas à Becket's Tempters, Mrs Ransom is an image
projected from Ransom's own mind—though she tended to
become all too solid flesh on the stage, especially in her
blank verse manifestations.

Isherwood's description of Lawrence—appearing after the
latter's death and after the creation of Ransom—had much
in common with that of the Marxist critic, Christopher
Caudwell. Like Auden, but to very different effect, Caudwell
compared Lawrence and Lenin. Lawrence, he said, was a
'bourgeois hero', strangled by his own consciousness whereas Lenin acted from an understanding of social causality.[19]
Isherwood, too, saw Lawrence as the embodiment of the
neurosis of a generation: a man who, although his highest
ambition was literary, had failed as a writer because he 'had
been unable to bring himself to record the full history of the
"deep cleavage" in his own nature'.[20] These neurotic
features of Lawrence are reflected with particular clarity in
Ransom's crisis in the monastery and also when his mother
tempts in rhyme:

> Michael, you shall be renowned,
> When the Demon you have drowned,
> A cathedral we will build

> *When the Demon you have killed. . . .*
>
> *A saint am I and a saint are you. . . .*   [p. 55]

Since the desire for sainthood is axiomatically counterproductive and 'Mrs Ransom' is herself the Demon, Michael Ransom's situation is as introverted as Thomas à Becket's when the Fourth Tempter voices his inmost desires. Mrs Ransom is here the symbolic figure through whom the ineluctable female influence, that deadly flaw in Nature, is dramatized. As Forster remarked in his review of the play, 'Mother-love, usually sacrosanct, becomes a very nasty customer.'[21]

The authors' divergent views of Lawrence may have been a source of the perplexing double motivation given to Ransom. When he first agrees to lead the expedition, Ransom is motivated by a complex of mother-fixation, sibling rivalry, Oedipal longings and the desire for adulation. Having been made fully aware of these corruptions in his nature, he resolves to abandon the climb. His resolution is short-lived, however. 'I must choose for myself alone', he says, but almost immediately accedes to the wishes of his companions and goes on up the mountain. This is the turning point of the plot and also its most obscure moment. Ransom's mother has nothing to do with this second decision, which so obviously violates his own better judgement. It proceeds from an obscure conflict within himself that is focused on his fellow climber David Gunn.

With one great exception, Ransom detaches himself from the wretched failings of humanity. The exception is David Gunn, whose very obvious flaws—including kleptomania, cowardice, greed and womanizing—Ransom indulges. No wonder that Shawcross, besotted as he is with Ransom, is driven to suicide by his idol's preference for the worse man.

The relationship between Ransom and Gunn was rather teasingly dramatized in the first (prematurely published) edition.[22] At the crisis of the play, when Ransom must decide whether to continue the climb, he has a conversation with Gunn that breaks off before Gunn can fully grasp the meaning of it:

RANSOM: Now I come to think of it, I remember that I never even asked you if you wanted to join this expedition. I asked all the others. I suppose I took you for granted.

GUNN: I should hope you did! I should like to see anybody trying to get up F6 and me not there!

RANSOM: But supposing, at the same time, somebody else had asked you to climb another mountain, twice as high as F6 and twice as difficult? Then would you have gone with him instead:

GUNN: Of course not! Oh, well, perhaps—I don't know.

Ransom's drift is not crystal clear. Is he worried that he may be abusing Gunn's affection, and that Gunn, unlike the others, has not had the chance to weigh up the balance of danger and reward; that he is unworthy of the trust Gunn places in him; or that Gunn may *not* be on the mountain for the sake of his leader but merely for the adventure? In any case the quality of Gunn's attachment to Ransom is the crucial factor and a little later, the solution to the mystery is imminent:

GUNN: . . . what this expedition would be like without you I simply can't imagine—

RANSOM: Listen, David. There's something I must tell you, now—[23]

What the something is we never learn. It is not that Ransom is going to take Gunn on the final assault. That decision is yet to come. The audience would have been to left to guess Ransom's urgent meaning.

In the revised text the passage was changed to make Gunn's purity of motive the issue:

RANSOM: You've thought enough about the ascent of F6 no doubt; about the couloirs and the north buttress and the arête. . . . Have you thought about the descent, too: the descent that goes down and down into the place where Stagmantle and my Brother and all their gang are waiting? Have you thought about the crowds in the street down there, and the loudspeakers and the posing and the photographing and the hack-written articles you'll be paid thousands to sign? Have you smelt the smell of their ceremonial banquets? Have you loathed them, and even as you were loathing them, begun to like it all? (*Becomes hysterically excited.*) Have you? Have you?

GUNN: (*Scared*) M.F., what on earth do you mean?

RANSOM: Don't lie to me now, David. Are you corrupt, like the rest of us? I must know. (*Seizes Gunn by the wrists and stares into his face.*) Yes. Yes. I see it! You too. How horrible! (*Throws him violently aside.*) Get out of my sight!   [pp. 77–8]

As a confession of his own horror of publicity and fascination with it, Ransom's fury is convincing enough. But why is he made to spend his passion on Gunn who, of all the climbers, is so obviously open to *all* the world's temptations? The puritanical Shawcross would make a much more fitting punchbag; or anyone but Gunn, about whom there is no question whatsoever that he is corrupt and, as audiences invariably felt, very attractively so. Ransom cannot now be discovering the frailty that he has already acknowledged and chosen to accept.

The dramatic situation created by Isherwood is quite clear: Shawcross is passionately devoted to Ransom and jealous of Gunn, while Gunn is insensitive to others' feelings, including Ransom's for him. This situation remains inert, presumably because the emotional triangle is a homosexual one. So, instead of the concreteness of the theatre, we have Ransom's not quite intelligible mental anguish. One consequence of this is that the authorial sympathy seems to be loosely and oddly associated with the outward and priggish aspect of the character.

Unlike such Left-wing writers as John Cornford, Christopher Caudwell, Cecil Day-Lewis and Rex Whistler, all of whom linked political and sexual emancipation, Auden and Isherwood concentrated, in their plays, on the negative (and heterosexual) aspects of the relation between social and sexual life. In Auden's poems a positive attitude to love found expression, but in the theatre, where the sex of the lover could not be left indefinite, he and Isherwood faced a particular test of sincerity. Had they focused on the crisis (as it appears to be) of a high-principled man who discovers that his social love is, after all, an extension of a repressed homosexual one—a love of which he is ashamed and that would alter everybody's view of him—they might have written a powerfully tragic play. It might also have been a banned one, of course, and they would certainly have had to have been a good deal more circumspect about alluding to T. E. Lawrence. As it was, the lack of concreteness in the portrayal of Ransom led critics to dwell on its unintelligibility. *Punch* guessed that Ransom had been 'scarred by a difficult childhood'.[24]

In the writing of *F6*, there was a clear division of labour between Auden and Isherwood. Auden wrote the 'woozy' passages: Ransom's opening speech; his dialogue with his mother; his soliloquy on the skull; the Abbot's big speech; and the passage about the death of Gunn. He also contributed the verse dialogue of Mr and Mrs A and the choruses. Isherwood was the main author of the plotting and the dialogue in scenes set in the Colonial Office and the inn; at the monastery; on the arête; and at Camp A—scenes that he later described as 'full of surreal parody, satire and pastiche'. The ending of the play, which the authors were never satisfied with, was joint work.[25]

Auden's part in the composition was the more abstract and universal. Social and spiritual despair, the quest for salvation, and the death wish were the main themes developed by him. Isherwood's part was the more concrete and satirical and included the drawing of most of the secondary characters. He cast the Establishment group in a Shavian mould: the neat complementarity of this rather endearing quartet of Edwar-

dian rascals recalls Shaw's dramaturgy and Lord Stagmantle
is particularly reminiscent of Shaw's Undershaft. There is no
hint of the savagery that went into the making of some of
the caricatures of *The Dog Beneath the Skin*.

The climbers belong to a different stylistic genre. They are
partly allegorical figures, as the names Ransom, Lamp and
(with phallic connotations) Gunn, indicate; but they also
have something of the realism of the characters in R. C.
Sherriff's *Journey's End*, or of another play about the First
World War, J. R. Ackerley's *Prisoners of War*.[26] Sherriff's
play deals with the intense pressures endured by soldiers at
the front; Ackerley's, which Isherwood particularly admired, dramatizes the emotional strains, including those
arising from homosexual rivalry, among a group of captured British officers. Isherwood was less serious than
Sherriff and not as bold as Ackerley in portraying the
emotional cauldron of the expedition but his dramatic
structure is similar to theirs: as the pressures of isolation,
exertion and danger increase, conventions are winnowed
away and the elemental passions of the climbers are
revealed.

The stylistic incongruities between the main groups of
characters—Mr and Mrs A, the Establishment gang, and the
climbers—were not themselves the result of collaboration.
And, far from being unfunctional, they produce an abrasive
energy. Auden spoke of the difficulty of integrating 'characters at different levels of reality' but the authors' main
difficulty was with the characterization of the hero himself
and consequently with the ending of the play.

In the first edition, the play closed with the Establishment
making political capital out of Ransom's triumphant death.
The scene is set in the broadcasting studio from which a
final tribute is being aired. Ransom reached the summit and
his body has been recovered by the Ostnian expedition,
whose leader, rather surprisingly, is in the studio with Sir
James and his gang. The broadcast ends in a mildly
surrealistic manner:

JAMES: Honour—
STAGMANTLE: Service—
GENERAL: Duty—
ISABEL: Sacrifice—
STAGMANTLE: England—
BLAVEK: Ostnia—
THE OTHERS: England! England! England!
    [*The stage box is darkened.*]
MR A: (*Regarding the monument with proprietary pride*) He
    belongs to us now![27]

It is left to the director and the actor to decide how ironical
the final lines are to be.

In the next published version (which went to press before
the play was staged), material from this broadcasting scene
was incorporated into Ransom's phantasmagoria on the
mountain (which now included Mr and Mrs A) but the
original broadcasting scene was *also* retained despite the
repetition or perhaps in error.[28] At the Mercury Theatre it
was intended until the last moment to play the broadcasting
scene but the first performance actually ended on the mountain. Ransom was supposed to be lost in a blizzard and the
success of his attempt on the summit to be as doubtful as
Mallory's on Everest. For the first performance, the phantas-
magoric trial of Ransom was cut and the last part of the play
was enlivened by a jazz scene in which Hedli Anderson sang
the magnificent blues number, 'Stop all the clocks. . . .' On
other evenings other endings were tried.

Lots of advice about the ending of the play was forthcoming. Forster was insistent that the phantasmagoria should be
restored and at the Arts Theatre it was, at least in part.[29] At
the Arts Theatre, too, Mr and Mrs A were given the last
words.[30] Forster also considered that something should be
done about the final appearance of the mother in a rocking
chair, which he found theatrically inadequate, though
psychologically right.[31] Yeats proposed that it would be
'good theatre' for the mother to be revealed, finally, as

'Britannia from the penny'. He was quite serious, he assured
Doone:

> Remember the English expedition is racing that of
> another country because the one who gets first to the top
> will, the natives believe, rule them for a thousand years;
> remember also what the Abbot said about will and about
> government. Britannia is the mother.[32]

Yeats's nationalist mythologizing, even ironically applied, was
doubtless too 'high', but his suggestion had the great merit of
being a concrete resolution of the public and private themes,
conflating the natural evil of motherhood and the political one
of the ruler of the waves. Unfortunately, the authors never got
to hear of it.

In the Old Vic revival of 1939, the final BBC scene was
restored in an abbreviated form, and other endings were tried
later. In a 1945 modification, by Auden, Mrs Ransom gently
and firmly detached herself from her son:

> *Willing to know, unwilling to be known*
> *You dreaded what you wished, to be alone,*
> *And fought that dread with nightmares of your own. . . .*
>
> *Open your eyes now to the Revelation*
> *That dissipates all myths of self-creation*
> *And gives what it demands: self-realisation.*[33]

As well as reworking the ending, Auden and Isherwood
made other changes before the first performance, some of
them in response to criticisms of the published text,
particularly those by Stephen Spender and F. R. Leavis.

A line appearing in the first published version but not
spoken on the stage, was Ransom's 'You haven't changed
much, have you Ian, since you were Head Prefect and Captain
of the First Fifteen?' Ignoring its sarcastic tone, Leavis
exhibited the speech as symptomatic of a fundamental
weakness. None of the climbers had 'changed much since they
were at school—at their Public School' and the authors

obviously assumed that their audience had not changed much either, since

> we are unmistakably expected to feel towards the school hero (the school, of course, being of the class in which mountaineering is a normal interest) the respect and awe felt by his school-fellow followers.[34]

Leavis identified Auden with the immature group consciousness of the climbers, attributing the poet's 'failure ... to mature' to 'the habits of the group world' that had entrapped him:

> The present is a time when the young talent needs as never before the support of the group, and when the group can, as never before, escape all contact with serious critical standards.

He drew no inference from the self-destructiveness of the group of climbers, nor from Ransom's attempt to escape from it into authentic self-hood, but in these ways the play actually embodied the social criticism that Leavis made.

The new political tendency observed in *F6*, particularly in the characterization of the hero, was frequently a cause for alarm or reassurance according to the political outlook of the observer. An anonymous contributor to the *Group Theatre Paper*, though, took a feebly neutral position in describing Ransom as 'a complex study of the hero of action ... who reminds us of ... T. E. Lawrence, or the dictators of the continent'. Obviously no slur on Lawrence was intended since the writer added that 'the pleasant and easy task of lampooning and caricaturing the dictator is here abandoned in favour of an attempt to understand the springs of his conduct'.[35]

Day-Lewis criticised the authors' concern with the 'interpretation of motives', which led to a morality that was 'at best Oxford Group and at worst Fascist'.[36] G. M. Trevelyan, on the other hand, approved the concentration on individual motivation. It marked an advance on the 'immature philosophy' of *The Dog Beneath the Skin*. Auden and Isherwood had now learned that

> the tragedy of modern life is not, as most Marxists assume, the result of something external, but of an interior failure on the part of men themselves.[37]

Quite inconsistently, he added that the play's real weakness was that Ransom's failure was 'not related to the tragedy of Mr and Mrs A'. He wanted both tragedy *and* social causality.

In their revisions the authors made Ransom less a would-be Fascist leader, more a would-be saviour who is brought to recognize his self-deception. In the first edition he sees himself as a

> *small gesticulating figure on the dais*
> *Above the swooning faces of the crowd*
> *Amid the torrential gestures of assent....*[38]

In the played version the blank verse became prose and the Fascist vision was modified. Through Ransom's eyes the crowd was now seen disgustingly close up:

> Was it to me they turned their rodent faces, those ragged denizens of the waterfronts, and squealed so piteously: 'Restore us! Restore us to our uniqueness and our human condition.'

There was also a clear distinction made between saviour and artist:

> Was it for me the prayer of the sad artist on the crowded beaches was indeed intended? 'Assassinate my horrible detachment. My love for these bathers is hopeless and excessive. Make me also a servant.'   [p. 70]

The artist who loves the bathers clearly alludes to the author of *The Dance of Death*, who could still entertain the pathetic—as it now appears—ambition of restoring the communion between artist and people.

The revision of Ransom's interview with the Abbot was consistent with the new emphasis on the failed saint. In the earlier version Ransom's self-deception was the issue; in the later one the Abbot shows Ransom the folly of trying to defeat the Demon and 'save mankind' by an act of will. Since the will comes from the Demon the aim is self-defeating. Ransom is presented with a miserable and stultifying paradox:

> Because men desire evil, they must be governed by those who understand the corruption of their hearts, and can set bounds to it. . . . But woe to the governors, for, by the very operation of their duty, however excellent, they themselves are destroyed.   [pp. 73–4]

He might have accepted the Abbot's offer and become a neophyte in the monastery, seeking 'complete abnegation of the will'. But, as Isherwood put it, Ransom is 'forced into going up the mountain' by his followers; or by one of them.[39] Ransom, it dimly appears, gives all for love.

The revisions did not answer the fundamental criticism made by Spender. The playwrights 'did not conceal the fact that their hero is a Fascist type', he said, nor was there anything wrong in dealing with this type sympathetically. The fault lay in the absence of an adequate objectification of the most important element in Ransom's character: the fact that he is a 'colossal prig'.[40] In the revised text Ransom was made to apply the term to himself but that did not neutralize the force of Spender's criticism. Ransom's priggishness remained as the outward expression of an obscure inner turmoil.

Notwithstanding the difficulty with the characterization of the hero, the play's construction was compared favourably with that of The Dog Beneath the Skin. Isherwood himself considered F6 'much maturer' than its predecessor and 'more of a unity'.[41] Even Day-Lewis and Spender saw a distinct advance in its authors' stagecraft. Auden and Isherwood had apparently heeded Eliot's recent advice in New Verse. Good dramatic construction, Eliot had learned, demanded that 'the interest should be one interest throughout, not merely a succession of interests'.[42]

Significantly, the advancement of this classical tenet—in unconscious opposition to Brecht's 'non-Aristotelian' principle of 'each scene for itself'—coincided with Eliot's abandonment of the notion of the committed audience. 'We need not assume', he now wrote,

> that the possible audiences represent one class rather than another, or one political tendency rather than another. So far as the dramatic artist is concerned 'the people' is everybody except the present occupants of the stalls at the more expensive theatres.

But, as Eliot was well aware, the dramatist's form did embody assumptions about the political outlook of playwright and audience. In his own search for an appropriate form he was turning to the conventions of the well-made drawing-room comedy, concentrated in time and place, unified in plot, illusionistic in manner, uninterrupted by music or choreographed movement and employing an unobtrusive poetic metre.

Although Eliot did not name *The Dog Beneath the Skin*, it was clearly in his mind as a play that comprised 'a succession of interests'; or, to put it another way, exhibited many of the formal characteristics associated with Leftist theatre: episodic structure, the repudiation of illusionistic techniques for presentational ones that lent themselves to didactic interpolations and parable, and an emphasis on the virtuosity of the performers. Such a form asserted the reality of the here and now both as to the immediate theatrical context and as to the contingent social setting. By contrast, the form that Eliot now advocated implied the unreality of the stage, which stood as a symbol of a world elsewhere.

With *The Ascent of F6* Auden and Isherwood said as much about the modification of their political feelings through the *form* of the work as through its theme. They compressed time and place, and focused on the central symbols of mountain, mother and hero. Despite the use of caricature and other Expressionist devices, the formal tendency of the work was towards the kind of symbolic structure that would become conventional for poetic drama in England.

The irregular blank-verse dialogue of Ransom and Mrs Ransom was a new departure for Auden. There is not much of it but enough to indicate a heightened interest in poetry *in*, rather than *of*, the theatre. Even more telling are Ransom's soliloquies. If burlesque was intended then William Devlin, who created the role, was cruelly deceived. He was hired for the part on the strength of his reputation—largely the result of his Lear—as a tragic actor and speaker of Shakespearian verse. Some thought that in *F6* Devlin hit the authentically tragic note, but Julian Symons had sport at his expense:

> The part of Ransom is played appallingly badly by William Devlin who gets, very early in the evening, the idea that he is acting in *Hamlet*, and does not abandon it. . . . He sits inside the monastery and asks gloomily, 'How many tins of malted milk?' making a bitter rhetorical question out of those ordinary words; he rants and roars whenever he decently can; he stands aloof from the conversation of the rest at all times, particularly in the monastery scene where he leans against the wall, thinking about Difficult and Important Questions, temptation and so on. . . .[43]

The playwrights were partly to blame, said Symons, for putting Shakespearian pastiche into Ransom's mouth: verse such as,

> *O senseless hurricanes*
> *That waste yourselves upon the unvexed rock,*
> *Find some employment proper to your powers. . .* [p. 106]

Much more of this and Auden would have been justly proclaimed a new Stephen Phillips! Happily there is not much more, though it is disconcerting to find that Ransom, when he speaks in blank verse, has much the same kind of thing to say, and much the same way of saying it, as Mildred Luce in *Dogskin*.[44] In such verse Auden seemed to be working both sides of the stylistic street. If it was taken at face value as the language of poetic tragedy (as it often was) well and good; if not, the bolt hole of burlesque had been prepared. Alec Guinness coped with the extravagance of the verse by playing it quietly.

Part of the reason for Auden's ambivalence and surprising poetic ineptitude in *F6* was that he was now using verse in the context of realistic characterization and dialogue whereas he had earlier limited its use to interpolated poems, songs and choruses. But the ambivalence of the play was confined neither to the verse nor to Auden's part in the writing. Isherwood in the theatre was a novelist on holiday but his much later observation that *The Ascent of F6: A Tragedy* was so called in mockery of 'established theatrical values' overestimates the clarity of intention and the sophistication that went into the writing of the play.[45] Despite the pastiche and parody, *F6* was played as a tragedy and received as a flawed one.[46]

For Ashley Dukes the play was the confirmation that 'a living poetic drama' had arrived and, incidentally, the occasion of 'the replacement of comedy by tragedy'. Auden, said Dukes, had achieved the 'highest language of the theatre' and as an example of it he quoted,

> O you, *who are the history and the creator*
> *Of all those forms in which we are condemned to suffer;*
> *To whom the intelligent and necessary is also the just;*
> *Show me my path.* . . .[47]

As it happened, the playwrights did not share Dukes's high opinion of this quasi-liturgical passage, which was rewritten as prose before it was heard on the stage of the Mercury. And it was not spoken verse but the combination of words and music that made *F6* impressive in the theatre.

In his music for the play, Benjamin Britten had to accommodate the stylistic incongruities of the text and, in so far as it could be done, resolve the emotional ambivalences. His score, arranged for two pianos and percussion, included atmospheric music for the mountain and monastery scenes and a number of songs: Gunn's 'I've got a date with love!'; the Mother's song; and the blues numbers. The last were strongly reminiscent of Weill's settings of Brecht. Isherwood himself found the singing of 'Stop all the clocks . . .' by Hedli Anderson 'overwhelming'; while the *New Statesman* reviewer called 'Dance John, dance!', which she also sang, quite 'devastating in its blend of vitality and spiritual death'.[48]

The music was written and rehearsed under trying conditions. At times, Britten found Doone 'really beyond all endurance' and was dismayed by 'his appalling vagueness . . . completely impractical for all his talents'. He made anguished protestations at Doone's cutting of 'a lot of the best music' (some, at least, of which was restored) and was exasperated by the director's demands: Doone 'saying in dozens of places "we must have more music here & here & here"—regardless of the fact that it takes time to write & rehearse music'.[49]

From Britten one gets the sense of the feverish urgency with which the production was mounted; the shortage of time and money, the inadequacy of the Group Theatre organization; and, underlying the local conditions, the desperate struggle to respond fast and effectively to the social and political changes that were threatening to engulf all of them artistically and otherwise.

In performance, Verschoyle found Britten's music 'unnecessary and unpleasing' and Porteus thought the play would have been better without the 'nicely . . . chosen' music, but these were eccentric judgements.[50] The music was extensive, integral and (as a performance at the 1980 Aldeburgh Festival made obvious) extraordinarily powerful. It gave the play a wild, harsh energy and brought it together as a disturbing, multi-faceted but emotionally coherent collage.

For the tiny stage of the Mercury, Medley produced a simple design: a pair of curtains on curved tracks demarcated locations in the downstage corners of the BBC studio on one side and Mr and Mrs A on the other. A raised platform in the centre of the stage represented, with the addition of a few properties, the Pillar Rock, the Wastdale Inn, the room in the Colonial Office, the camps and, finally, the summit. On the summit Mrs Ransom, in a white veil and seated, became part of the geological formation—at least in symbolic intention. The chessboard of Ransom's phantasmagoria was reluctantly abandoned, but despite this important compromise with the limitations of the Mercury, the staging was often admired. Yeats thought it 'almost flawless' and even Verschoyle admitted that, as he put it, 'Rupert Doone managed to avoid the flashier tricks of modernist staging until quite near the end.'[51]

F6 followed the revival of *Murder in the Cathedral* at the Mercury. It opened on 26 February (a week later than had been announced) and enjoyed good houses before it was transferred to the Arts Theatre, Cambridge, on 22 April, by an arrangement between Dukes and Keynes. The play was well received in Cambridge, though Keynes himself was 'angry that being so good it should not be better'.[52] From the Arts Theatre the production went to the Little Theatre. This was a very small house but still it could be said that Auden and Isherwood had now arrived in the West End.

The Ascent of F6 was the Group Theatre's biggest theatrical success but the rejoicing was tempered by the fact that this was not, in a full sense, a Group Theatre production. Even this circumstance, however, was a less serious sign of things to come than the theme of the play itself, which proclaimed that, for Auden and Isherwood, the charms of the 'group world' had vanished. In the play they had tried out new social attitudes that they were not yet ready to confess even to themselves. It was after the completion of *F6* that Auden realized that he would eventually have to leave England and one can see how this decision might have been made as he and Isherwood attempted to isolate and dramatize the failure of Ransom.

10
Louis MacNeice and the Group Theatre

The poet is likely to find bits of himself . . . on
the stage which he would never notice
among the books and papers in his study.[1]
LOUIS MACNEICE, 1938

Playwriting was a means by which Louis MacNeice attempted
to steer past the whirlpool of introspection and affirm his
existence as a social being. He had a 'hankering for some sort
of group life' and saw this as 'a desire doomed to
disappointment' as far as modern poets were concerned,
though it might be enjoyed by artists who were inevitably
involved in collaboration, such as 'playwrights, actors and
musical executants'. Predisposed as he was to the kind of
collaboration that the Group Theatre stood for, MacNeice
immersed himself in collective creation more fully than any of
its other playwrights, though it was not with the Group but in
the BBC that he 'found this missing group experience' in a
valid form.[2]

Not only the contingent circumstances of playwriting but
the very use of dramatic form served MacNeice as a way out of
self-absorption. By contrast with Eliot and Spender, he turned
to playwriting more as a relief from the intensity of poetry than
to find another medium for it. In the 'mere fact that one's
words issue from other people's mouths', as a playwright he
found 'a welcome release from . . . involuntary egotism'.[3] The
kind of plays he liked best were 'a mixture à la
Shakespeare—comic relief sticking out in the middle of

tragedy, rant, jokes for the groundlings, and slapstick'.[4] Delighting in the inherent vulgarity of the stage, he was so willing to meet the audience half way that he often overemphasized incidental theatrical effects at the expense of the overall dramatic structure.

If the desire to 'connect' was MacNeice's dominant motive for playwriting, its antithesis—the world's assault on the self—was his great dramatic theme. In his plays, a barrage of bills, bombs and busybodies prevents the self from getting on with what it supposes to be its own business. Intrusive 'persons from Porlock' masquerade as creditors and predatory women, politicians and planners, broadcasters and bailiffs, but ironically they turn out to be mere parrots with nothing to say that their victim, the self, has not taught them. MacNeice could not escape the self, even in the objectivity of the theatre.

Auden took to the theatre as a form of corporate communion: for MacNeice it was a Saturnalia, an opportunity to turn the psyche inside out and make a wild social game out of private terror. All the Group Theatre playwrights described their work in formulations similar to Doone's 'realistic fantasy, fantastic realism' but it was singularly apt for MacNeice. 'Single-plane' writing was almost bound to be a falsification, he said:

> The fact that there is method in madness and the fact that there is fact in fantasy (and equally fantasy in 'fact') have been brought home to us not only by Freud and other psychologists but by events themselves.[5]

In the world in which 'Mussolini . . . surpasses the wildest fantasies of Swift', MacNeice found confirmation of his fundamental doubts about supposed distinctions between mind and its objects; and he seized on the theatre, and later the radio, as means of expressing the inextricability of substance from fantasy.[6]

At the beginning of 1934, MacNeice, who was then a 27-year-old lecturer at Birmingham University, had five books in progress or planned.[7] One of these was a play on which he had already made a good start. In January it was 'in fair shape', in March he revised it completely and by the end of June, or thereabouts, it was finished.[8] MacNeice had begun the play with a view to its performance in Dublin but, like Sean O'Casey before him, MacNeice found that for practical purposes he had overdone the Irishness. It 'wouldn't be allowed' in the Free State, he thought, since President De Valera 'would take it personally'. He was confident, though, that it would 'look very well on the stage'.[9]

It was this play, *Station Bell*, that MacNeice sent to Doone early in 1934, when he heard about the existence of the Group Theatre from Auden. What Auden had in mind, he told Doone, was that MacNeice should make a translation for the Group of a play by Aeschylus or Aristophanes—a natural combination of MacNeice's avocations of scholar and poet—so the submission of an original play by another aspirant poet-playwright was something of a surprise; but not, in the event, an especially pleasant one for Doone.

Station Bell is an Aristophanic, political fantasy in prose rather reminiscent of the plays of Denis Johnston. It is set in the waiting room of a Dublin station and its protagonist is the new Fascist dictatress of Ireland. Her stratagems include the demolition of a train full of passengers and elopement with a lunatic posing as a vicar. Among the minor characters are such exotics as a bearded lady and two carnival giants, members of the dictatress's propaganda corps. It is 'all very Olympia Circus', as MacNeice said, and full of the 'old and vulgar tropes' that he relished.

Doone rejected *Station Bell* but MacNeice was not put out since he himself thought its Irishness 'a bit much' for the Group Theatre. He hoped to persuade the Dublin Gate Theatre to produce the play and, in the meantime, planned to write another one that would be 'less of a compromise between two traditions' and more suitable for the Group.[10]

The new play, first called *The Rising Venus*, progressed very slowly and, in 1935, MacNeice put it aside to begin work on a translation of *The Agamemnon*. Then, in December of the year, came the great upheaval in his personal life caused by the elopement of his wife. After this, the translation assumed high priority and in March 1936 MacNeice was hurrying to get it finished before he left for a visit to 'still peaceful Spain'. From a draft prologue it may be gathered that his own recent experience was very much on his mind.[11] He stressed the importance of Helen's elopement as an antecedent to the action and darkly observed that it was 'to be noticed that both Menelaus and Agamemnon are ruined by their wives'.[12]

MacNeice was aiming to produce an actable English version that would come as close as possible to Aeschylus' meaning. He deliberately sacrificed 'the liturgical flavour of the diction and the metrical complexity of the choruses', though he did not altogether avoid archaic constructions, inversions, congested phrasing and other traces of translatorese.[13]

When he returned to England in mid-April, MacNeice found Doone unenthusiastic. Doone seemed to think that *The Agamemnon* was not 'topical enough for his chaps' though he was 'going to get them to work on the choruses and see if they think them feasible'.[14] It was probably at this stage that MacNeice refined his translation and made it more pointedly contemporary in its diction.

Without straying from the sense of the original, MacNeice sharpened the analogy between past and present. The Herald's speech, for example, evoked the First World War:

> *If I were to tell you of our labours, or hard lodging,*
> *The sleeping on crowded decks, the scanty blankets,*
> *Tossing and groaning, rations that never reached us—*
> *And the land too gave matter for disgust. . . .*
> *Continuous drizzle from the sky, dews from the marshes,*
> *Rotting our clothes, filling our hair with lice.*   [p. 31–2]

Later in the play, the Chorus utters the fear that Clytemnestra and Aegisthus 'are going to set up a dictatorship in the state' (p. 59) and the verbal suggestiveness was underscored in performance by having the soldiers give the Nazi salute.[15]

But MacNeice and Doone need not have been concerned that the play would seem irrelevant. As one reviewer remarked:

> The lesson that evil produces evil, that blood begets blood, is worth repeating; and the killing of Iphigeneia, in exchange for a favourable wind for ships of war, is no mere fable of the past, when every day munitions factories flourish and populations starve.[16]

Two assumptions that MacNeice asked his audience to adopt for the occasion had particular bearing on the contemporaneity of the play. One was that 'war is a disaster, caused by the stupidity of a few and ending in the suffering of many'.[17] For the performance, MacNeice foreshadowed this general suffering by tacking on to *The Agamemnon* the first chorus of *The Choephoroe*, and so ending with a descent into chaos no less pertinent to the Europe of 1936 than to the house of Atreus:

> *The house is down, the sun shines no more*
> *The master is fallen and the house is dark*
> *The authority of kingship is gone but fear survives. . . .*[18]

A second Aeschylean assumption that the audience was asked to make was that sin is not only real but 'punished in this world' by a chain of cause and effect.[19] It was an assumption that invited some reflection on the contemporary political situation and denied any such transcendent consolation as that offered by *Murder in the Cathedral*. Like Auden and Isherwood in *The Ascent of F6*, MacNeice was offering *The Agamemnon* as a corrective to Eliot's play; this time through a strictly temporal perspective of ritual murder. In the production, though, Christian analogies undermined Aeschylean rigour.

The speech from *The Choephoroe* was also intended by MacNeice as a reminder of the incompleteness of the action of *The Agamemnon*, for which some compensating device was required. Somehow the audience had to be informed of both the antecedent events and the rest of the *Oresteia* if they were

to grasp the significance of the play being presented. One of the
solutions proposed, and rejected, was the prologue already
mentioned. Another suggestion, coming from Auden, was that
the Atreid family tree be depicted on a stage cloth.[20] MacNeice
entertained this idea but decided that the facts of the story and
the assumptions embodied in it should be given together. The
weak device eventually adopted was a programme note. It did
not forestall the general complaint that, in isolation from the
rest of the *Oresteia*, *The Agamemnon* was not fully compre-
hensible.

Like Doone, MacNeice was anxious that the staging should
not be too static. He supposed that the stage direction would
compensate for the lack of intrinsic physical action with
'marchings and countermarchings and things' and he included
tentative stage directions to this end.[21] The first chorus might,
he suggested, be accompanied by 'women moving round
silently, nunlike, doing obeisance at the altar or altars'. He
wanted Agamemnon and Cassandra to enter in two chariots
'to martial music'. Aegisthus' guards might confront the
Chorus with 'stylized threats and counter-threats approximat-
ing to a dance'.[22]

MacNeice also interested himself in the design of the
costumes, wanting something of the gorgeousness that the
Greeks expected in the theatre: 'Not . . . that you should do it
at all archaeologically,' he told Doone,

> but I think the production ought to tend towards the
> statuesque and rather larger-than-life. I think the classical
> Greek dress (tunic and much too flowing *peplos*) ought to
> be avoided; it is too vague and incoherent. Best to create
> your own costumes with hints from the Mycenean age
> etc. and archaic statues and vase paintings. E.g. I think
> you might use the very precise, elaborate coiffures of the
> archaic period. Clytemnestra might have a very lofty one.
> Also I don't think she should have a flowing unbusiness-
> like dress but a fairly fitting one like some of the
> goddesses; or possibly a highly flounced skirt like the

Cretan snake priestesses; ear-rings; plenty of colour. Agamemnon might wear a cloak such as some of the Homeric heroes have on the vases—very patterned, all over stars and rosettes.[23]

Medley followed MacNeice's suggestions for the costuming of the principal characters and his designs for their dresses (especially Clytemnestra's, with its brilliantly coloured, geometrical pattern) were often admired. But there were also some dissenting opinions and much mockery of the clothes worn by the Chorus.

The *Time and Tide* reviewer was one who took exception to the design of the costumes overall:

> Aeschylus, it seems, would be dead unless modernized. So we had the curious spectacle of a chorus dressed in dinner-jackets and goggles . . . a watchman as a hooded monk. Clytemnestra with a headdress of a Chinese mandarin backed by a scroll, Agamemnon with a jester's cap, slaves in purple tarbushes and veils and close-fitting black tights, more slaves dressed like the Klu Klux Klan, Cassandra as an Arab from the shores of the Euphrates, with an Elizabethan ruff, and lastly Aegisthus in a Christmas cracker helmet and black evening cape. This might be thought enough; yet undoubtedly the *pièce de résistance* was the almost universal gloving of the cast.[24]

The reviewer disliked the choreography almost as much, hazarding the opinion that in Greek drama 'the actors should be simply clothed in togas, almost statuesque in action'. MacNeice defended the director and designer from this 'dear simple Greeks' attitude, but the dinner-jackets and the masks of the Chorus of Old Men he did not approve; on the contrary he diplomatically applauded Doone's integrity in recognizing them as a failed experiment that was abandoned after the first performance.[25]

The advance publicity had made a point of mentioning the novel masks, made of cellophane panels. Auden explained that,

> Just as the Greek has to be translated into modern
> English, so the visual effects have similarly to be
> translated. The chorus masks in combination with the
> modern jackets are intended to give the effect of a timeless
> formality, the masking resembling a leaded head in a
> stained-glass window.[26]

This was indeed the effect that Doone was aiming at but the
masks did not much resemble stained glass because the faces
behind them, though whitened, did not reflect enough light to
make the cellophane transparent. The *Stage* found them
redolent of seaside holidaymaking.[27]

Quite apart from the practicalities, there was a fundamental
confusion in the attempt to express 'timeless formality'. As
MacNeice insisted, the action of the play took place *in* time,
not out of it. The implicitly Christian analogy, which was
doubtless an echo of, or a response to, the production of
Murder in the Cathedral was altogether misleading in this
respect. Given the assumptions that the audience was asked to
make, the meaning of the murder of Agamemnon was utterly
different from that of the martyrdom of Thomas but the
'stained-glass' effect was designed, it seemed, to make the two
events congruent.

The dinner-jackets, Doone explained, were intended to
make a connection between the actors and the audience by
putting the Chorus in the 'uniform' of the latter. This being the
Group Theatre production, however, the audience was not 'in
uniform'—so the point was rather lost. In practice, the onstage
dinner-jackets were distracting and tended to separate the
Chorus from the main action.

The murder of Agamemnon, like that of Thomas, took place
on the stage; and the animal masks in the dance that followed
it were a visual counterpart to the verbal imagery of horror
that Eliot had put into the mouths of the Women of
Canterbury. Here and elsewhere neither Doone's choreography nor Britten's music met with approval. *The Times* thought
that Doone had, in general, carried the formalism too far,

making 'a ritual dance of death' out of the play; while Peter
Burra, writing in the *Group Theatre Paper*, considered that the
theatrical conception wobbled between 'naturalism' and
'style'. As for the acting, the impassioned performance of
Vivienne Bennett as Cassandra came in for praise but Veronica
Turleigh's Clytemnestra was found too mild and Robert
Speaight too liturgical. Whether the criticism of Speaight was
founded on his actual delivery or a more tenuous impression, it
was not surprising that there should have been, or have
appeared to be, some convergence of his Sunday portrayals of
Agamemnon's suffering with his weekday ones of that of
Thomas à Becket.[28]

One of those most acutely disappointed by the production
was MacNeice's friend Professor E. R. Dodds, whose fury had
not abated when he recalled it many years later:

> Doone was determined at all costs to display his originality
> and he made a dreadful hash of *The Agamemnon*, on
> which I was supposed to act as adviser. 'Aeschylus', said
> Doone, 'was static, I am dynamic, so fuck all.' Some of his
> more eccentric 'Dooneries' were eliminated at rehearsals,
> like his proposal to have Cassandra, as Louis described it,
> 'gibbering unseen in a sort of portable bathing tent'. But on
> the first night of the show the Chorus were still dressed in
> dinner-jackets, to demonstrate how 'contemporary' and
> 'relevant' Aeschylus was. Small wonder that the aged
> Yeats who was sitting in the stalls murmured to me at the
> interval, 'We are assisting, my dear Dodds, at the death of
> tragedy.' But he had the grace to add that the translation
> deserved a better producer.[29]

Dodds was partial and seems to have disapproved entirely of
MacNeice getting mixed up with Doone. And it was, after all,
MacNeice himself who had told Doone that 'the trouble with
this play is it is so static'.[30]

There was, too, an element of compromise in MacNeice's
own attitude to the production, which he wanted to be neither
an adaptation nor a museum piece. He was asking his audience

to make certain assumptions about Aeschylean morality and religion while expressing his own scepticism about them not only in the programme note but in the translation itself. Edmund Wilson, who admired MacNeice's version, nevertheless observed that, by contrast with the original, it presented a 'catastrophe unilluminated by philosophy or religion'.[31] The implications of this bleak perspective were only partly brought out on the stage.

Yeats's remark about 'the death of tragedy' may have been intended, as Dodds suggested, as a condemnation of the production; but it also intimated, as Yeats's remarks so often did, the passing of a cultural phase; and Yeats himself would shortly attempt to give tragedy its *coup de grâce*.[32] Doone's methods of production had subverted stage tragedy but so had public events. What theatrical presentation would not have fallen short of the sense of tragedy of life as it was felt in the winter of 1936? If the Group's *Agamemnon* marked the death of theatrical tragedy, the production was, perhaps, more at fault for not registering that event more deliberately, for not being 'contemporary' enough.

Eliot saw the effect of his influence on the production and was influenced in his turn. In his new play, *The Family Reunion*, he was making use of *The Choephoroe* not as translator but as a modernizer whose work of adaptation would be so radical as to leave the 'original' almost undetectable. As he confronted the problems of how to integrate the chorus and how to present the Eumenides, the example of *The Agamemnon* was useful, and not wholly negative. He decided to put the Eumenides in evening dress, like the Chorus in the *Agamemnon*. He afterwards considered this a mistake, but his Chorus, similarly clothed, was insinuated into the everyday world of the play with more success.[33]

Early in 1936 MacNeice had resumed work on *The Rising Venus*, which had been 'stuck' for some time. Shortly after he saw *The Dog Beneath the Skin* he reported to Doone that

Venus was once again 'evolving rapidly' and to judge from what evolved *The Dog Beneath the Skin* had acted as a strong tonic.

MacNeice worked at *Venus*, at the translation of *The Agamemnon* and at yet another play (probably *Blacklegs*, designed expressly 'for the people in Dublin') simultaneously.[34] In July he sent Doone a draft of *Venus*, with the news that Eliot was planning to publish the play in the spring, to coincide, if possible, with its production. In fact, the play was not published until June 1937 (by which time the title had been changed to *Out of the Picture*) and it did not reach the stage for another five months. In the meantime *The Agamemnon* had received its two Sunday performances, *The Ascent of F6* had enjoyed its run, and the Group Theatre had been through the convulsions of reorganization.

MacNeice's commitment to Doone never wavered and his solidarity was essential since, after the staging of *F6* under Ashley Dukes's management, the Group Theatre's main hope of regaining its independence lay with *Out of the Picture*. It was also important that the Group should find an alternative to Sunday performances and some effort was made to do so. Eliot tried to arrange for a first production of MacNeice's play at the Arts Theatre, Cambridge, but Keynes was unwilling. He agreed with his wife's verdict that *Out of the Picture* was 'too . . . much an unhappy reaction against life'.[35] So the Group reverted to its old practice and gave two Sunday performances of *Out of the Picture* at the Westminster Theatre, on 5 and 12 December 1937.

Ironically enough, *Out of the Picture* was seen as a consolidation of the Group's celebratory style and collaborative methods. Like *The Dance of Death* and *The Dog Beneath the Skin*, it depended on the virtuosity of the performers and its open structure left room for the contributions of the director-choreographer and the composer. With the performance of MacNeice's play, wrote Dilys Powell, the Group's productions had ceased to be isolated oddities in the theatre and attained the accumulated force of a 'valuable development'.[36] But the development had come too late.

Out of the Picture was not only stylistically indebted to the earlier productions but borrowed from *Dogskin* more particularly: Portright's crush on the vacuous film star echoed Alan Norman's weakness for Lou Vipond, and the auction-as-liturgy recalled the surgery scene in *Dogskin* from which the liturgical element had been cut in performance. MacNeice's wireless interludes were derived from Auden's Box and Cox in *The Dance of Death* but it was a coincidence, irritating to him, that they were structurally similar to the broadcasting scenes in *F6*.[37] Written under the spell of Auden, *Out of the Picture* was nevertheless an original piece of work overall and the first half of the play indicates how a distinctive form might have been brought to maturity if a Group ensemble and its poet-playwrights had managed to work together consistently.

Four big themes are interwoven in *Out of the Picture*: art, love, war and death. The hero, Portright, is an artist in whom it would be difficult not to see a mocking self-portrait of the playwright as lost soul. 'The trouble with me, dearie,' MacNeice wrote to a friend, 'is that I am all form and no content'—and that is one of Portright's difficulties, too.[38] He wants 'just to create' but has no special content in mind. He foists on to his landlady a burlesque version of Eliot's idea of artistic impersonality—'The Pure Form crank says that he makes works of art in order to escape the emotions of life'—and immediately answers it: 'Now I do the opposite. . . . I go to Art to *find* the emotions of life. In an intenser form'.[39] Instead of finding life's emotions in art Portright discovers a great discrepancy between the aesthetic and the sensual. He uses the real woman who loves him as the model for a statue of Venus which, having made, he loves. Looking then for the incarnation of this ideal beauty he is attracted not by the model but by the film star, Clara de Groot. Venus incarnate is also a character in the play, but she appears only to the audience, to whom she confides in monologue the secret of life's grand illusion.

Portright suffers 'tradesmen's bills, landlady's anger, little boys' laughter, critics' contempt, the War Office'—which sends him his call-up papers—and other slings and arrows, but his most serious problem is paranoia:

> Perhaps I am ill. Perhaps I am mad. I know what you want. You want to set the psychologists on me to dig me to pieces with scalpels. Or you want to set the Communists on me to make me a cog in a gearbox. Or you want to set the storm-troopers on me to make a man of me with truncheons. Don't you now, don't you?[40]

The context of this speech is an intellectual farce in which Portright, as he gets out of bed, becomes enmeshed in the web of his difficulties with art, underwear, the gas, and impecuniosity. Preoccupied with these, he pays no attention to the news of impending war that comes over the radio. Bailiffs descend and carry off his statue of *The Rising Venus*. Moll O'Hara, the model of the statue, comes to dun him for her fee, stays out of love for him and arranges to meet him at the auction sale at which the *The Rising Venus* is to be sold.

The action shifts to the office of Dr Spielmann, a psychiatrist, who is with his patient, Clara de Groot. In the course of this scene, which is devoted to broad satire of the matched inanities of therapist and film star, Dr Spielmann has to contend with the interruptions of his very knowledgeable parrot. He prescribes art collecting as Clara's therapy and arranges to take her to the auction. Thus the two elements of the farce converge.

The auction scene is a surreal, ecclesiasticized extravaganza in the course of which Spielmann makes a puckish experiment in mass hypnosis. Under his spell all the bidders are made to fall in love, as the *Venus* is unveiled, with the person they next lay eyes on. Portright and Clara become the central figures in a waltz of the newly paired couples that ends the first part of the play.

The broadcast at the opening of the play had introduced the theme of war and one at the end announces the first onslaught of bombing. These two broadcasts are merely heard; between them MacNeice placed three interludes of radio made visible,

in which the Listener-In is not a passive auditor, like Mr and
Mrs A in *F6*, but licensed to answer back:

RADIO ANNOUNCER: You are going to be out of a seat soon.
LISTENER-IN: What seat?
RADIO ANNOUNCER: That study chair of yours. They won't let
    you hang on to that.
    (LISTENER-IN *does not answer but backs into the chair*.)
    Hi! Did you catch what I said? It was a warning.
LISTENER-IN: Take your damn warning. I'm going to sit in my
    chair while I have time.
    (RADIO ANNOUNCER *returns to the microphone*.)
RADIO ANNOUNCER: (*Into microphone*) Hm! Get a move on
    there. Turn the bloody knob.
LISTENER-IN: Oh no I don't. Shut up. I'm not listening in this
    evening.[41]

The role of the Announcer offered scope for the virtuosity of
John Glyn Jones, whose earlier performance as Cox of the BBC
in *The Dance of Death* was probably part of MacNeice's
inspiration. His mimicry, complete with radio atmospherics
and multilingual snatches of broadcasts picked up across the
wavebands, earned much laughter and excellent reviews. More
seriously, MacNeice made the business of transmission and
reception a reflection of the world's madness and the disorien-
tation of the individual. The broadcasts were the key to the
overall image of disintegration.

MacNeice also used these interludes as catch-alls for sketches
and poems, some of which were cut in performance. The talk by
'Mr MacDonald the famous veteran hurdler' went, and so did
the ode 'Pindar is Dead'—good things in themselves but too
digressive. The more relevant recitation, 'What's become of the
glory and the grandeur of the gold-men and gunmen' survived.

In his published text MacNeice had distributed the songs
among various characters and a most important revision made
for performance was to gather them into a continuous part for a
chorus of five singers. This brought the practical advantage that

it was possible to use real singers. The change also added a
sinewy strength to the play's structure, which anticipated that
of *On the Frontier*. The songs themselves were the most
brilliant part of MacNeice's text: limpid in sense, diction and
imagery, rhythmically interesting and very settable. 'Riding in
cars' was one of them:

> *Riding in cars*
> *On tilting roads*
> *We have left behind*
> *Our household gods,*
> *We have left behind*
> *The cautious clause,*
> *The laws of the over-*
> *rational mind.*[42]

In Britten's setting, the songs counterpointed the tragic farce
with a sense of deep longing and loss, the title song focusing
these emotions.

   MacNeice also added for the performance a long choral
recitative on the impotence and irresponsibility of a society
journeying to war. It begins:

> *Nobody,*
> *Yes,*
> *Nobody's done,*
> *Nothing at all, Never at all.*
> *We sit in a train,*
> *And we ride for a fall,*
> > *Yes, Yes,*
> *We shift in our seats*
> *And we puzzle our brains*
> *For something to do*
> *(The telephone posts*
> > *Go past to the past. . . .*[43]

This became part of an intricate balletic and musical
elaboration of the scene in which Portright, waiting for Moll
outside a tourist agency, collides with a number of puppet-like

citizens. What, in the text, had been a too tangential satire of escapist travel (reminiscent of the Fifth Avenue scene in Eugene O'Neill's *The Hairy Ape*), became, in performance, a lively image of the stampede into war. MacNeice's songs, Doone's choreography and Britten's music combined to make this a high point of the production and one of the most effective scenes ever created by the Group Theatre.

As the play unfolds, it becomes apparent that Portright's malaise—the lack of a content for his art and his incapacity for love—is connected with the imminence of war. His 'artistic block' comes from an ill-defined sense of the futility of attempting to contribute to a civilization that is about to go down the drain; and, since he will be one of the victims of the general destruction, there is not much future in love, either. Moll, perceiving his impasse, finally makes his quietus for him.

As performed (in a version very different from the published text) the second part of the play takes place in Clara's flat. Sir Sholto Spielmann, twin brother of the psychiatrist, has come to relax with his mistress while he waits for his resignation as Minister of Peace to take effect. He falls asleep. Moll arrives to steal back the statue. Portright, hot with lust, turns up with Clara. During further farcical comings and goings Portright shoots Sir Sholto. Since Portright's number is now clearly up, Moll kindly administers poison to him and tries to make his last moments happy ones. She dresses in Clara's clothes and goes off with him to make love in the adjoining bedroom. While Portright is loving and dying, the real Venus steps on to the empty stage, to outface the sculpted travesty of herself and reveal the reality behind the world of appearance:

> Let not man be contriving a frozen beauty;
> While he is here and now let him deal in the here and now
> Work and fight for meat and love,
> Gallant approximation, bravado of defeat.
> I am Venus and principle of unity and division,
> Multiplication by pain,
> Spawning of worlds from a discord

Always recurring
I am the attempt to cover the abyss with grass
And to spangle the grass with flowers
And to put there cattle grazing the grass
And young men picking the flowers,
And to make believe through elaboration of pattern
That life goes on forever. . . .[44]

In performance, the incarnation of Venus did not take the elaborate form that MacNeice at first intended. In the published text *The Rising Venus* is a painting and the divine personage steps out of the canvas. This effect was difficult to capture on stage and there was some advantage in substituting the more emphatic statue. But the change destroyed, of course, the most obvious reference in the title.

In the published version, MacNeice had been reaching for the symbolic disappearance of the artist out of his picture through a contrivance of moving walls that would mysteriously immure Portright. In performance, the approach of universal destruction replaced this rather obscure symbolism. At the end of the play, a troop of super-police, under their 'leader', disposed of the bodies on stage as the aerial bombardment of London began. The dialogue was punctuated by screaming shells, with lighting effects to match. This effect was a mixture of the desolation of O'Casey's *The Plough and the Stars* and the destructive ecstasy of Shaw's *Heartbreak House* in their final moments, though MacNeice's combination of satire and farce was more extreme than that of his fellow Irishmen.

For performance, the second part of the play was radically revised by MacNeice. He greatly improved his published version but the close plotting of this second part remained in startling contrast, stylistically, to the open structure of the first part and contained serious faults in itself. According to one reviewer, Vivienne Bennett, playing Moll, was ready to give a tragic conclusion but lacked the material.[45] This was certainly the case as far as the material was concerned. The tragic point, such as it was, lay in the song 'I gave him poison. . . .' When this was cut, Moll became a strangely laconic euthaenasist. Venus, too, was weakly accommodated into the play's structure. Her soliloquy was essential to the theme, her presence irrelevant to the plot. Here MacNeice was probably attempting to graft a love and art theme from *The Rising Venus* on to the theme of impending war that dominates *Out of the Picture*.

The production was better received than the play itself. Medley had to design a set that would fit in front of the one for *Mourning Becomes Electra*, then running at the Westminster. With great ingenuity, he used the space between the pillars of the *Electra* mansion. Curtains on curved tracks (as for *F6*) and interchangeable panels represented the various locations, and conveyed an appropriate sense of the sterility and impermanence of the modern world. For the staging and acting the Group Theatre earned more praise than for any of its earlier efforts. MacNeice himself did not think much of the play but found that on the stage 'it took on a unity and drive . . . which it lacked on paper'.[46] Even Kenneth Allott was satisfied with the production, while Dilys Powell thought it put the West End to shame, despite the unfavourable circumstances.[47]

Although it did nothing to strengthen the Group Theatre as an organization, the production of *Out of the Picture* was one of the Group's most successful experiments. MacNeice's inclination toward collaboration and his taste for the theatrical made him just the kind of poet-playwright the Group had wanted. But *Out of the Picture* marked the end of the Group's broadly collaborative phase.

There was a certain consistency in MacNeice's attempts to use the theatre to mediate between his sense of the illusoriness and absurdity of existence on the one hand and, on the other, of the reality of pain. But he never found a form in which he was at ease. *Blacklegs* and *Station Bell* and the second part of *Out of the Picture* were in his 'Irish' manner, in which the characters themselves are licensed by their eccentricity to speak and act fantastically within a unified, melodramatic plot and in prose dialogue. The first part of *Out of the Picture* was in his 'Group Theatre' manner: a looser structure in which interludes and plot are juxtaposed and placed in a more direct, Expressionist relation with reality, and in which he found a place for songs and poetry. MacNeice's third approach to the theatre, as the translator of *The Agamemnon*, was bedevilled by the conflict between an inclination to modernize and a literary conscience that prevented him from doing so. He was to have tried his hand with a second Greek play for the Group Theatre in 1939 but the war eclipsed his projected version of *The Hippolytus* of Euripides before he had progressed very far.[48]

In 1938, MacNeice was enthusiastic about the suitability of radio drama as a medium for poets and he soon proved it for himself. Radio suited him partly because it lent itself to fluid transitions between actual and imagined worlds. But though MacNeice's talents as a dramatist were realized in such radio plays as *Christopher Columbus* and *The Dark Tower*, he never lost his ambitions for the stage. He wrote three plays for the theatre after the war; one was abandoned, another was briefly staged and later adapted to television and the third, *One for the Grave*, was published and produced posthumously.[49] This last was not only a development of the parable form that MacNeice had explored as a radio dramatist but, in an extraordinary way, recalled the pre-war efforts of the Group Theatre.

One for the Grave is 'a modern morality play' in which, said MacNeice, 'topical allusions are important' but its essential modernity lies in the morality itself. Unlike the medieval *Everyman*, MacNeice's protagonist is not caught up in a struggle between good and evil but in the search for an identity. 'In production', said MacNeice,

> a very delicate balance must be preserved between [the play's] primary content, which is serious, and the revue or music-hall elements (sometimes pretty near slapstick) which are introduced not primarily for their own sake but

for satirical purposes, the modern Everyman's world
being one which cannot be properly treated *without*
satire.[50]

This modern world is a midden of spurious politics, spurious
science, pretended passion and commercialized everything;
and MacNeice's all-embracing figure for modern existence is
the television studio. The action of the play takes place there
'because it is the fate of the twentieth-century Everyman to live
in a world of mass media'.[51] In its revue style, its adaptation of
a morality play, its use of broadcasting as a symbol of failed
communion, *One for the Grave* recalls *The Dance of Death*
and *Out of the Picture*. The hero, too, has much in common
with Portright, as a confessionally drawn portrait of a man
living and dying in the midst of cruel illusion. MacNeice
attempts to grasp this reality by insisting that the performance
is nothing but a performance. The elegy spoken over his
Everyman is by way of being a summary of the kind of reality
he tried to present:

> As I warned you, this show was really more like a
> rehearsal. For Everyman, for me—and for you. And
> Everyman, remember, was only an amateur. As I imagine
> most of you are. So please don't be too critical of this
> performance.[52]

MacNeice's sense of life itself as mere show informed his view
of the theatre. For him, the theatre was not so much a mirror
held up to nature as the reflection of a mirage. In this way he
was a lively forerunner of the dramatists of the absurd.

11
Stephen Spender's *Trial of a Judge*

Of bullets and bombs as the true works of art.[1]
On the Frontier, 1938

Spurred on by Auden's example, Stephen Spender began to write a play for the Group Theatre in 1933. The Group hoped to present it the following year but it was not until 1938 that *Trial of a Judge* at last appeared. By this time, the Group Theatre had become a compact artists' collective operating occasionally rather than regularly and Spender himself was its Literary Director. During the long period of his play's gestation, Spender was able to observe the experiments of the Group and of his fellow poets but only Eliot's influence was discernible in the dramatic form that Spender conceived. As to its substance, the embryonic work was strongly affected by the rapid transformation of political actuality and the changes in Spender's own political attitudes.

Spender was writing *Trial of a Judge* intermittently in 1933 and 1934, in 1935 during his stay in Sintra, and in the spring of 1936, when he was in Barcelona. By 1936, he was also writing *Approach to Communism* (which was to become *Forward from Liberalism*) for the Left Book Club and, at this time, there was a convergence of the ideas in the treatise—which asserted a connection between 'the truths of political justice' and 'poetic truth'—with those embodied in the play.[2] The last stage of the evolution of *Trial of a Judge* spanned the period in 1937 during which Spender was a member of the Communist Party. From Party membership and its demands, Spender withdrew to the position that MacNeice derisively

called 'redeeming the world by introspection' and Spender
described as 'one of the most creative, realistic and valid
positions for an artist in our time'—that of the politically
liberal poet encountering within his own mind the great
political conflict taking place in the world.[3] *Trial of a Judge*
was a defence of this position, a transposition of objective
events to a mental realm where a connection between justice
and poetry might be forged.

The actuality on which the play was based was the murder
of a Polish Jew by Nazis and the interference by the Nazi
confederates with the trial of the murderers. This incident took
place in Silesia in 1932 in the general context of the Weimar
Government's ambivalent attempts to come to terms with
Hitler. In *Trial of a Judge*, the conviction of the Blackshirts lies
in the immediate past. In the present, the Judge who had
sentenced them reluctantly sentences three Communists to
death for the crime of carrying firearms. At the same time, he is
urged to reprieve the convicted Blackshirts by his wife and by a
Government Minister who thinks that the Nazis must be
appeased if they are to be controlled.

Acceding to pressure, and in an effort to retain a semblance
of legal authority, the Judge rescinds the sentence on the
Blackshirts. He later recants this second judgement and is
himself 'tried' and shot, along with the Communists. The
Minister also comes to see the futility of the attempt to ride the
Fascist tiger, but too late to do anything except ensure his own
destruction. The play ends with a Chorus of Red Prisoners
whispering:

> We shall be free.
> We shall find peace.[4]   [p. 115]

Since the Communists have abandoned their pacifist stance,
they may be understood as hoping for the 'peace' that comes
with the extirpation of their enemies; but whether in this sense
or otherwise, peace is a very forlorn hope indeed.

The transmutation of Spender's material from political
reality to poetic symbol was partly done for him by the

rapidity of the historical process itself. Had *Trial of a Judge* appeared within a year or two of the Silesian incident, the theme of complicity between Government and Blackshirts would have been a resonantly topical one in Britain, for in 1934 it was possible to see Mosley's Fascists and their supporters as a real menace. By 1938 the threat of collusion between the Establishment and the Fascists had receded in Britain and there was no distinction between them in Germany. Hitler's rise to power, the suppression of the Communists and the *unofficial* victimization of the Jews belonged to a completed political phase. The question asked in the play, whether the idea of Justice might be sustained by pliancy to Fascism had become a rhetorical one.

If Spender had begun the play with the idea of impressing on its audiences the immediate dangers in the political situation —and he could hardly not have done so—that motive soon became irrelevant. To be sure, *Trial of a Judge* is about a kind of appeasement and that was a very lively issue in 1938, but Spender was so far from stressing such immediate political applications that he cut out of a draft version an episode in which foreign ambassadors, complaisant to Fascist power, were introduced.[5] In the interests of the imaginative autonomy of the tragedy he avoided everything that smacked of mere propaganda.

Refining actuality into symbol, Spender filtered out specific identifications. Place is barely mentioned and time is fluid. The only personal names used are 'Petra' for the murdered Jew (who does not appear in the play) and 'Hummeldorf' for 'the Home Secretary'. The Judge is unnamed and other characters are identified by relationships: the 'Wife' (of the Judge), and the 'Mother', the 'Brother' and the 'Fiancée' (all of Petra). The 'Black Leader' and the 'President of State', important offstage characters obviously alluding to Hindenburg and Hitler are also unnamed. Such abstraction of place, time and person was a convenient way of avoiding the hazards of censorship but Spender's essential concern was an artistic, idealizing one. It is for the sake of the symbolic pattern that the Fiancée is

pregnant and the Wife childless, for instance; and the
Blackshirts were intended to be 'too idealized to be dismissed
simply as bullies' [p. 15].

In the effort to assert and define a permanent world,
transcending time and history, Spender carried the process of
abstraction deep into the structure of the play. The five acts
work on different levels of reality, two of them taking place
within different minds. In the second act, which is mostly in
prose, Spender came nearest to realism, in the characterization
of Hummeldorf. He later thought that he had made the
mistake of overemphasizing the Minister's public persona,
'which is incredible in real life (though true) and therefore
doubly incredible on the stage'.[6] But Spender's caricature of
the Wife, in whom the vacuum left by the denial of the
maternal instinct is filled by a pathological, Fascist hatred for
life, was a stylistically intrusive, Audenesque satire that
strained credibility much further.

In the third and fifth acts the 'real' world is presented in a
frankly stylized way. In Act 3, the Reds and the Blacks
confront each other from opposite sides of the stage and the
Red Leader is ritualistically shot. Here, the combination of
tableaux and densely poetic dialogue is reminiscent of the style
of *The Rock*. Act 5 is more fluid. In an unrealistic prison
setting, the Judge and the Reds debate their positions, and the
Blacks rejoice in their triumph. The executions of the Judge
and the Reds take place offstage and the prison gives way to an
indefinite location in which Petra's Mother and the Judge's
Wife speak elegies on their dead from their respectively
Christian and Fascist viewpoints.

Stylization is used to different effect in the first and fourth
acts, which are dream sequences. Act 1 is the Judge's dream, in
which he relives the trial of Petra's murderers. Act 4 is
Hummeldorf's nightmare, in which he sees himself as a stooge
of the Blackshirts and has to pass judgement on the Judge, now
that 'lawlessness / Itself made into a law' rules. It is easy to
forget that the stage represents the contents of the Judge's
mind in Act 1 and of Hummeldorf's in Act 4. And since the

characters' dream worlds are not much differentiated from the stylized presentation of the objective world in Acts 3 and 5, the various levels of reality tend to merge into an authorial dream world.

Spender looked to the staging of his play to demarcate the boundaries between minds and world, but in Doone's production the attempt partly misfired. In the opening scene, for instance, the Judge lay on Petra's coffin—as in a dream he well might—but the dream did not register as such and some members of the audience were bewildered. In keeping with the dream structure, Spender's stage directions called for a cinematographic fluidity. In practice, John Piper's abstract Expressionist setting—his first design for the theatre—was anything but dreamlike. The brightly coloured, severely geometrical screens and the simple, stylized balcony helped to create a powerful—even terrifying—image of cruel and implacable forces bearing down upon vulnerable individuals.[7] What emerged from the staging was an Expressionistic treatment of actuality rather than the series of elisions between objective and mental strife.

At the beginning of the play, the Reds are idealists, like the dead Petra:

> *Inferior of physique, he coughed*
> *His guts out, whilst about the room he crept*
> *And wove his plots from sterile cleverness.*
> *To judge from books and papers spread around,*
> *Petra was like an angel, without food*
> *Existing singly from his light of mind.*   [p. 17]

This is not just the Blackshirts' contemptuous view. Petra's brother sees the victim in a similar, though approving, light:

> *He's dead. His living was one word*
> *Influencing the surrounding speech*
> *Of a crowd's life, printless until*
> *The words of all his time were frozen*
> *By all our deaths into a winter library*
> *Where life continually flows into books.*   [p. 23]

The value of such idealism is upheld by the Reds until Petra's Brother is also murdered. Then their attitude changes. They sternly abandon ideas in favour of bullets and put love aside to make room for 'the necessary killing hatred' [p. 103].

The newly belligerent Reds are different from the Blacks in two ways: their recourse to force is pragmatic, as an evil that contradicts their ultimate ends but is nevertheless necessary; and they are ineffectual. The Blacks, by contrast, are consistent and successful; and, as commonly happens with the devil's party, they get some of the best speeches. In the words of their Leader they are an

> *enormous tide*
> *Whose tall, wordless movement does not resemble history*
> *Taught in their libraries. For we are in no sense ideas:*
> *We do not discuss and cannot be discussed.*
> *Indivisible we ARE, and by our greater strength of being*
> *Defeat all words.*   [p. 109]

Preferring to work in the medium of flesh and blood rather than in words, the Blackshirts despise the Judge for his verbalizing idealism:

> *Yet this Judge, in the last analysis believed*
> *That an argument would govern the state which drew its*
>   *form*
> *From the same sources as the symmetry of music*
> *Or the most sensitive arrangement of poetic words*
> *Or the ultimate purification of a Day of Judgement.*
> *When, for example, Petra's battered corpse seemed unspeak-*
>   *able,*
> *Simply, he failed to perceive how far we were serious.*
>   [p. 110]

The Nazis cannot tolerate disorder, weakness and ugliness: Fascist seriousness insists on the imposition—unimpeded by moral scruple—of order and idolizes the realized beauty of 'the nordic / Sunhaired head ... matched against cloud drifts'.

Nevertheless, there is much talk about words in the play and, even when words are not the subject of discourse, Spender draws attention to them by the density, the intricacy and, frequently, the obscurity of the language used:

> *A lawyer's a man well-trained in memory*
> *Of cases, precedent, repartee, speeches,*
> *So now my words like birds fly after me.* [p. 14]

So says the Judge, through whom, chiefly, his author addresses the task of making words mean something in a world in which only action seems meaningful. This is the problem in theory: in practice it is to find the *right* words and, unfortunately, Spender's often sound as though they belong neither to his characters nor himself. We hear Eliot in 'When Spring the tiger, / Breaks the bones with clawing roots . . .' [p. 69]; Shakespearian pastiche in 'The sun, which lost our empire, now does rise' [p. 59] or 'The workers' salt undifferentiated, fretting sea' [p. 25]; and your typical Jacobean dramatist in 'I am sent to make you mad' [p. 105]. Apart from pastiche and echoes, the most remarkable feature of the verse is the density produced by syntactical inversions, elaborate metaphors and imagery, repetition and other devices.

In terms of action, the Blackshirts are the Judge's main antagonists: in terms of debate, the Reds. Spender had criticized *Murder in the Cathedral* for confining 'the real theme of the play'—spiritual pride versus God's will — within Becket. Since there was no character equal to disputation with the Archbishop, the crucial question was not, Spender thought, properly dramatized: 'In a Greek tragedy the chorus would have discussed it with him.'[8] In *Trial of a Judge*, the Reds have such a role and their arguments are at least as good as those given to the Judge.

The Judge's credo is,

> *That if we reject the violence*
> *Which they use, we coil*
> *At least within ourselves, that life*

Which grows at last into a world.
Then, from the impregnable centre
Of what we are, we answer
Their injustice with justice, their running
Terroristic lie with fixed truth.   [p. 103]

This, say the Reds, is an egotistical and self-indulgent idea,

                         built upon a lie
Which is the suffering of many that the enlightened few
May pick truths out of chaos. . . .   [p. 102]

They mock the Judge's quasi-Christian motive:

Even in death you sign the martyr's truce
Of Christians who have let themselves be killed,
Clasping the lovely flowering crown and white
Innocence of a saint's winding sheet. . . .   [p. 103]

The reiterative hovering over the idea of Christian martyrdom is attributable to Eliot's overshadowing influence and it is not a loose accretion to Spender's theme. If the Judge were a Christian, his intellectual and linguistic problems would have been much less acute; as would those of the poetic dramatist in search of a permanent symbolic world. In terms of his theme, as well as his method, Spender was the first of Eliot's close followers in poetic drama even though—unlike Christopher Fry, Anne Ridler, and Norman Nicholson—he did not use the form to affirm Christian belief. In *Trial of a Judge*, indeed, Christianity is mere escapism. Its sole representative, the Mother, looks to God for redress rather in the way she begs money from her son's murderers, in a spirit of weak desperation.

The Judge is scrupulously, if mysteriously, agnostic:

And I believe
That in our acts we are responsible
Before a final judgement, whether indeed
Those legends of belief which made
The traditional sky fluid with prayer

Freeze time suddenly into a single crystal
Where history is transparent; or whether
Each generation is the outpost
Of a total spiritual territory
And defeats, even of necessity,
Are defeats indeed. . . .   [p. 104]

The Judge searches for an adequate expression of the *poetic* idea of 'a final judgement'. Analogously, Spender was attempting to establish a connection between poetry and justice, a humanist equivalent to the link that Eliot had forged between poetry and Christianity. The Judge's tragedy is that he does not manage to articulate a metaphysical basis for justice and the big question was whether the dramatization of this failure transcended it.

In an article published a week before *Trial of a Judge* opened, Spender defined his own approach to poetry on the stage by way of a commentary on the plays of his fellow poets. He disagreed with the suggestion that Eliot had once made that poetry might be restored to the theatre by the adaptation of the techniques of music-hall and such popular forms. This, he thought, was 'only an ingenious restatement of the position of the Victorian poets who wanted to capture the stage for poetry'. It was 'not the tactics of poets' that would restore poetic drama but the world situation.

Like the Elizabethans, said Spender, contemporary poets and their audience were intent on politics and history, and these were matters for which poetry was the best medium. There was 'an unwritten poetry' in present conflicts that demanded a form of expression with the power to generalize, the descriptive means to set a large scene economically, without elaborate décor or stage machinery, and the sinuosity to evade censorship. At a far remove from literary Marxism, Spender wanted to replace 'the whole apparatus of the Expressionist stage, a hastily constructed improvization' with 'a calmer, more permanent form'; and, he asserted, 'the form that should take the place of Expressionist experiments is poetic drama'.[9]

Trial of a Judge was an attempt not only to realize this 'more permanent form' but to justify it thematically. Whereas many Leftist writers were very conscious of the effort required to reconcile art with action, Spender perceived quite a different problem. With its monstrous *aesthetic* pretensions, Fascism offered to make action itself the supreme art, deploying humanity itself as the plastic material. Poetry, issuing from the realm of ideas, necessarily opposed this Fascist pretension. But Spender's polarization of a Fascist aesthetics of action and the poetic idea of justice left out of account a major factor; as did his lyrical theory of 'poetic drama'.

The Reds in his play are idealists gone sour. At their best they regard words as a medium by which ideas get into, and can be got out of, books. Like the Blackshirts and the Judge, they ignore the social, sensuous and celebratory functions of poetry—the very functions that Auden, MacNeice, Doone and the Group had emphasized. Significantly Spender ignored the possibility of the kind of interaction between artists and audience that the Group Theatre had tried to develop.

Of all the Group Theatre plays, *Trial of a Judge* came nearest to being a closet drama. The play was not a product of theatrical collaboration but of a single mind, requiring interpreters. The actors' essential function was to speak the verse. Characterization was a secondary matter, even in the role of the Judge, and the choric roles scarcely required ensemble technique since they were made up of individual speeches. The director was required to create tableaux rather than to choreograph movement and, since the poetry was self-sufficient, no musical complement was called for. As for the audience, its presence was ignored.

For the production, the Group Theatre made an arrangement with Unity Theatre to use the latter's premises, the only occasion on which it did so; and, uniquely for a Group Theatre production, *Trial of a Judge* was staged before it appeared in print, so that most of the critics were concerned with the play in performance. The reviews ranged from the *The Times*'s cool respect for a not altogether successful work of 'distinction' to contemptuous dismissal in one of the two reviews that appeared in *Twentieth Century Verse*.[10] Geronwy Rees was not alone in preferring the poetry to the politics, without caring much for either:

> Sterility . . . can have great beauty, and *Trial of a Judge* proves it, but politics are not concerned with beauty, nor is the political writer, except as a by-product of his main purpose. His primary task is to transcend personal and subjective conflicts so that he may give a picture, as truthful as possible, of the objective conflicts . . . and this is not possible if the writer, however great his sympathy and understanding, describes not the world of action but the mind that mirrors it.[11]

It was precisely in perceiving the relation between politics and beauty in Fascism that Spender was most original. But it was not surprising that Rees and others focused on what appeared to be Spender's unregenerate, and perhaps solipsistic, political liberalism.

The play ran for its allotted time at Unity Theatre from 18 to 26 March 1938. Nominally and by virtue of the fact that Spender, Piper and Doone were members, it was a Group Theatre production, though it was frequently misattributed to Unity.[12] This was displeasing to both parties. It was one thing for Unity to make a contribution to the prevailing policy of the United Front by housing a play by a Communist author, produced by the Group Theatre; it would have been quite another matter for Unity actually to have produced a poetic drama of such doubtful political tendency. The nonce alliance between the Group Theatre and Unity certainly appeared afterwards to have been a mistake from Unity's standpoint, as was indicated by a discussion of the play held in the Group Theatre Rooms on the evening after the last performance.

Trial of a Judge had not offered Unity Theatre members the participatory role they were accustomed to in their theatre and in the discussion they partly made good the deficiency. It was an 'exhilarating' and not untheatrical occasion, according to

Louis MacNeice. Spender responded vigorously to the sharp criticism and heckling to which he was subjected until, in the last stages of the debate,

> an old man got up, very sincere, very earnest, very toilworn. There was one thing about the play, he said, which especially worried him; of course he knew S. could not have meant it, there must have been a mistake, but the writing seemed to imply an acceptance of Abstract Justice, a thing which we know is non-existent. S. deliberately towered into blasphemy. Abstract Justice, he said, of course he meant it; and what was more it existed.[13]

After *Trial of a Judge* Spender continued to work for the Group Theatre on one of its most promising projects. He and Geronwy Rees completed a translation of Georg Büchner's *Dantons Tod* and Medley made highly original designs. But approach of war brought the Group Theatre to an end shortly after the production was announced.[14]

12
On the Frontier

The case for the prosecution rests on the
fallacious belief that art ever makes anything
happen, whereas the honest truth, gentlemen, is
that if not a poem had been written, not a picture
painted, not a bar of music composed, the
history of man would be materially unchanged.[1]

W. H. AUDEN, spring 1939

When *On the Frontier: A Melodrama in Three Acts* appeared
in print and on the stage late in 1938, many people thought
that the play had been overtaken and dwarfed by real events.
One of them explained how this had come about:

> It was . . . written . . . some eighteen months ago, when
> Austria was still independent, Czechoslovakia entire, the
> Jews in Germany an oppressed but not desperate
> minority, and the gas mask familiar only from photo-
> graphs in the papers or on the screen. If we had seen this
> play immediately after its composition, we should have
> gone home profoundly disturbed by the imminent
> prospect of war, which for most imaginations seemed
> inconceivable until the actual crisis. As it is, the authors'
> dismal prophecies have been fulfilled, and as a result the
> scenes in the Ostnia–Westland sitting-room became
> emotionally insignificant beside our own experience in
> September.[2]

The play had not been written quite as long before it was
staged as the writer supposed: the first version had been

completed a little over a year earlier and it had been revised since. And the description of it as fulfilled prophecy was interestingly imprecise. Reasonably enough, the reviewer was equating Westland with Germany and Ostnia with Austria (and Czechoslovakia) but he was overlooking the fact that the German victories had so far been gained without recourse to war. In that respect *On the Frontier* was narrowly ahead of events. Still, the delay in its appearance was crucial to its reception.

The play opened at the Arts Theatre, Cambridge, on 14 November. By this time, even those who had felt some relief at the concluding of the Munich Agreement in September knew that there was no health in it. To a public deeply sceptical about the efficacy of appeasement; humiliated—as many people were—by the Anglo-French sacrifice of Czechoslovakia; not only alive to the fear of war but aware of the degradation to which that fear itself might lead; to such a public the play brought the 'news' that war was disastrous. The timing could hardly have made its authors look more out of the picture.

Auden and Isherwood had intended to make a start on the piece in mid-1937, about two weeks after Auden returned from Spain and saw *F6* at the Mercury. Ransom-like, they were going to retire to the Lake District to write their 'new revue'—or so it was reported.[3] But both of them were soon preoccupied with other matters and, if they even began *On the Frontier* at that time, they did not make headway with it.[4] It was not until the middle of August 1937, shortly after the miserable Group Theatre conference at Fawley Bottom, that *On the Frontier* was begun in earnest—in the 'frontier' town of Dover, suitably enough.

Like *F6*, the new play was written very rapidly. In two weeks the work was 'ahead of schedule'; in four it was 'finished' and there were already good prospects for its production, since Keynes had declared an interest in presenting it in Cambridge. Keynes's interest became strong enthusiasm when he read *On the Frontier* in October 1937. He was amazed to find that the authors had not been tempted 'into being clever', as they had before. 'You have kept it crude and obvious throughout; and that is very successful,' he told Auden.[5]

Keynes's only suggestion for improvement was that there was 'room for a few more of the interludes'. Auden took this to imply that 'the poetic side of the play' was 'lightweight', and he admitted that it was. He countered, though, with the assurance that 'the fact that the interludes are sung, and, except for the last one, will have quite an elaborate musical accompaniment, will give them both length and weight'.[6] This dependence on music made the play a 'melodrama' in the pure sense as well as the common one: an 'operatic melodrama', Britten called it.[7] The separate choric role for a group of trained singers and the abandonment of any other kind of chorus was a major development of the 'Group Theatre method' already seen in the performed version of *Out of the Picture*.

Keynes proposed that the Group Theatre production of *On the Frontier* should open for a short run in Cambridge and then be transferred to a West End theatre. It was a proposal that accorded well with the playwrights' ambitions and overcame the general dissatisfaction with Sunday performances. Negotiations to this end went along amicably but not smoothly. Initially, Keynes thought it might be feasible to mount a two-week programme of Group Theatre productions that would include revivals of *F6* and *The Agamemnon* but he was soon informed that the Group was in no position to mount three productions in such a short time. Worse, he discovered that the Group Theatre not only had no money but was not even a legal entity capable of entering into contracts. Unravelling its organizational incoherence, Keynes devised a generous arrangement by which the Group Theatre would be responsible for the artistic side of the production while he would underwrite its cost and bear any financial loss. But no sooner was this agreed than he encountered a further obstacle to the proposed spring opening.

Keynes had assumed that the authors would be on hand 'to make sure that the words and music and production all click as they are meant to' and was much put out when they announced their intention of going abroad before the play was staged.[8] Having taken the point that the 'poetry' was to lie largely in the *combination* of music and words, he was worried that the words might be sacrificed to the music. Auden and Isherwood were quite content that Spender, Britten and Keynes himself should 'keep an eye on things' for them — 'things', it appears, being a euphemism for 'Doone'. Keynes, however, was neither willing nor well enough to supervise the production; and, since it was the very fear that Britten's settings might obscure the words that most vexed him, the composer's supervision was not the answer, either.[9]

Keynes's misgivings were confirmed when he heard a broadcast of Britten's settings of Auden's poems or, rather, 'did not catch a single line and heard of the poetry only an occasional word here and there', despite good transmission and his hard concentration. After this Keynes adopted the old Group Theatre stand that 'in an experimental theatre, of this kind, the intimate association of the authors with the production is surely essential'.[10] Auden and Isherwood were unwilling to delay their departure for China—where they were going to observe the Sino–Japanese War—and so the proposed production was put off against their return.

One of the consequences of the delay was that there was time for rewriting. In October, Auden had revised the last scene and in the following June, on the crossing from Japan to Vancouver, he and Isherwood made further modifications. These included the excision, or possibly the transformation, of a character that had been dear to Isherwood, 'an American gangster called "Babyface"—about 19 years old'.[11] Keynes liked the new version, which he did not regard as radically different, but Doone and Medley were less well pleased.[12]

In July 1938 Auden and Isherwood arrived back in London—just in time to attend Berthold Viertel's Group Theatre production—and preparations for *On the Frontier*

were resumed.[13] Keynes was still confident about the play
although he was having difficulty in finding a London theatre
to transfer the production to. After Munich his views changed.
'Do you still feel you can go ahead with it in precisely its
present form without feeling at all silly?' he asked Isherwood.
He himself would have welcomed some 'new inspiration' that
would have modified the play 'without any change to the main
fabric'.[14] He must have realized, though, that minor revision
could scarcely bring the plot and, more important, the
authors' attitudes up to date. Auden did make one very
important change when he substituted for the last interlude a
new one implicitly critical of the kinds of quasi-journalism
found in On the Frontier, and the forthcoming Journey to a
War, as species of voyeurism. But this new material could not
alter the general tenor of the work.

The focus of attention in On the Frontier is the 'frontier'
between Ostnia and Westland but most of the play takes place
in Westland itself. Unlike the country of the same name in The
Dog Beneath the Skin, Westland in On the Frontier satirizes
Germany from three distinct angles of vision. The foreground
plot is an extravagant, often frivolous, caricature of the
country's leaders. Valerian is an armaments manufacturer. To
his villa, overlooking the Valerian Works, comes the Westland
Leader, an emotional windbag whom Valerian despises and
manipulates. The Leader's function, in Valerian's scheme of
things, is to fool the people and stoke up bellicosity towards
neighbouring Ostnia, but to stop—or be stopped—short of
war. This brinkmanship creates an excellent market for
Valerian armaments in both countries. But a border incident
triggers an emotional response from the Leader and unharnes-
ses the fury of both the Westland and Ostnian populations.
War is declared. Eventually, the gruelling international
conflict is halted by insurrection within both belligerent states.
The Leader is assassinated (offstage) by some of his disaffected
soldiers and Valerian is shot (on stage) by one of them. But the
popular uprisings and the deaths of these villains do not make
a happy ending.

A second window on Westland is the sequence of a prologue
and three interludes, with musical settings, constituting an
Expressionistic montage somewhat in the manner of *The
Dance of Death*. These interludes present, in turn: a chorus of
workers with revolutionary sentiments: a chorus of political
prisoners, not specifically identified with the first but representing their fate; ballroom dancers trying to waltz away their
fears while Left-wing agitators harangue them; and Westland
soldiers fraternizing with the enemy.

The gulf between this montage and the foreground plot is
very great, in terms of both subject matter and political feeling.
The prisoners in the first interlude, for example, display their
understanding and spirit in a song sung (at Auden's insistence)
to the air of 'Sweet Betsy from Pike':

FIRST PRISONER: 'If you're foolish enough', they declare, 'to
    resist,
    You shall feel the full weight of fieldboot and fist.'
    They beat us with truncheons, they cast us in jail,
ALL: But all their forms of persuasion shall fail!

SECOND PRISONER: They boast: 'We shall last for a thousand
    long years,'
    But History, it happens, has other ideas.
    'We shall live on for ever!' they cry, but instead
ALL: They shall die soon defending the cause of the dead!

THIRD PRISONER: They talk of the mystical value of Blood,
    Of War as a holy and purifying flood,
    Of bullets and bombs as true works of art.
ALL: They'll change their opinion when shot through the
    heart![15]

[pp. 40–1]

In the foreground, Valerian and the leader are not merely blind
to the kind of reality portrayed in the interludes: they seem to
be characters in a different kind of play altogether. The Leader
is not the Hitler-figure evoked by the song. He has nothing to

say about the mystique of blood, a thousand years of supremacy or any of that stuff. He is merely a piece of theatrical stock-in-trade, and a rather moth-eaten one at that. Eliot remarked that Hitler was 'not the simpleton that the authors made him out to be', but it was not the descent to buffoonery in itself, so much as the geniality of the caricature, that was so at odds with the reality of the times; and also with the feeling of the interludes.[16] The reason for this discrepancy was not difficult to find.

Much of the ambivalence in *On the Frontier* may be attributed to the authors' difficulties in reconciling their attitudes to the political scene with their ambitions for the theatrical one. Westland was based on Germany but it aspired to the charm of Ruritania. In a certain way, Isherwood recalls, the Valerian scenes were too successful:

> What became evident in performance was that Wystan and Christopher had made their two villains, Valerian and the Leader, more entertaining, more sympathetic even, than any of the other characters. The play was overbalanced by Valerian's charm and humour and the Leader's clowning.[17]

In the scenes in which these characters appear, Westland is a genial region located somewhere in the West End, its real frontier is a proscenium and its residents ingratiating actors.

When Doone read *On the Frontier* he congratulated the authors on a 'much more professional' piece of work than their earlier plays; and that, Isherwood says, 'was also its epitaph' for, by this time, he and Auden had acquired a 'boring kind of know-how' about the stage.[18] The pity of it was that they had fashioned a theatrical form that was anything but boring and had themselves undermined in the attempt to be 'professional'.

The text of *On the Frontier* was, in effect, an 'acting edition', replete with detailed directions for the setting, the lighting effects, the movements of the actors and their gestures, intonations and facial expressions. In his long opening monologue, the actor playing Valerian is to go 'thoughtfully up to the window', to pick up 'a signed photograph of the Leader' and so on. The 'Notes on the Characters' reveal the authors' theatrical ambitions all too clearly. Manners, Valerian's manservant, is described, *tout court*, as 'a stage butler' and many of the dramatis personae are stage something-or-others. Janet Adam Smith remarked that 'the smell of the theatre' had 'sometimes been too much for' the playwrights and that 'their characters and situations' were sometimes 'simply parodies of Shaftesbury Avenue'.[19] The kind of imitation involved, however, was more straightforward than parodic, and not quite Shaftesbury Avenue.

In the foreground plot, some familiar Shavian masks were borrowed along with Shaw's technique of turning stock characters upside down. Valerian is a refined bachelor with a neo-Nietzschean self-image:

> The truth is, Nature is not interested in underlings—in the lazy, the inefficient, the self-indulgent, the People. Nor, for that matter, in the Aristocracy, which is now only another name for the Idle Rich. The idle are never powerful. With their gigolos and quack doctors, they are as unhappy as the working classes who can afford neither, and a great deal more bored. The world has never been governed by the People or by the merely Rich, and it never will be. It is governed by men like myself—though, in practice, we are usually rich and often come from the People.
>
> [pp. 24–5]

Undershaft, the armaments tycoon in Shaw's *Major Barbara*, is more inclined to talk to others than to himself in this way but Shaw's fictional character rather than the real Krupp was clearly the prototype for Valerian. Hence the whimsicality of the Valerian–Lessep relationship. Valerian knows his secretary is a spy but, since he gets better secretaries that way, he is quite content for Lessep to serve his Ostnian masters so long as he does not interfere in the running of the household. In

Shaw the situation would have been developed: here it is mere
decoration.

While Shaw presided over the Valerian scenes, there was a
strong 'whiff of Barrie in his *Mary Rose* mood' in the
supersensory meetings of Eric and Anna.[20] Here, the
conception of unrealized love (which may have been modelled
on Owen's 'Strange Meeting') was potentially moving but the
coyness of the treatment was embarrassing. In performance,
these 'mystical love scenes', said MacNeice, 'made one long
for a sack to put one's head in'.[21] Eric and Anna are the most
important figures in the third element of the play's structure; a
middle-ground presentation of Ostnia and Westland in which
the characters are writ smaller than those of Valerian and the
Leader. The dominant image of the play came from the
presentation of this middle ground.

Scenically, the 'frontier' in the play was defined by the
'Ostnia–Westland Room', which comprised the living rooms
of a family in each country set side by side on the stage with no
wall between them. Medley's design divided the upstage into
architecturally distinct halves, which opened into a unified
downstage space. It was a strong statement of the fundamental
unity underlying self-imposed division. The dialogue of the
two families is dovetailed structurally and thematically, and
they are almost mirror images of each other: a father, a
mother, an aunt and a son on the Westland side; a grandfather,
a mother, an uncle and a daughter in the Ostnian family.
Totally reactionary, except for their youngest members, these
representative families are drawn to the brink of war by their
stupidity, their xenophobia and their private neuroses; by the
exhortations of the Westland Leader and the Ostnian King;
and by their conditioned responses to the effusions of the press
and radio. War comes by accident but it is not an unwilled one.

The inhabitants of the 'Ostnia–Westland Room' are
familiar Auden types. The Westland aunt is an ingrown virgin
suffering from religious mania, which is iconographically
projected onto her Leader. The uncle on the other side is a
drunken stage Ostnian who 'might even speak with an Irish

accent' [p. 11]. The Westland father is a rigid pedant: the Ostnian grandfather an equally rigid Blimp. The Westland mother is devoted to fortune-telling: the Ostnian one to her family's social and military distinction.

Eric, the Westland son, and Anna, the Ostnian daughter, pass from the level of ordinary reality to a higher plane beyond the 'frontier', where their 'strange meetings' take place. It was a theme that germinated in Isherwood's misery at his enforced separation from Heinz and may also have been informed by the mystical experience of *agape* that went into the writing of Auden's 'Out on the lawn I lie in bed. . . .'[22] In a privileged, psychic dimension—defined for the audience by special lighting effects and verse dialogue—Eric and Anna envision the love that frontiers and war preclude. In the real world, where they never meet, Anna becomes a nurse and dies of the plague, while Eric is imprisoned for his pacifism. Eric later comes to realize that he is not exempt from the 'necessary wrong of killing' and is himself killed, presumably as a revolutionary, 'at the barricade' [pp. 120–1].

Latent in the image of the 'Ostnia–Westland Room' was a wholly unintended irony. The Room figured the absurdities of frontiers, the futility of war and the essential likeness of neighbouring peoples. By the time the play appeared, some real European frontiers had been eliminated, without war and under the pretext of social integration. Ostnia is not a specific caricature of Austria as Westland is of Germany: its family names (Vrodny and Hussek) give it a Slovak coloration; its Royal broadcasts (which were seen as parody of those by the late King George V) and its Ostno-Irish uncle a British one.[23] But even though Ostnia is a composite fictional caricature, the facts that the frontier was down between Austria and Germany and that Germany had swallowed a piece of Czechoslovakia left Auden and Isherwood looking like apologists for appeasement and, as Keynes said, rather silly.

Even in 1937 or early 1938 an audience might well have taken exception to the even-handed depiction of the two states threatening *each other*. Had the authors turned a blind eye to the abortive *Anschluss* of 1934? Did they see Austria, Britain or any other country in such a tit-for-tat relation with Germany as Ostnia is with Westland? In some superficially Marxist way they did. All wars were 'bosses' wars', engendered by capitalists on both sides, distractions from the reality of the class struggle. But in their attempt to distinguish Fascist aggression from German aggression and illusory national interests from real class interests, Auden and Isherwood (like many others on the Left) had flown directly into the nets of history.

As for the class struggle, one reviewer found the presentation lopsided in that 'the underdogs' were merely 'allotted the interludes, speaking ... before the curtain'.[24] In fact the 'underdogs' sang, and Britten gave them their poetic due, though it was significant that the authors looked to Britten to imbue the play with political feeling. Nothing could be done, however, to prevent the last Westland interlude from ringing hollow. To the tune of 'Mademoiselle from Armentiers', the soldiers sing the horrors of war:

> *The subaltern's heart was full of fire,*
> *Now he hangs on the old barbed wire*
> *All blown up like a motor-tyre. . . .*
>
> *Fritz was careless, I'm afraid.*
> *He lost his heart to a parlour-maid.*
> *Now he's lost his head to a hand-grenade. . . .*
>
> *We're sick of the rain and the lice and the smell,*
> *We're sick of the noise of shot and shell,*
> *And the whole bloody war can go to hell!* [pp. 99–100]

The fraternization between the Westland soldiers and the offstage Ostnians that concludes the episode was 'hardly in keeping', as the *Stage* remarked, 'with a play which does not relate to the war of a generation ago'.[25] The reviewer might have said worse. The recourse to historical indignation was an easy way out of emotional and intellectual engagement with the present.

The fraternization interlude serves as the prelude to the last Valerian scene, dealing with revolution. Valerian, ill informed for once, hears the latest news from a business associate. The soldiers on both sides have stopped fighting each other and have turned against their governments. Not too disturbed by these developments, Valerian apostrophizes the absent revolutionaries:

> You don't know what you're letting yourselves in for, trying to beat us on our own ground! You will take to machine-guns without having enough. You will imagine that, in a People's Army, it is against your principles to obey orders—and then wonder why it is that, in spite of your superior numbers you are always beaten. You will count on foreign support, and be disappointed, because the international working-class does not read your mosquito journals. We shall expose your lies and exaggerate your atrocities, and you will be unable to expose or exaggerate ours. The churches will be against you. The world of money and political influence will say of us: 'After all, they are the decent people, *our* sort. The others are a rabble.'
>
> [p. 108]

In this speech, which has the authority of soliloquy, can be heard an oblique authorial commentary on the Spanish Civil War. In relation to *this* situation Valerian's confidence would not be ill placed and the playwrights' pessimism, running against the ideological grain, is understandable.

In making popular revolution the consequence of war the authors were dutifully Marxist but in a distinctly morbid way: morbid because the revolution is the prelude to worse disasters, not a better future. Instead of representing the uprising in Westland with some uplifting song of revolutionary fervour, as the logic of the interlude sequence and the plot—but not political actuality—seemed to demand, the final interlude was the digressive satire on journalism, to which we shall return.

In the foreground plot, Valerian is shot by Corporal Grimm
because Valerian probes Grimm's intense maternal fixation.
So the only close-up of an insurrectionary soldier depicts a
pathological case. In the middle ground of the 'Ostnia–
Westland Room' comes the plague that scrapes any residual
gilt off the revolutionary gingerbread. Eric's spinster aunt has
read the future in the Book of Revelation and the authors' own
vision of it seems to have come more from this source, too.
International Communism may be round the next corner but it
is more likely that the four horsemen will appear. A
perfunctory ideology is overshadowed by a genuine despair.

Plausibly, Julian Symons described *On the Frontier* as
expressing 'Auden's Communism in a clearer and more useful
way (for Communists) than any other of his writings', and
Kenneth Allott attributed to it 'the simplicity of a *Daily
Worker* editorial'.[26] On the other hand, the *New English
Weekly* declared the play 'so free from anything resembling an
idea that it might have been lifted straight from *The Times*'
and wondered at the authors' conservatism:

> What can have happened? Has success dammed up the
> stream of ingenuity? Are the rebels so immured in their
> good reputations that they cannot break the locks and
> rebel again? We know of course that red when exposed to
> sunlight will fade to a gentle strawberry and that with
> authority and increasing years most pinks tend towards
> blue. But, good gracious, Auden and Isherwood are not
> so old as all that! It is too soon for them to wear the
> bottoms of their trousers rolled. Or for a pair of such St
> Georges to proceed against the Dragon with a furled
> umbrella.[27]

That the play could be seen as Chamberlainesque and Marxist
at the same time was remarkable but not incomprehensible.
The confusions of desperate international diplomacy were
making strange political bedfellows and these ambivalences
were compounded by the more personal ones of the
playwrights.

Westland and Ostnia alluded to actualities with which the audience was acutely concerned. Having engaged this interest, the authors moralized their invented countries. But between the actuality and the parable the difficult issues were glossed over. Eric's dilemma is whether to engage in passive or active resistance to Fascism. But if pacifism was obviously anti-Fascist *in Westland* what did it mean elsewhere? Were the authors merely offering an otiose platitude about the Germans? If not, what might be the application elsewhere of the parable? Eric's explanation of why he ceased to be a pacifist has an air of authoritative generality:

> *Believing it was wrong to kill,*
> *I went to prison, seeing myself*
> *As the sane and innocent student*
> *Aloof among practical and violent madmen,*
> *But I was wrong. . . .*
>
> *we must kill and suffer and know why.*
> *All errors are not equal. The hatred of our enemies*
> *Is the destructive self-love of the dying,*
> *Our hatred is the price of the world's freedom.*
> *This much I learned in prison. This struggle*
> *Was my struggle. Even if I would*
> *I could not stand apart.*   [pp. 120–1]

This speech is very much in the manner of *Trial of a Judge* and, as in Spender's play, versification signals elevated abstraction. Whether an *Ostnian* (or British) anti-Fascist would be bound to 'stand apart' as a pacifist, or fight against his rulers at the barricades, or fight for them against a Fascist nation, are questions too prosaic, as it were, to be raised. And the very structure of the plot helps evade them. As Eric's Ostnian counterpart, Anna is conveniently exempted by her sex from such choices. The conventional theatricality of the sexual equation obfuscates the unevenness of the political one.

The *New Statesman* reviewer, deeply impressed by the play in performance, tortuously explicated its political parable as meaning

> that national frontiers are artificial nonsense and the real struggle is between common people and those who rule them by money and fraud; that the individual who understands this is confronted with a terrible choice of evils and may be compelled to submit to the 'necessary wrong' of killing his friends; but that he can always remember what he is fighting for and who his real enemies are; so that when the chance does come, hands may be joined across the trenches and a new world be founded out of common suffering and bitter experience. . . . The civilization we know may die but a new one will arise and those who would build it must take the path that brings them into contact, even though it is the contact of murder, with their friends in the trenches opposite them.[28]

The 'necessary wrong' is apparently a pragmatic acceptance of the need for an 'Ostnian' to fight against a Fascist 'Westland', even though the people of 'Westland' are not 'his real enemies'. But it was precisely this particular 'choice of evils' (which would have been acutely interesting for the members of the New Peace Movement, to which advertising for the performance was sent) that the authors shied away from dramatizing —and for good reason.

During and after the composition of *On the Frontier*, Isherwood was discovering where he stood with respect to frontiers, pacifism and the 'necessary wrong'. His 'uncomplicated hatred' of the Nazis changed, he recalls, when Heinz became 'an unwilling part of the Nazi machine'. Since he could do nothing that might harm Heinz and since, even in a Nazi army committing the worst atrocities, 'every man . . . could be somebody's Heinz', he was 'forced to recognize himself as a pacifist'. This extension from particular to universal love had its limits, however, since Isherwood's 'dead secret, basic reaction' to Munich was, 'What do I care for the Czechs?'[29]

Auden's political convictions were also much less Leftist than Julian Symons and others supposed. But the difficulty with *On the Frontier*, as he perceived it at the end of 1938, was not a matter of his personal attitudes. It was intrinsic:

> A political subject is a mistake because history is always now more terrible and more moving than anything you can possibly invent and much more extravagant than anything you can imagine.[30]

In France, in 1940, *On the Frontier* certainly seemed to be such a mistake to the critic Louis Bonnerot:

> Jugé d'après la réalité de la tragédie que nous vivons, il apparait comme une oeuvre sans consistance, sans portée et sans émotion.[31]

For Auden, *On the Frontier* was a decisive experiment, though he may not have drawn the right conclusion from it. He had begun to write for the theatre on the assumption that performance was essentially a mode of action, implicating and conditioned by its circumstances, and had given the Group Theatre a strong lead in this direction. After *On the Frontier* he adopted, and tenaciously maintained, the dogma of a categorical distinction between art and action. It was a change of attitude that had already been registered in a late revision of the play itself.

The weakest part of the published text was undoubtedly the last interlude, an inert prose sketch about five English newspaper readers whose minds and dress match the politics of their papers. Before the performance, Auden substituted the new interlude, in verse, that has already been mentioned. This interlude is a meeting of four ghoulish Journalists, parodic counterparts of the Witches in *Macbeth*.[32] The Journalists,

> Visit violence for the sake
> Of the public when they wake.
> Justify their party creeds.
> Each according to his needs.

The sentiment and mood of the interlude are summed up in a Kiplingesque song:

> *We fly to a cabinet crisis*
>   *We motor out to the wars*
> *Where the General's temperature rises*
>   *Or the little orator roars*
> *Where over the tyrannous waters*
>   *The flag of revolt is unfurled*
> *You will find us, the ace reporters*
>   *Presenting the world to the world.*
>
> *When cholera threatens a nation*
>   *Or troops open fire in the rain*
> *Whenever there's want or inflation*
>   *We meet each other again*
> *When bombs bring down babies and plaster*
>   *Or stones at policemen are hurled*
> *We meet over death and disaster*
>   *Showing the world to the world.*

Some of the allusions in the new interlude brought the play more up to date:

> FIRST JOURNALIST: Where have you been?
> SECOND JOURNALIST: Watching the frightened die
>   As bombs fell from the Asiatic sky,
>   And untrained peasants facing hopeless odds.

This satirical reflection of the authors' recent visit to China and on the indecency of making human misery marketable conveyed some sort of apology for the vein of opportunism in the play itself and the confessional tone was intensified by the allusion to evil ambition in *Macbeth*.

As Auden had calculated, the songs lent the performance poetic and emotional weight. Keynes had feared that Britten's music would swamp the words. His assessment afterwards was that, though the play had serious defects, 'the music was a little masterpiece'.[33] And the reviewers tended to think better of the performance than of the play. They praised Doone's direction, Medley's setting and also the acting of Wyndham Goldie and Ernest Milton in the 'star' roles of Valerian and the Leader (or 'Guidanto' as—at the suggestion of the censor—he was called).[34] The play had been written to attract such stars and the Group Theatre made no bones about claiming that it had retained 'a full West End cast' for the production.

The West End was as much the goal of the production as of the writing of the play, and it was in the expectation of a good London run with proper salaries that the actors agreed to perform in Cambridge at reduced rates.[35] But the critic who thought that the play displayed 'a sense of the middle-class art market and timing of delivery of goods as accurate as Noël Coward's was proved to be mistaken.[36] The timing, at least, of the production was hopelessly off. All Keynes's efforts to get London bookings came to nothing and when, at last, in February 1939, Doone found a large Shaftesbury Avenue theatre, it was for one Sunday performance only. Nor were the playwrights there to see their play in the West End setting it aspired to. They had crossed their frontier and were already in America.

13
Conclusion

Acrobatics of all kinds are popular and are
poetry's natural allies. It is the pure West-end
drama that is talk without action.[1]

W. H. AUDEN, 1934

There are so few things—that is unfortunate—that
people on the stage can do: they can sing, they can
dance, they can gesticulate, they can talk.
Gesticulation is much more suited and subtle on the
screen and the most important thing they can do is
talk. The spoken word is the basis of drama.[2]

W. H. AUDEN, 1938

The idea that inspired the founders of the Group Theatre was
not a new one. The attempt to create a theatre in which actors,
dancers, singers, musicians, designers, poets and a 'participating audience' would engage in collaborative creation informed
the European theatre at its very beginnings and has eluded it
ever since. If such a 'total theatre' is impossible to achieve it
may be because—as theorists from Aristotle to Brecht have
explained—the consuming reality of ritual actions is incompatible with a thoroughly self-conscious art; which is not to say
that the pursuit of the idea has not been a productive means of
jolting the theatre out of the too restrictive conventions of the
moment.

Taking a shorter perspective, the founders of the Group
were not only dedicated to a high old ideal but acutely aware
that the English theatre lagged far behind the most interesting
developments in Europe. The resistance to theatrical experiment in England was not only a matter of artistic provincial-

ism and social conservatism but the result of entrenched economic interests. The Group Theatre, setting about to change this situation, as others had before it, became part of a distinctly new wave in the theatre. As the need for general social renewal became more acute, the theatre assumed a key, even dangerous role. It was perceived, rather atavistically, as a possible means of re-engendering social unity, whether that unity was to be based on political or religious grounds. In so far as performances could be made not merely representational but real acts, the theatre might foster some modern equivalent to the communities from which it had arisen. As the reformers' ambitions for the theatre grew, so its actual state seemed correspondingly dismal.

The Group Theatre always saw the economic obstacles to the attainment of its aims as the main ones but it is most doubtful that, even with much more managerial expertise and sincerity than it was able to muster, it would have been able to build and sustain the kind of artistic community it envisaged. Quite apart from the intrinsic impossibility, as it may be, of achieving such an ideal, there was the fact that the most active and talented members of the Group were young, and developing individually as artists in ways that were bound to cause strain in any collective enterprise. Political feelings and commitments, moreover, exerted intense and rapidly changing pressures on members of the Group: conditions were decidedly unconducive to any calm and systematic attempt to resolve the basic problems of collaboration of the arts in the theatre. But vexed as it was by such pressures, by lack of time, lack of money, poor organization and unsuitable physical conditions, the Group's most serious weakness, at crucial moments, was the opportunism of its leaders.

Nevertheless, the Group Theatre's productions showed certain patterns of development. Major influences were absorbed and some synthesis was achieved; notably in the ways in which verse, prose and song were combined. In the Group's early days, Diaghilev's extravagent theatrical collages and the zealous purification of the theatre undertaken by

Copeau were the great, contrary, inspirations. With *The Dance of Death*, Auden and the Group achieved an extraordinary synthesis of elements from medieval theatre, from the emergent political theatre, from Cocteau and from Brecht. *Die Dreigroschenoper*, especially, remained a major model for the Group; not one that was closely imitated but an example of a kind of mixed theatrical genre that the Group aspired to create. It was a genre that lent itself to serious political engagement as well as to a celebratory kind of theatricality.

The political and Brechtian influences in the Group were very strongly counteracted by Eliot, as a successful poet-playwright who was as closely associated with the Group and as helpful to it as he could be, short of becoming artistically involved with it. In opposition to the sensuousness, didacticism and immanence of Brechtian theatre, Eliot emphasized the word and the symbolic relation of the stage to reality. Under his influence, Group Theatre plays and productions tried to accommodate poetry and symbol on the one hand with song, dance and parable on the other. Auden's position on the theatrical see-saw was critical.

Having begun with an aversion to 'talk' on the stage, Auden gravitated towards it, but he did not find, as Eliot did, a satisfactory form of poetic dialogue. Auden himself gave a reason for this failure late in 1938, in a talk on poetic drama: 'You cannot have poetry', he said, 'unless you have a certain amount of faith in something, but faith is never unalloyed with doubts and requires prose to act as an ironic antidote.'[3] The 'ironic antidote', in the verbal structure of his and Isherwood's plays, was far stronger than the 'faith'.

Given his own approach to the theatre, Eliot's opinion of the relative merits of the Group Theatre plays was not surprising. 'I do not feel,' he said,

> that the plays of Messrs Auden and Isherwood have been on the main line of development: they have tended to be rather prose plays interspersed with verse than real

dramatic poetry. The most promising play so far is, in my opinion, the *Trial of a Judge* by Stephen Spender, a play which has faced all the difficulties of being all in verse. . . . The play has serious technical defects, and I do not think that the author has a perfect control of his medium, but the possibilities of development are obvious.[4]

Spender's play also impressed Isherwood as, of all the plays written for the Group Theatre, the one most fully entitled to be called 'poetic drama'.[5] Interestingly, Spender himself, diverging from Eliot after the production of *Trial of a Judge*, saw Büchner's *Dantons Tod*—which he was then translating for the Group—as 'a play suggesting a solution of nearly all the problems of a modern poetic drama' that he, Eliot, Auden and the Group had been wrestling with.[6]

In MacNeice's *Out of the Picture* and the later plays of Auden and Isherwood, it was Britten's music that contributed most of the 'poetry' and 'faith'; and it was Britten and Doone, above all, who kept the Group Theatre's plays in the realm of the sensuous. Since the plays are now known merely by their published texts it is easy to overlook the essential role of music in them. It is even easier to forget that dance was part of the conception itself of all the Group Theatre productions except *Trial of a Judge*.

That the combination of dance, music and drama became the signature of Group Theatre productions and plays is largely attributable to Doone and his ambition for 'total theatre'. And the manner in which they were combined was, to a considerable extent, the expression of Doone's intuition, incoherence, and, perhaps, genius. His dominant role in the Group Theatre is, after all, the hardest to assess: his complex artistic personality impossible to describe with any confidence. As his leadership of the Group Theatre proved, Doone was not a 'builder'. Nor was he a polemicist, like Craig, or a memoirist, but totally a man of the theatre, creating for the moment with tremendous intensity. And one thing about his work does emerge clearly: Doone, more than any other English director, combined the arts of the theatre in the harshly and energetically justapositional manner that was characteristic of 'modernism' in the non-theatrical arts. In this respect, at least, Doone's contribution to the English theatre was a rare and valuable one.

Appendix A
The Superior Landlord

The typescript scenario of *The Superior Landlord* in the library of King's College, Cambridge, is bound up with other papers relating to the Sweeney fragments, the condition in which it was received as part of a bequest from Eliot's friend John Hayward.[1]

The other papers include a version of the 'Prologue' and a carbon copy of it, and a carbon copy only of the 'Fragment of an Agon'. These two items correspond very closely to the published fragments of *Sweeney Agonistes* but are not identical with them.

There is also the two-page holograph outline for the play described in chapter 4 above (pp. 91–92) and a typescript headed 'Homage to Aristophanes: A Fragment'. This typescript gives an alternative title, 'Fragment of a Comic Minstrelsy' and contains five quotations, two of which were printed with the fragments as epigraphs. A note by Eliot reads: 'My typing probably precedes the fragments themselves.' There is nothing to suggest that this note was meant to include all the typescripts now bound together.

The Superior Landlord is a scenario consisting of five typescript pages and the carbon copies of them. They have been bound in the wrong order but the right order is indicated by pagination in pencil. The title-page bears the signed inscription, by Eliot, 'Early typescript'.

The typed title of the scenario is PEREIRA / OR / THE MARRIAGE OF LIFE AND DEATH / A DREAM but this has been crossed out and, on the ribbon copy, a new title, THE SUPERIOR LANDLORD, pencilled in. On this title-page appears a quotation from *Julius Caesar* that occurs nowhere else in the papers nor in the published fragments:

> *Between the acting of a dreadful thing*
> *And the first motion, all the interim is*
> *Like a miasma, or a hideous dream.*

This epigraph may be a slight clue to the date of the scenario and to an experience that it renders, since the lines were those that went through Eliot's head, as Robert Sencourt recalled, when he put into the post the documents that would give him a legal separation from his wife.[2] This fateful mailing was made early in 1933 in America. The lines might well have occurred to Eliot at any time, or many times, of course, but we know that they were emotionally laden ones in 1933. To which it may be added that the climax of 'The Marriage of Life and Death' is a quarrel between Sweeney and Mrs Porter that leads to her murder and her resurrection. It may not be too fanciful to see in the fictional severance and reunion an image of the spiritual condition and the spiritual destiny of Eliot and his wife, as Eliot perceived them.

The typescript of *The Superior Landlord* is clearly not work that 'precedes the fragments themselves', since there is a sentence in it that reads: 'Badinage between Sweeney and Doris leading up to the conversation of Fragment II'. The scenario was obviously written not only after the writing of the fragments but after Eliot had decided that they *were* fragments and so, probably, after *Sweeney Agonistes* was published as 'Fragments of an Aristophanic Melodrama'. There is no reference in *The Superior Landlord* to the first fragment, of which, in 1933 at least, Eliot did not think highly.

Given the fact that the scenario was written after the fragments, given the resemblances (notably the use of Intruders, 'Casey Jones', Mendelssohn and a balletic interlude) to Auden's *The Dance of Death*, and given Eliot's expressed intention of starting 'something new of the same kind' as *Sweeney Agonistes* after finishing *The Rock*, I conclude that the scenario probably dates from 1934.

There were several moments when Eliot had an incentive to take up *Sweeney Agonistes* again. One was at the time of Hallie Flanagan's production in 1933 and another, when she declared an interest in seeing a fuller version, in February 1934. This was shortly before the date of the proposed performance of *Sweeney Agonistes* in Cambridge by the Group Theatre, which might also have been an incentive for Eliot to have considered an elaboration of the Sweeney material. But he was engrossed with rehearsals for *The Rock* until the end of May and the likeliest time for him to have turned his hand to Sweeney again was in July 1934, after *The Rock* was finished and before he accepted the Canterbury commission. On 25 July he was contemplating a new play, was indefinite about when it would be finished and was entertaining the idea that it might be produced by Doone and the Group Theatre. The most economical hypothesis is that *The Superior Landlord* represents his work on this new play.

Whether or not Eliot took up the Sweeney material again in July 1934, or made any progress with it, he had a further reason to do more with it when he agreed, in October 1934, that *Sweeney Agonistes* should be part of a double bill with Auden's *The Dance of Death* in the projected Poets' Theatre season. And in November his interest in *Sweeney Agonistes* was certainly heightened by the Group Theatre production of the fragments in the Rooms. For this, Doone made all the characters projections from Sweeney's mind, a feature of the production of which the encompassing dream of the 'Tenant Downstairs' in the scenario may be an echo. In certain other details, too, *The Superior Landlord* coincides with the production of *Sweeney Agonistes* in the Group Theatre Rooms: the dancing to the music from a gramophone; the singing by Klipstein and his companions shortly after their entrance; and Sweeney drawing a weapon with murderous intent. None of these things occurs in the published fragments.

The plan for the Poets' Theatre was abandoned in March 1935 and after this Eliot, busily finishing *Murder in the Cathedral*, would have had neither time nor a strong motive to continue work on *The Superior Landlord*, but it is possible that he did so with a view to the Group Theatre production of *Sweeney* as part of a double bill with *The Dance of Death* in October 1935.

Appendix B
The Poets' Theatre

On 20 October 1934, W. B. Yeats invited Rupert Doone, with whom he had been in correspondence some months earlier, to dine at his club.[1] A week later, he and Doone had apparently come to some sort of agreement, since Yeats reported to his wife that 'a little gathering of friends at Dulac's last night decided that "The Group Theatre" should act and produce' his plays. Some of them objected, said Yeats, to his working with Auden and Eliot on the grounds that 'comparison with rival schools prevents proper understanding', but he had other views.[2] The mention of Eliot indicates that Yeats knew that the Group Theatre had permission to produce *Sweeney Agonistes*. He had probably heard also that it expected to produce Eliot's new play.

The friends Yeats consulted included the actress Margot Collis, a beautiful, humourless woman with high artistic and intellectual ambitions, who had recently been the lessee, with her husband, of two provincial theatres.[3] In September 1933 she had written to Yeats, out of the blue, to propose the foundation of a poets' theatre. Yeats met her in London in October and became her lover. He decided that she had the beauty and the intellectual passion to be a great actress and began to execute her idea with gusto and with a view to advancing her career. 'Organizing is like a bumble-bee in a bottle,' he said. 'One tries all directions until one finds the neck'.[4] This activity must have reminded Yeats of the foundation of the Irish Literary Theatre many years before and his strong appetite for it confirmed, perhaps, the effectiveness of his recent Steinach operation.

It was Yeats's own idea to include 'the poetical Left' in the proposed new theatre. He explained to Margot Collis that he wanted Eliot to be part of the scheme because he represented 'a movement that had grown all over the world and is strong at the universities'.[5] Yeats also sought the collaboration of Frederick Ashton and Ninette de Valois. De Valois had created the role of Fand in his *Fighting the Waves* and Yeats wanted a new production of this play with music by Constant Lambert. Lambert, de Valois and Ashton were otherwise engaged, however, and Yeats eventually dropped the play from his list.[6]

A few days after the 'gathering' at Edmund Dulac's, Yeats had lunch with Eliot, who came away from their meeting conscious of an increased liking and admiration for the old poet and having agreed to collaborate in 'Yeats's theatre season'.[7] The next day, Yeats informed his wife that Ashley Dukes, with whom he had doubtless discussed the matter earlier, had offered the Mercury Theatre and had undertaken to meet production expenses for the proposed season.

By mid-December it had been decided that the Mercury season should open with a triple bill of Yeats's plays. He was then at work on *A Full Moon in March* (a rewriting of *The King of the Great Clock Tower*) in which he had mentally cast Margot Collis as the Queen. Dulac was to compose the music for this play and to design *The Player Queen* in which, Yeats assumed, Margot Collis would play the title role. The third play was to be *The Resurrection*. Yeats's plays were to run for a week and to be followed by a double bill consisting of *The Dance of Death* and *Sweeney Agonistes*.[8] By February, at Dukes's entreaty, the Auden–Eliot double bill was replaced by two new full-length plays, each of which would run for a week, Auden's *The Chase* and Eliot's *Murder in the Cathedral*. Henry Moore was suggested as the designer for *Murder in the Cathedral*.[9] Eliot agreed to this and also to the later substitution of Medley for Moore, and he arranged for *Murder in the Cathedral* to appear in the Poets' Theatre season before it was to be presented at Canterbury. It was to be a Group Theatre production directed by E. Martin Browne.[10]

When he read *A Full Moon in March* to Doone, Yeats was pleased with the latter's 'most strange and imaginative suggestions' for the staging of the play.[11] He also approved Doone's suggestion that Tyrone Guthrie be asked to direct *The Resurrection* and *The Player Queen*. Guthrie agreed but he subsequently discovered that he could not 'visualize' *The Player Queen*.[12] His vision may have been clouded by the designs already made by Dulac, or by Yeats's insistence that Margot Collis play the lead. Guthrie was one difficulty. Another was the role of the Group Theatre, which Yeats did not question until Dukes sounded the alarm. Was Doone to be 'just a producer called in' for a 'season of poetic plays by Yeats, Eliot and Auden' or was the season to be under the aegis of the Group Theatre?[13] To put it another way, was the Group Theatre to usher in a new phase in the English theatre or was it to be Dukes, acting as producer as well as backer?

Privately Dukes hoped to form a small, permanent company of his own at the Mercury but Doone was adamant that the Auden and Eliot plays, *A Full Moon in March* and *The Resurrection* (directed by Guthrie) were to be Group Theatre productions, with actors drawn, as far as possible, from the Group; and he insisted that the Group Theatre should be billed as producer. Dukes acceded to this arrangement but he also wrote to Yeats, who was only infrequently in London, about the dangers of a Group Theatre 'label' and Group Theatre control. Dulac did his best to clear up the confusion but it was too late. Yeats's suspicions were aroused:

> I care nothing about labels. What I care about is that I must approve the cast, producer and method of production of my own plays. A play is written for a certain method of production. Now if all are 'Group Theatre', according to label, will Doone feel impelled to interfere? His name is associated with a certain method. . . . I certainly will not find in the Group the chief players for 'The Player Queen' and perhaps not for my other plays. I know 'The Group' can dance, I know that they are adepts in concerted movement. I selected them for these reasons. I do not know that they can act.
>
> Doone of course must not produce 'The Player Queen'. He has the wrong training. . . .[14]

At this time, Yeats still hoped to persuade Guthrie to direct *The Player Queen*, not knowing that Guthrie had withdrawn from the scheme altogether.

Dukes tried to retrieve the situation with the suggestion that the opening of the season be postponed and another director found to replace Guthrie. But there were other problems. Dukes was not prepared, after all, to give full backing but was still looking for guarantors. Doone considered the rehearsal time scheduled at the Mercury was insufficient and, exasperated by the loss of Guthrie, himself withdrew.[15]

Eliot, the only one of the major collaborators who had been consistently constructive, wrote consolingly to Doone, thanking him for his suggestions for *Murder in the Cathedral*:

> I am afraid that the whole thing has been badly muddled. Whether the issue would have been more successful had Yeats been able to be in London I do not know. And also, unless there was someone behind such a scheme with the time and influence to get adequate support it could come to nothing. This end of it was obviously not your business and I don't consider it was mine.
>
> I am sorriest on account of Auden, and I hope that you will be able to make arrangements with the Westminster Theatre to give him a show in the Autumn. As for myself, I want to assure you that I have found your criticisms very valuable, and but for this abortive undertaking I should not have had the benefit of them. . . .[15]

Eliot turned his attention to the Canterbury production of *Murder in the Cathedral*. In collaboration with Isherwood, Auden undertook a wholesale revision of *The Chase*. Doone began to plan a Group Theatre season at the Westminster. Yeats bitterly blamed 'false, fleeting, perjured Ashley', whom he later described as 'a swamp' that he and Margot Collis had 'got mired in'.[17] Dukes obtained the rights to *Murder in the Cathedral* and had a great critical and financial success with its production (after the Canterbury one) at the Mercury. As for Margot Collis, she eventually acted the role of the Player Queen, but for one understudy performance only, at the Little Theatre. Two years later she was committed to a lunatic asylum.[18]

Appendix C

Members of the Group Theatre, 1933–5

The following list is a composite of the three lists published by the Group Theatre that I have been able to discover. That some of the most active members of the Group do not appear on the list is probably because they did not pay a subscription in the years in question or because they joined after 1935. They may even be masquerading under typographical errors that I occasionally suspect but cannot confirm. In 1935–6 the membership may have grown considerably as a result of the Group Theatre's Westminster Theatre season and the campaign connected with it. Whether the membership expanded or contracted (as seems likely) in the later pre-war years I do not know.

	1933	1934	1935
MARION ADAMS			x
ELIZABETH ADDISON	x	x	x
COLIN AGNEW	x	x	x
RICHARD AINLEY	x	x	
ELSPETH AITCHISON			x
BARBARA ALLEN			x
ERNEST ALLEN			x
JOHN ALLEN	x	x	x
MARJORIE ALLEN	x	x	x
NANCY ALLEN	x	x	
PERCY ALLEN			x
RAYMOND ALLEN	x	x	x
ELIZABETH ALLISON			x
MRS G. C. ANDERSON	x	x	x
HEDLI ANDERSON		x	x
HELIN ANREP	x	x	x
IGOR ANREP	x	x	x
G. LEE APPLEBY			x
KATHERINE ARBUTHNOT	x	x	

	1933	1934	1935
GABRIELLE ASTON			x
W. H. AUDEN	x	x	x
JANE BACON			x
HARLEY GRANVILLE-BARKER			x
CLIFFORD BAX			x
LINDSAY BAXTER		x	x
KEITH BAYNES	x	x	
ANNE GRAHAM BELL	x	x	x
FRANK GRAHAM BELL	x	x	x
VANESSA BELL	x	x	x
FRANCIS BIRRELL	x	x	
DAVID BLAIR	x	x	x
MERVYN BLAKE		x	x
F. S. BOAS	x	x	
DENISE BOWER			x
JOCELYN BRAITHWAITE			x
R. A. BRANDT			x
GRACE M. BROOKE	x	x	

Name	1933	1934	1935
G. H. P. BUCHANAN		x	x
IRENE BULLER		x	x
GUY BURN	x	x	
HELEN BURRA	x	x	
ERIC BURROWS	x	x	x
BASIL BURTON	x	x	x
CHRISTABEL BURTON			x
BASIL BURWELL		x	
MUNDY CASTLE	x	x	x
PAT CAVENDISH		x	x
LADY CLWYD	x	x	x
CATHERINE COCKERELL			x
NEVILL COGHILL			x
NANCY COLDSTREAM	x	x	x
WILLIAM COLDSTREAM	x	x	x
WILLIAM COLLINS		x	x
ROSALIND COLVILLE			x
JANE CONNARD		x	x
PETER COPLEY	x	x	x
ANNE COVENTRY		x	x
KATHLEEN CRAMPTON	x	x	
MARGARET CRASKE	x	x	x
LESLEY CREASE			x
KATHLEEN CROFTON		x	
OONAGH CUNNINGHAM			x
AILEEN CURRAN		x	
ELSPETH CURRIE			x
VERA CURTIS	x	x	
ROSEMARY DALE		x	x
NICOLETTE DEVAS	x	x	x
EVE DISHER	x	x	x
JESSICA DISMORR			x
BONAMY DOBREE			x
JOHN DODGSON	x	x	x
ANTON DOLIN	x	x	x
RUPERT DOONE	x	x	x
EILEEN DOUGLAS	x	x	x
RALPH DRESCHFIELD	x		x
DAPHNE DU GRIVEL	x	x	
AILEEN DUNLOP	x	x	
R. O. DUNLOP	x	x	
GEOFFREY DUNN	x	x	
COLIN EATON		x	x
MARY EDE			x
KATHLEEN EDWARDES		x	x
T. S. ELIOT			x
HAVELOCK ELLIS	x	x	x
ARTHUR ELTON	x	x	x
R. H. ERRINGTON		x	x

Name	1933	1934	1935
LILIAN ESPENAK			x
JOAN EVANS	x	x	
RAYMOND FARRELL		x	x
DOROTHY FERGUSON		x	
SYBIL FERRITA		x	
GERALDINE FITZMAURICE			x
ROBERT FLEMYNG	x	x	
PATRICIA FLETCHER		x	x
CONSTANCE FOLJAMBE	x	x	x
RICHARD FORD			x
NORMAN FRANKLIN	x	x	x
JEAN FRASER			x
ANNE FREEMANTLE			x
LESLIE FRENCH	x		
HELEN FULLER		x	x
JANE GALE	x		
NELLY T. GALLON			x
ROLLO GAMBLE	x	x	x
SUSAN GAMBLE		x	
VERNON GARDNER			x
ELEANOR GARLAND	x	x	
JEANNE GARMAN	x	x	
JOHN GARRETT			x
MISS H. M. GASKELL			x
JOAN GEARY		x	x
MARGARET GERSTLEY	x	x	
MARK GERTLER			x
DOROTHY GIBSON	x	x	x
JILL GILL			x
M. C. GILMOUR	x	x	
CECILY GIMINGHAM	x	x	
NORA GIMSON			x
VIOLET GOLDFRAP	x	x	
COMMANDER V. GOLDSMITH	x	x	
FRANCIS GOODWIN			x
R. M. GOODWIN			x
IRENE GORDON	x	x	x
MOLLY GORDON		x	x
MARIUS GORING		x	
DUNCAN GRANT	x	x	
HUGH GRANT	x	x	x
JANET GRANT	x	x	
LORNA GREENWOOD	x	x	x
ORMEROD GREENWOOD	x	x	x
MARGARET GRIEVE		x	x
GEOFFREY GRIGSON			x
BRYAN GUINNESS			x
JUDITH GUTHRIE	x	x	x
TYRONE GUTHRIE	x	x	x

Name	1933	1934	1935
ANMER HALL	x	x	x
DR T. E. HALL		x	x
BETTY HARDY	x	x	
MARGERY HARPER	x	x	x
JOY HARRINGTON	x	x	
LADY FRIEDA HARRIS	x	x	
PHILLIP D'ARCY HART	x	x	
ARTHUR HEWITT		x	
DIANA MURRAY HILL		x	
JOHN HILLIARD		x	
PETER HOAR	x	x	
MARGARET HODGES	x	x	
CLARE HOMFRAY	x	x	
HELEN HORSEY	x	x	x
WINIFRED HOWE	x	x	
MRS ST JOHN HUTCHINSON			x
MARJORIE ILLINGTON			x
NELSON ILLINGWORTH			x
JANET IMAGE			x
J. L. IRVINE			x
JOHN JOHNSON			x
PAMELA KEILY		x	
JOAN KEMP-WELCH		x	x
BARBARA KENT		x	x
DAVID KENWORTHY	x	x	x
RENATA KUH			x
BARBARA LAMB			x
LYNTON LAMB	x	x	x
HOPE LAMBRICK			x
CONSTANCE LANE			x
JOHN LAYARD			x
DAPHNE LEA	x	x	x
MRS A. LEAHY		x	
EILEEN LEAHY		x	
MARY LEAHY			x
JOHN LEDWARD	x	x	
MISS LEIGH-HUNT	x	x	
ANNE VAN LENNEP			x
ETHEL LEWIS	x	x	x
DAVID LEY	x	x	x
ANNE LONG			x
P. S. LONG-INNES			x
ELINOR LORING	x		x
ANGELA LOWIS			x
CYNTHIA LYALL			x
GILL LYALL	x	x	x
LEONARD LYALL			x
MURRAY MACDONALD			x
W. MACELROY		x	x
BARBARA MACKENZIE-SMITH	x	x	

Name	1933	1934	1935
TESSA MACNAMARA	x	x	
OLIVE MANGEOT	x	x	
ELSPETH MARCH	x	x	
DIGBY MARRIOTT		x	
HUGH MARTINDALE	x	x	
JOHN MASEFIELD			x
OLIVE MATHEWS			x
LADY MATTHEWS	x		
GRETA MAY			x
ANGUS MCLEOD		x	
MRS A. G. MEDLEY	x	x	x
ANNE MEDLEY		x	
J. C. MEDLEY	x	x	x
ROBERT MEDLEY	x	x	x
NORAH MCGUINNESS			x
SYLVIA MELLAND	x	x	
CLARICE MOFFAT			x
E. V. MOLTENO			x
G. N. MONK			x
JOHN MOODY	x	x	x
ROBERT MOODY	x	x	x
ENA MOON	x	x	x
HENRY MOORE	x	x	x
MRS HENRY MOORE	x	x	x
ENID MORGAN			x
HAROLD MORLAND			x
KATHERINE MORLEY			x
PETER MORRIS	x	x	
ELIZABETH MORWOOD		x	
BEATRICE MOSES		x	x
MRS MURRAY	x	x	
HERBERT MURRILL	x	x	x
MRS E. NASH	x	x	x
BETTY NEAVE		x	
MAUREEN NEWBOLD			x
ROBERT NEWTON		x	x
ELIZABETH NICOLLS			x
JOHN NICOLLS			x
NANCY NICOLLS	x		
HAROLD NICOLSON			x
IRENE NICHOLSON			x
VERONICA NOBLE			x
MARGARET NOEL-PATON			x
JOAN NOELS		x	
ANNE NORTHCOTE			x
MRS HILDA NUNN	x	x	x
RALPH NUTTALL-SMITH	x	x	
MAUREEN O'MOOR	x	x	x
GRETCHEN OLIVAE		x	
MAURICE J. ORME	x	x	x

	1933	1934	1935
DOUGLAS ORR			x
NANCY OSBORNE		x	x
RUTH WYNN OWEN		x	
SUE PALMER	x		
J. GOWER PARKS	x	x	x
STEPHEN PASSMORE	x	x	x
VICTOR PASMORE	x	x	x
WINIFRED PASSMORE	x	x	x
GEORGE PARKER			x
SORAB PATUCK		x	x
RUTH PENNYMAN			x
STELLA PETTIWARD		x	x
BARBARA PHILLIPS	x	x	
EMILIA PHILLIPS			x
MARGERY PHIPPS-WALKER	x	x	x
ALISON PICKARD	x	x	
W. H. PLATTS			x
BRIDGET PLOWDEN		x	x
VERA POLIAKOFF	x	x	x
DEREK PRENTICE		x	x
JOHN PUDNEY		x	x
MARY DE QUINCEY		x	x
BEATRICE RADLEY	x	x	x
MRS L. B. RADLEY	x	x	x
ROSEMARY READ		x	x
JOHN REDMOND		x	
MICHAEL REYNOLDS	x		
OLIVER REYNOLDS	x	x	
SIBYL A. RICHARDS			x
GORDON RICHARDSON			x
JEAN RICHARDSON	x	x	x
VALENTINE RICHMOND			x
SHUMLA RIDOUT			x
J. DORYNNE RIVERS	x	x	x
MERVYN ROBERTS	x	x	x
FLORA ROBSON	x		
ALAN ROLFE	x	x	x
YVONNE RORIE	x	x	x
ENID ROSE	x	x	
JEAN ROSS	x	x	
PATRICK ROSS		x	x
SITIEL ROWDEN			x
MRS GILBERT RUSSELL			x
NANCY RUSSELL	x	x	
MABEL RYAN	x	x	x
MICHEL SAINT-DENIS			x
MRS E. HILDA SCAIFE	x	x	x
GILLIAN SCAIFE	x	x	x
ISOBEL SCAIFE	x	x	x
JEAN SCOTT-ROGERS			x

	1933	1934	1935
RUPERT SCOTT	x		
PHILLIDA SEWELL	x	x	x
BARBARA SEYMOUR	x	x	x
RICHARD SEATON	x		
JOAN SHARP			x
GEOFFREY SHAW	x	x	x
RUPERT SHEPHARD	x	x	x
DOROTHY SHORT	x	x	x
C. A. E. SHUCKBURGH			x
MARY SKEAPING		x	x
ELSIE SMART	x	x	x
HELEN GUY SMITH			x
BETTY SMYTH	x	x	x
AGNES SNAPE	x	x	
STEPHEN SPENDER	x	x	x
NEVILLE STAFFORD		x	
NANCY STENNET		x	x
DAVID STEWART		x	
MARJORIE STEWART	x	x	x
ADRIAN STOKES	x	x	x
OLWEN STUART	x	x	
DORRIE STURGEON			x
HARRY STURGES	x		
GRAHAM SUTHERLAND			x
MARY SYMONDS	x	x	
KATRINA TAMAROVA			x
KATHLEEN TAPLAY	x	x	
JOHN TEED	x	x	
CLEGHORN THOMPSON		x	
MOLLIE TOMKINS			x
GEOFFREY TOONE	x		
MRS E. TOYE	x	x	
PHYLLIS TRAILL	x	x	x
FELIX TROTT	x	x	x
ANTONY TUDOR	x	x	x
W. J. TURNER		x	x
ANNE TWIGG	x	x	
MRS A. TYLOR	x		
ETHEL TYLOR		x	x
YOLANDE UPWARD			x
JEANNE VALLEE		x	
PATRICIA VILLERS			x
RUTH WAINEWRIGHT			x
SHIRLEY WAKEFIED	x	x	
ANTHONY WALTER-ELLIS		x	x
DESMOND WALTER-ELLIS		x	x
PRUDENCE WALTER-ELLIS			x
M. PICKERING WALKER			x

	1933	1934	1935		1933	1934	1935
HUGH WALPOLE			x	J. H. WHYTE	x	x	x
OCTAVIA WARE	x	x		R. GOWANS WHYTE			x
PAMELA WARE			x	RUTH WHYTE	x	x	
C. A. WARNER	x	x	x	PATRICIA WILDING	x	x	
RONALD WATERS	x	x	x	BRUCE WILLIAMS		x	x
ELISABETH WATSON	x	x	x	PETER WILLIAMS			x
MARJORIE WATSON	x	x		ANGUS WILSON	x	x	x
IRENE WEBB		x		BEATRICE WILSON			x
ROBERT WELLINGTON	x	x	x	JUDITH WOGAN	x	x	x
ALAN WHEATLEY	x	x		RICHARD WOOD		x	x
ANTONIA WHITE			x	MISS B. WOODWARD			x
JOAN WHITE	x	x		ANGELA WORTHY		x	x
JOHN WHITEHEAD	x	x		EDITH YOUNG	x	x	x
NANCY WHITELOCK		x	x	RACHEL YOUNG			x

Cast Lists of Group Theatre Productions

3 April 1932: Everyman Theatre, Hampstead

The Provok'd Wife by Sir John Vanbrugh

The producer, cast, etc., are not identified on the programme.

Produced by Rupert Doone
Musical Director and Composer: Herbert Murrill

CONSTANT	J. Gower Parks
HEARTFREE	John Allen
SIR JOHN BRUTE	Oliver Reynolds
RASOR	Ormerod Greenwood
BELINDA	Isobel Scaife

Other members of the cast are not known.

27 June 1932: Kenton Theatre, Henley-on-Thames

The Man Who Ate the Popomack: A Tragi-comedy of Love by W. J. Turner

Produced by R[upert] D[oone]

MAN-ABOUT-TOWN	Gervase Lambton
OLD MAN	Ormerod Greenwood
WOMAN	Jean Richardson
ANOTHER WOMAN	Barbara Seymour
FIRST YOUNG MAN	John Allen
SECOND YOUNG MAN	Robert Newton
LORD BELVOIR	Frederick Peisley
MURIEL RAUB	Ena Moon
HARRINGHAM	Jean Richardson

LADY OLIVIER	Mary Duff
LADY PHILO PHARON	Barbara Seymour
SIR PHILO PHARON	Ormerod Greenwood
MANDARIN	John Allen
CHINESE GUEST	Gervase Lambton
NOSEGAY	Alan Rolfe
HON. RUPERT CLAVELLY	Gervase Lambton
CAPT. ANTHONY	Gervase Lambton

29 January 1933: Westminster Theatre

An Experimental Reading of Ibsen's *Peer Gynt*, translated by William Archer

Produced by Rupert Doone and Gillian Scaife
Grieg's music played by Herbert Murrill and Frances Petersen
Design by Robert Medley
Stage Direction and Lighting by John Moody

PEER	Robert Speaight
AASE	Gillian Scaife
TWO OLD WOMEN	Eleanor Garland
	Elspeth March
ASLAK	Anthony Eustrel
KITCHEN MASTER	Rollo Gamble
SOLVEIG'S FATHER	John Moody
SOLVEIG	Isobel Scaife
HELGA	Daphne du Grivel
INGRID	Vera Poliakoff
THE BRIDEGROOM	Ormerod Greenwood
HIS FATHER	Jan Bussell
HIS MOTHER	Eleanor Garland
THE GREEN-CLAD WOMAN	Frances Petersen
THE OLD MAN OF THE DOVRE	Jan Bussell
THE BOYG	Frank Arundel
KARI	Eleanor Garland
ANITRA	Jean Shepheard
NORWEGIAN SKIPPER	Frank Arundel
STRANGE PASSENGER	Robert Newton
PASTOR	Waldo Wright
BUTTON MOULDER	Richard Ainley

LEAN MAN   Evan John

WEDDING GUESTS, TROLLS, VOICES IN THE AIR, ETC.: Guy Burn,
Constance Foljambe, Rollo Gamble, Hugh Grant, Ormerod
Greenwood, Margery Harper, Joy Harrington, David Kenwor-
thy, Elinor Loring, Elspeth March, John Moody, Beatrice
Radley, Rupert Shephard, Anne Twigg, Ronald Waters, John
Whitehead.

There was at least one more performance, for which the following
cast changes were made:

INGRID   Betty Hardy
ANITRA   Ena Moon
PASTOR   Anthony Eustrel
ASLAK   Stuart Bull
NARRATOR   Rollo Gamble

19 March 1933: Everyman Theatre, Hampstead

Fulgens and Lucrece by Henry Medwall

Producer and choreographer: Rupert Doone
Music by Herbert Murrill
Costumes designed by J. Gower Parks

A, AN INTRUDER   J. Gower Parks
B, AN INTRUDER   Oliver Reynolds
FULGENS   Ormerod Greenwood
LUCRECE   Daphne Lea
PUBLIUS CORNELIUS   John Teed
GAIUS FLAMINIUS   John Moody
LUCRECE'S MAID   Margery Phipps-Walker
MUMMERS:
DEATH   Mary Skeaping
THE JESTER   Rupert Doone
THE SINGER   Margery Harper
MUSICIAN   Joan Sharp

23 April 1933: Westminster Theatre

Fulgens and Lucrece by Henry Medwall

Production and cast as for 19 March 1933

1 July 1933: Melford Hall, Long Melford, Suffolk

The Group Theatre in Songs, Dances and a Play

Square Pegs, a play by Clifford Bax
HILDA   Ena Moon
GIACONDA   Irene Gordon

Waltz from *Les Sylphides*
Choreography by Rupert Doone
Dancers: Rupert Doone and Mary Skeaping

Songs directed by Tyrone Guthrie: 'King Herod and the Cock';
    'Bridgewater Fair'; 'Why dost thou turn away, fair maid?'; 'O
    dear, what can the matter be?'
Singers: John Allen, Jane Connard, Anne Coventry, Irene Gordon,
    Margery Harper, John Hilliard, Margaret Hodges, Helen Horsey,
    Daphne Lea, Ethel Lewis, Beatrice Radley, Jean Richardson, Alan
    Rolfe, Isobel Scaife, Richard Wood.

Dance: 'The Chinese Actor'
Choreographed and danced by Rupert Doone

Songs directed by Tyrone Guthrie: 'Mylechraine'; 'Weaving Lilt';
    'Mouse's Den'.

'Spring Dance'
Choreography by Rupert Doone to music by Paradies.
Dancers: Kathleen Crofton, Rupert Doone, Mary Skeaping.

Song: 'The Gipsy Laddie'.

24 July 1933: Croydon Repertory Theatre

The Group Theatre in Songs, Dances and a Play

Lancelot of Denmark

Produced by Rupert Doone
Costumes and scenery by Robert Medley
    LANCELOT   John Allen
    SANDEREEN   Isobel Scaife/Daphne Lea
    LANCELOT'S MOTHER   Eleanor Garland/Ethel Lewis
    THE KNIGHT   J. Gower Parks

FOREST RANGER   Alan Rolfe/M. J. Orme
REYNALD   John Moody

Songs and Dances
Songs produced by Tyrone Guthrie
Dances choreographed by Rupert Doone
Costumes by Margery Phipps-Walker and Robert Medley

'Pavane to a Dead Infanta', music by Ravel
Dancers: Mary Skeaping, Kathleen Crofton, Rupert Doone

Songs directed by Tyrone Guthrie: 'King Herod and the Cock';
    'Bridgewater Fair'; 'O dear, what can the matter be?'
Singers: John Allen, Jane Connard, Constance Foljambe, Irene
    Gordon, Molly Gordon, Margery Harper, Tristram Hilliard,
    Margaret Hodges, Daphne Lea, Ethel Lewis, John Moody, J.
    Gower Parks, Beatrice Radley, Jean Ricardson, Alan Rolfe, Isobel
    Scaife, Elizabeth Sadler, Richard Wood.

Dances:
'The Chinese Actor''
Choreographed and danced by Rupert Doone
'Witch Dance'
Choreographed and danced by Mary Skeaping

Songs directed by Tyrone Guthrie: 'Mylechraine'; 'Weaving Lilt';
    'Mouse's Den'.

'Spring Dance'
Choreographed by Rupert Doone to music by Paradies
Dancers: Kathleen Crofton, Rupert Doone, Mary Skeaping

Songs: 'Why dost thou turn away, fair maid?'; 'The Gypsie Laddie'
Singers: Jane Connard and Richard Wood.

'The Dance of Death' (from the Group Theatre production of
    Fulgens and Lucrece)
Music by Herbert Murrill
Choreography by Rupert Doone
Costumes by J. Gower Parks
Dancers:
    DEATH   Mary Skeaping
    A GIRL   Kathleen Crofton

MUSICIAN	Joan Sharp
THE MAN	Rupert Doone

Epilogue by W. H. Auden

27 November 1933: Maddermarket Theatre, Norwich

Fulgens and Lucrece by Henry Medwall

Production as for 19 March 1933, with the following cast changes:

A, AN INTRUDER	Colin Eaton
B, AN INTRUDER	Ormerod Greenwood
FULGENS	Maurice Orme
LUCRECE	Isobel Scaife
PUBLIUS CORNELIUS	Robert Newton
LUCRECE'S MAID	Constance Foljambe

25 February 1934: Westminster Theatre

The Deluge from the Chester Mystery Plays

Produced by Rupert Doone
Costumes, masks and setting by Robert Medley

GOD	Desmond Walter-Ellis
THE UNEMPLOYED FAMILY:	
NOAH	Ormerod Greenwood
MRS NOAH	Margery Phipps-Walker
SHEM	John Moody
MRS SHEM	Isobel Scaife
HAM	Patrick Ross
MRS HAM	Jean Richardson
JAPHET	Peter Copley
MRS JAPHET	Ruth Wynn Owen
ANIMALS:	
LION	Raymond Farrell
LAMB	Constance Foljambe
BEAR	Neville Stafford
CAT	K. Tamarova
COCK	Elizabeth Allison
GOSSIPS:	

Mrs Empire Builder	Margery Harper
Mr Capital Profiteer	Joan Kemp-Welch
Miss Old Lily	Jane Connard
Tory Stateman Esq.	Pamela Keily
Rev. Googles	John Allen

The Dance of Death by W. H. Auden

Produced by Tyrone Guthrie and Rupert Doone
Music by Herbert Murrill
Designer: Robert Medley
Death's mask by Henry Moore
Orchestra: Herbert Murrill (piano); D. Blatchley (banjo); Edith Gordon and Mary Skeaping (drums)

Death	Rupert Doone
Announcer	John Allen
The Manager	Stefan Schnabel
Miss Annabelle Eve	Betty Hardy
'Stage Hands'	Desmond Walter-Ellis
	Colin Eaton
The Doctor	Patrick Ross
Sir Edward	Peter Copley
Box	Desmond Walter-Ellis
Cox	Digby Marriott
Karl Marx	Marius Goring

Death's Attendant Nurses: Isobel Scaife, Valentine Richmond, Mary Skeaping, Edith Garland.

Principal singers: Hedli Anderson, Jane Connard, Daphne Lea, Ethel Lewis, Maureen O'Moor.

Nameless parts: Betty Aitchison, Hedli Anderson, Lindsay Baxter, Irene Buller, Basil Burwell, William Collins, Jane Connard, Peter Copley, Anne Coventry, Elspeth Currie, Rosemary Dale, Raymond Farrell, Pat Fletcher, Constance Foljambe, Eleanor Garland, Joan Geary, Ormerod Greenwood, Margery Harper, John Hilliard, Pamela Keily, Joan Kemp-Welch, David Kenworthy, Daphne Lea, A. Leahy, Ethel Lewis, Gill Lyall, Eve Morley, Maureen O'Moor, Margery Phipps-Walker, Vera Poliakoff, Derek Prentice, Mary de Quincey, Rosemary Read, Jean Richardson, Alan Rolfe, Barbara Seymour, Rupert Shephard, Neville Stafford, Nancy Stennet,

Donald Stewart, John Teed, Prue Walter-Ellis, Nancy White-
lock, Bruce Williams, Richard Wood, Angela Worthy, Ruth
Wynn Owen, Rachel Young.

17 April 1934: Westminster Theatre

Lancelot of Denmark and 'Dance of Death'

A charity matinée for Kingsley Hall. This 'Dance of Death' was the
mumming from the Group Theatre production of *Fulgens and
Lucrece*.

9 June 1934: Fulham Palace

Fulgens and Lucrece by Henry Medwall

The performance was given as part of a *Garden Fête and Housing
Exhibition*.

14 June 1934: Wadham College, Oxford

Fulgens and Lucrece by Henry Medwall

Produced by Rupert Doone
Music by Herbert Murrill
Costumes by J. Gower Parks
Choreography by Rupert Doone

A, AN INTRUDER	Colin Eaton
B, AN INTRUDER	Ormerod Greenwood
FULGENS	Richard Wood
LUCRECE	Isobel Scaife
PUBLIUS CORNELIUS	Peter Copley
GAIUS FLAMINIUS	John Moody
LUCRECE'S MAID	Constance Foljambe
MUMMERS:	
DEATH	Elizabeth Allison
MUSICIAN	Richard Wood
THE JESTER	Rupert Doone

August 1934: Suffolk Tour

East Lynne, a melodrama based on the novel by Mrs Henry Wood

2 August: Public Hall, Beccles
3 August: Victoria Hall, Sudbury
8 August: Finborough
10, 11 August: Southwold

?October 1934: Group Theatre Rooms

Midnight Cabaret

Decorations: Clarence Moffat, Nora McGuinness, Geoffrey Monk, Graham Sutherland
Compère: Desmond Walter-Ellis

Excerpts from *East Lynne*

ARCHIBALD CARLYLE	John Moody
LADY ISABEL	Ruth Wynn Owen
LITTLE WILLIE	Isobel Scaife
SIR FRANCIS LEVISON	John Allen
MISS CORNEY CARLYLE	Margery Phipps-Walker
JOYCE	Rosemary Dale
WILSON	Joan Geary
BARBARA HARE	Barbara Seymour

Narrative lyrics by John Allen

Songs by the Group Theatre Singing Waiters: John Allen, Rosemary Dale, Ormerod Greenwood, John Moody, Ruth Wynn Owen, Jean Richardson, Alan Rolfe, Barbara Seymour, Desmond Walter-Ellis
Hedli Anderson in old and new songs of satire
Rupert Doone: 'The Spirit of Cocaine'
Isobel Scaife and Jean Richardson: 'At It Again'
Desmond Walter-Ellis: 'The Man on the Flying Trapeze'
Rupert Doone and Renata Kuh: 'The Devil's Can-Can'
Finale: 'Can-Can'

11 November 1934: Group Theatre Rooms

Sweeney Agonistes by T. S. Eliot

Produced by Rupert Doone
Music by William Alwyn
Masks by Robert Medley

DUSTY	Ruth Wynn Owen
DORIS	Isobel Scaife
WAUCHOPE	Mervyn Blake
KLIPSTEIN	Desmond Walter-Ellis
KRUMPACKER	Ormerod Greenwood
SWEENEY	John Moody

1 October 1935: Westminster Theatre

Sweeney Agonistes by T. S. Eliot
Production as for 11 November 1934, except for the following cast changes:

WAUCHOPE	Richard Schjelderup
KLIPSTEIN	Peter Copley
KRUMPACKER	Stefan Schnabel

The Dance of Death by W. H. Auden
Production as for 25 February 1934, except for the musicians and the following changes in the dramatis personae named cast and chorus:

ANNABELLE EVE	Arabella Tullock
'STAGE HANDS'	Rupert Scott, John Glyn Jones
COMMUNISTS	Patrick Ross
	Rupert Scott
	John Glyn Jones
'STAGE MANAGER'	John Moody
BOX OF THE BBC	Rupert Scott
COX OF THE BBC	John Glyn Jones
CABARET SINGER	Hedli Anderson

(KARL MARX is omitted from the dramatis personae.)
DEATH'S ATTENDANT NURSES: Isobel Scaife, Anna Brunton, Lilian Espenak, Renata Kuh.
SINGERS AND DANCERS: Hedli Anderson, Colyn Campbell, Jane Connard, Kathleen Edwardes, Jack Endle, Ilona Ference, Rollo Gamble, Jeanne Garman, Ormerod Greenwood, Ronald Ibbs, John Glyn Jones, Daphne Lea, Will Leighton, Dorothy

Morland, Mary de Quincey, Jean Richardson, Alan Rolfe, Richard Schjelderup, Rupert Scott, Barbara Seymour, Marjorie Stewart, Christine Sheldon Williams, Richard Wood
  SPEAKERS IN THE AUDIENCE: Constance Foljambe, Robert Medley, Geoffrey Monk, Ruth Wynn Owen, Margery Phipps-Walker
Many of the above chorus of singers, dancers and speakers appeared in the 25 February 1934 performance where they are listed under the heading 'Nameless Parts'.

15 October 1935: Westminster Theatre

Lady Patricia by Rudolf Besier

Though part of the Group Theatre season, this was not otherwise a Group Theatre production.
Staged by John Wyse
Décor by Colonel George Hawes

LADY PATRICIA COSWAY	Phyllis Neilson-Terry
ELLIS	Jack Endle
BALDWIN	Craighall Sherry
WILLIAM O'FARRELL	Trevor Howard
DEAN LESLEY	Stanley Lathbury
MRS O'FARRELL	Gillian Scaife
CLARE LESLEY	Caryl Jenner
MICHAEL COSWAY	Nigel Clarke
JOHN	Drelincourt Odlum
ROBERT	Robert Tollast

29 October 1935: Westminster Theatre

Sowers of the Hills by Jean Giono, translated by Jolliffe Metcalfe

Staged by Michel Saint-Denis
Décor by Robert Medley
Costumes by Marie-Madelaine Gautier

CATHERINE	Vera Poliakoff
MARTHA	Jean Shepeard
BERTHA	Iris Ashton
MADAME DELPHINE	Sara Allgood

AUBERT	Marius Goring
MAÎTRE ANTOINE	D. A. Clarke-Smith
PAUL	Reginald Beckwith
AUGUSTE	Will Leighton
ALPHONSE	John Glyn Jones
DOMINIQUE	Harold Young
A PEDLAR	Harcourt Williams

19 November 1935: Westminster Theatre

Timon of Athens by William Shakespeare

Staged by Nugent Monck
Décor by Robert Medley
Music by Benjamin Britten
Choreography by Rupert Doone
Orchestra directed by Herbert Murrill

TIMON	Ernest Milton
LUCIUS	Peter Copley
LUCULLUS	Trevor Howard
ALCIBIADES	Torin Thatcher
APEMANTUS	Harcourt Williams
FLAVIUS	Frederick Piper
POET	Rollo Gamble
PAINTER	Richard Fleury
LUCILIUS	John Moody
FLAMINIUS	Will Leighton
THIRD SERVANT	Maurice Orme
FOURTH SERVANT	Ronald Ibbs
CAPHIS	John Glyn Jones
VARRO	Colin Eaton
ISIDORE	Ronald Ibbs
SENATORS	John Boddington
	Rupert Scott
BANDITS	Patrick Ross
	Colin Eaton
ALCIBIADES' FRIEND	John Allen
STRANGERS	Ormerod Greenwood
	Mervyn Blake
	Ronald Ibbs

PHRYNIA	Kathleen Edwardes
TIMANDRA	Isobel Scaife
THIRD COURTESAN	Olivia Windram
SOLDIERS	Patrick Ross
	Colin Eaton
	Mervyn Blake
	John Vaughan
	Noel Brophy
	Bruce Lancaster
AT TIMON'S FEAST:	
MASTER OF CEREMONIES	Rupert Doone
DANCING COURTESANS	Marjorie Stewart
	Jeanne Garman
	Renata Kuh
	Elizabeth Allison

14 December 1935: Westminster Theatre

A Programme of Dances and A Harlequinade

Nominally this was not a Group Theatre performance but the company was drawn from the Group Theatre and *A Harlequinade* was officially adopted as an afterpiece to *The Impresario from Smyrna*, which opened on 23 December 1935.

Dance Recital
Dances arranged by Renata Kuh, Mary Skeaping and Rupert Doone.
Dancers: Renata Kuh, Mary Skeaping, Zoe Randall, Christine Sheldon Williams, Eve Sheldon Williams.

A Harlequinade by John Allen
Produced by Rollo Gamble
Music by Herbert Murrill
Costumes by Jeanne Garman

PANTALOON	Alan Rolfe
CAPITANO	Peter Copley
ZANY	Tony Spurgin
HARLEQUIN	John Glyn Jones
SMERALDINA	Arabella Tulloch
YSABELLA	Isobel Scaife

PEDROLINO	Colin Eaton
COLUMBINE	Eleonora Marra
COCODRILLO	John Allen
THE CHILD	Jean Richardson

23 December 1935: Westminster Theatre

The Impresario from Smyrna by Carlo Goldoni, translated by Clifford Bax
Staged by John Fernald

BELTRAME	John Moody
COUNT LASCA	Alan Wheatley
CARLUCCIO	Max Adrian
LUCREZIA	Sylvia Coleridge
NIBIO	Douglas Seale
TOGNINA	Julia Crawley
PASQUALINO	Oliver Reynolds
MACCARIO	John Glyn Jones
ANNINA	Betty Hardy
ALI	Morland Graham
FABRIZIO	Noel Brophy
SERVANT TO ALI	Patrick Ross
SERVANT TO ANNINA	Ronald Ibbs
OLD LADY	Margaret Douglas
LAD	Noel Brophy
SERVANT TO LUCREZIA	John Allen
PAINTERS, ETC.	Ormerod Greenwood
	Alan Rolfe
	Colin Eaton

A New Harlequinade
Production as for 14 December 1935, except that CAPITANO was played by Douglas Seale.

12 January 1936: Westminster Theatre

The Dog Beneath the Skin by W. H. Auden and Christopher Isherwood

This performance was technically a private one, for members of the Group Theatre. For the first public performance see below.

Staged by Rupert Doone
Music by Herbert Murrill
Masks by Robert Medley
Pianists: Herbert Murrill and Anthony Spurgin

THE DOG, FRANCIS	Oliver Reynolds
ALAN NORMAN	John Moody
FIRST JOURNALIST, SECOND BOY	John Glyn Jones
SECOND JOURNALIST	Desmond Walter-Ellis
WITNESS	Veronica Turleigh
WITNESS	Robert Speaight
VICAR, TIGER JACK, SECOND LUNATIC, SURGEON, POLICE SERGEANT	Patrick Ross
GENERAL HOTHAM, SECOND PRISONER, FLAG LUNATIC, COLONEL, CABARET ANNOUNCER	Bryan Coleman
MRS HOTHAM, THE QUEEN OF OSTNIA, PROPRIETRESS OF YAMA THE PIT, SECOND MAD LADY, FIRST INVALID, SISTER, CHORUS	Barbara Seymour
IRIS CREWE, FIRST MAD LADY, INMATE, CHORUS	Betty Hardy
CURATE, LUNATIC WITHOUT FLAG, POET, ANAESTHETIST	Robert Eddison
SERGEANT, BARMAN, SECOND M. O., ATTENDANT, SECOND STUDENT, SECOND WAITER	Alan Rolfe
BUS CONDUCTOR, FIRST GUARD, LEADER'S VOICE, PAINTER, FIRST WAITER, CHORUS	John Allen
SCOUTMASTER, CHIMP EAGLE, CHORUS	Richard Wood
MILDRED LUCE, FIRST BEREAVED WOMAN	Constance Foljambe
FIRST BOY, MASTER OF CEREMONIES, FIRST TOUT,	Ormerod Greenwood

FIRST LUNATIC, FIRST LOVER, FIRST STUDENT, FIRST PAGE, CHORUS	
THIRD BOY, FOOTMAN, FISHERMAN	Noel Brophy
FOURTH BOY, THE KING OF OSTNIA, DOPEY JIM, PORTER AND MANAGER	Rupert Scott
DONOR OF THE WATCH, SECOND LADY-IN-WAITING, MADAME BUBBI, CHORUS	Hedli Anderson
FIRST LADY-IN-WAITING, MOTHER HUBBARD, NURSE, THIRD MAID	Kathleen Edwardes
THIRD LADY-IN-WAITING, SECOND TOUT, SECOND INVALID, SECOND PAGE, CHORUS	Jean Richardson
FOURTH LADY-IN-WAITING, INMATE, NURSE, FIRST MAID, CHORUS	Isobel Scaife
FIRST PRISONER, NAKED LUNATIC, FOURTH STUDENT	Henry Rayner
THIRD PRISONER, FIRST M.O., SHADOW BOXER, THIRD STUDENT, CHORUS	Ronald Ibbs
FOURTH PRISONER, PROFESSOR, THIRD WAITER	Maurice Orme
SECOND GUARD	Robert Medley
THIRD GUARD	Geoffrey Monk
FOURTH GUARD	Rupert Shephard
SECOND BEREAVED WOMAN, SECOND LOVER, CHORUS	Ilona Ference
THIRD BEREAVED WOMAN	Rosemary Bourne
FOURTH BEREAVED WOMAN, NURSE, CHORUS	Joan Geary
GRABSTEIN	Stefan Schnabel
VIOLINIST	Margaret Douglas
SECOND MAID	Christine Sheldon Williams
LOU VIPOND	Carmen Costa

| CHORUS | Betty Barr |
| CHORUS | Colyn Campbell |

30 January 1936: Westminster Theatre

The Dog Beneath the Skin by W. H. Auden and Christopher Isherwood

The production was as for 12 January 1936, except for some modification of the text and the following cast changes:

THE DOG, FRANCIS	Geoffrey Wincott
SECOND JOURNALIST*	Charles Hickman
WITNESS	Gyles Isham
VICAR, TIGER JACK, SECOND LUNATIC, POLICE SERGEANT	Patrick Ross
GENERAL HOTHAM, NAKED LUNATIC, SURGEON	Christopher Steele
IRIS CREWE, NURSE, CHORUS	Joan Geary
CURATE, LUNATIC WITHOUT FLAG, POET, ANAESTHETIST	Max Adrian
SCOUTMASTER, FLAG LUNATIC, CHIMP EAGLE, CHORUS	Will Leighton
DONOR OF THE WATCH, LADY-IN-WAITING, A GIRL OF THE QUARTER, MADAME BUBBI, CHORUS	Hedli Anderson
VILLAGER	Rosemary Bourne
VILLAGER	Rachel Young
GRAND VIZIER, A TOUT, FIRST LUNATIC, FIRST LOVER, FIRST STUDENT, FIRST PAGE, CHORUS	Ormerod Greenwood
THE SULTAN, COLONEL, PORTER, MANAGER	Eric Chitty
LADY-IN-WAITING, THE CLOCK, SECOND INVALID, SECOND PAGE, CHORUS	Jean Richardson
THE PROFESSOR, ATTENDANT, STUDENT, FOURTH WAITER	Noel Brophy
DOPEY JIM	Rollo Gamble
FISHERMAN	Maurice Orme

NINEVEH GIRL	Betty Barr
LOU VIPOND	Carmen Wincelma

* For some of the public performances, at least, John Glyn Jones remained in the role of one of the JOURNALISTS.

Merely nominal and very minor changes in the casting are not noted.

The following members of the 12 January cast did not take part: Colyn Campbell, Bryan Coleman, Robert Eddison, Betty Hardy, Robert Medley, Geoffrey Monk, Henry Rayner, Oliver Reynolds, Rupert Scott, Rupert Shephard, Robert Speaight.

26 March 1936: Westminster Theatre

Fulgens and Lucrece by Henry Medwall

Staged by Rupert Doone
Music by Herbert Murrill
Costumes designed by Robert Medley

A, AN INTRUDER	Desmond Walter-Ellis
B, AN INTRUDER	Ormerod Greenwood
FULGENS	John Boddington
LUCRECE	Isobel Scaife
PUBLIUS CORNELIUS	Robert Eddison
GAIUS FLAMINIUS	John Moody
JOAN	Margery Phipps-Walker
MUMMERS:	
DEATH	Mary Skeaping
JESTER	Rupert Doone
A SINGER	Hedli Anderson
MUSICIAN	Joan Sharp/Margaret Donnington

1 November 1936: Westminster Theatre

The Agamemnon of Aeschylus, translated by Louis MacNeice

Produced by Rupert Doone
Music by Benjamin Britten
Masks and costumes designed by Robert Medley
Choreography by Rupert Doone
Chorus mistress: Evelyn Bowen

CHORUS OF DANCERS:	Elizabeth Allison, Nesta Brooking, Kathleen Edwardes, Renata Kuh, Daphne Lawrence, Richard Ellis, Mark Baring, Nigel Henderson, Peter Garst
CHORUS OF CITIZENS:	Bethell Datch, Edward Dudgeon, Dennis Glenny, Ormerod Greenwood, Michael Lane, Stuart Latham, John Moody
A WATCHMAN	John Moody
CLYTEMNESTRA	Veronica Turleigh
HERALD	Francis James
AGAMEMNON	Robert Speaight
CASSANDRA	Vivienne Bennett
AEGISTHUS	Guy Spaull
SLAVES:	Evelyn Allen, Constance Biron, Kathleen Edwardes, Daphne Lawrence
PRIESTESSES:	Constance Foljambe, Elspeth Aitchison
SOLDIERS:	Nigel Henderson, Michael Law, Michael Brown, Geoffrey Monk
CHORUS OF WOMEN SLAVES:	Elspeth Aitchison, Evelyn Allen, Constance Biron, Margaret Dewar, Kathleen Edwardes, Constance Foljambe, Jill Gyngell, Barbara Seymour

Greek Commentary spoken by Louis MacNeice

26 February 1937: Mercury Theatre

The Ascent of F6 by W. H. Auden and Christopher Isherwood

Presented by Ashley Dukes in association with the Group Theatre
Produced by Rupert Doone
Music by Benjamin Britten
Costumes, masks and scene designed by Robert Medley
Musical Director: Brian Easdale
Instrumentalists: Frida Easdale, Vera Dart

MICHAEL FORSYTH RANSOM	William Devlin
SIR JAMES RANSOM	Raf de la Torre

LADY ISABEL WELWYN	Ruth Taylor
GENERAL DELLABY-COUCH	Erik Chitty
LORD STAGMANTLE	Edward Lexy
DAVID GUNN	Barry Barnes
IAN SHAWCROSS	Norman Claridge
EDWARD LAMP	Peter Ashmore
DR WILLIAMS	Philip Thornley
MRS RANSOM	Dorothy Holmes-Gore
THE ABBOTT	Evan John
MONKS	Alan Aldridge
	Michael Lane
	Robert Newport
MR A	Will Leighton
MRS A	Isobel Scaife
AN ANNOUNCER	Stuart Latham
THE SINGER	Hedli Anderson
BLAVEK	Noel Woolf

22 April 1937: Arts Theatre, Cambridge

The Ascent of F6 by W. H. Auden and Christopher Isherwood

Production as for 26 February 1937, except that: Eve Kifli replaced Vera Dart as instrumentalist; BLAVEK did not appear in the list of characters (nor Noel Woolf in the list of actors); AN ACOLYTE became a named character (played by Alan Aldridge); Alan Aldridge and Michael Lane were described as BROADCASTERS, but not MONKS; and Robert Newport did not appear in the cast. This production was transferred to the Little Theatre on 30 April 1937.

5 December 1937: Westminster Theatre

Out of the Picture by Louis MacNeice

Produced by Rupert Doone
Music by Benjamin Britten
Décor and costumes designed by Robert Medley
Musical director: Brian Easdale
Instrumentalists: Frida Easdale, Vera Dart, Frederick East

PORTRIGHT	Geoffrey Edwards
MISS HASKEY	Christine Silver
BAILIFF	John Moody
FIRST MAN	Peter Bennett
SECOND MAN	Robert Carrington
MOLL O'HARA	Vivienne Bennett
LISTENER-IN	Stuart Latham
RADIO ANNOUNCER	John Glyn Jones
CLARA DE GROOT	Elspeth Duxbury
DR SPIELMANN	Phillip Leaver
BILL THE PARROTT	John Moody
MRS FREUDENBERG	Isobel Scaife
COMMENTATORS:	Sophie Wyss
	Merial St Clair
	Nella Burra
	Ian Glenny
	William Grant
SALE ROOM ATTENDANT	Robert Christie
AUCTIONEER	Francis James
AUCTIONEER'S ASSISTANT	Peter Bennett
JENNY	Jane Vaughan
SIR SHOLTE SPIELMANN	Phillip Leaver
VENUS	Vera Poliakoff
UNIFORMED MAN	Robert Christie
THREE MEN	Noel Brophy
	Ian Henderson
	Christopher Cornford
PASSERS-BY, COLLECTORS, ETC.	Alice Bolster, Kathleen Edwardes, Constance Foljambe, Ruth Glover, Mary de Quincey, Violet Todd

18 March 1938: Unity Theatre

Trial of a Judge by Stephen Spender

Produced by Rupert Doone
Set designed and painted by John Piper
Chorus Mistress: Hilda M. Adams

THE JUDGE	Godfrey Kenton

THREE FASCIST PRISONERS	Peter Copley
	Aidan Turner
	Colin Eaton
PETRA'S MOTHER	Constance Foljambe
PETRA'S BROTHER	Moran Caplat
PROSECUTING COUNSEL	Julian Somers
THE FIANCÉE	Emma Trechman
A COMMUNIST	Kenneth Evans
THE JUDGE'S WIFE	Kathleen Boutall
HUMMELDORF	Evan John
MANSERVANT	Neil Gibson
TWO FASCISTS	Peter Bennett
	Bill Sykes
FASCIST TROOP LEADER	Julian Somers
JEWISH DOCTOR	Peter Bennett
COMMUNIST PRISONERS	George Windred, Richard Wordsworth, H. Dagnall, J. W. Maule, F. Spelling, L. White

17 July 1938: Westminster Theatre

The Human Voice: A Play in One Act by Jean Cocteau, translated by Carl Wildman, and a Song Recital by Marianne Oswald

Introduction by Stephen Spender
Songs by Cocteau, Prévert and Kosma, Bonheur and Kosma, Brecht and Weill, and Lenoir, sung by Marianne Oswald
Pianist: Youly Tepley

The Human Voice
Directed by Berthold Viertel
Setting by Geoffrey Monk
Acted by Beatrix Lehmann

14 November 1938: Arts Theatre, Cambridge

On the Frontier: A Melodrama in Three Acts by W. H. Auden and Christopher Isherwood

Presented by the Group Theatre in association with the Cambridge
  Arts Theatre Trust
Produced by Rupert Doone
Music by Benjamin Britten
Scenery and costumes designed by Robert Medley
Musical Director: Brian Easdale

LESSEP	Hugh Grant
MANNERS	Alan Rolfe
VALERIAN	Wyndham Goldie
ALVING	Nigel Fitzgerald
CORPORAL GRIMM	Ian Dawson
THE GUIDANTO	Ernest Milton
DR OLIVER THORVALD	Tristan Rawson
MRS THORVALD	Mary Barton
ERIC THORVALD	Eric Berry
MARTHA THORVALD	Everley Gregg
COLONEL HUSSEK	Cecil Winter
LOUISA VRODNY	Juliet Mansel
ANNA VRODNY	Lydia Lopokova
OSWALD VRODNY	John Moody
WESTLAND ANNOUNCER	Ian Glenny
OSTNIAN ANNOUNCER	Peter Pears
SINGERS AND DANCERS:	Nella Burra, Harold Child, Jane Connard, Ian Glenny, Cuthbert Matthews, John Moody, Peter Pears, Prudence Wood, Richard Wood.

12 February 1939: Globe Theatre

On the Frontier: A Melodrama in Three Acts by W. H. Auden an
Christopher Isherwood

Production as for 14 November 1938, except for some rearrange-
ment of the text and the following additions:
Musical Director: Brian Easdale
Instrumentalists: Brian Easdale, Frida Easdale, H. C. Morse, Sidney
  Ellison, Bernard Brown

27 June 1939: Old Vic Theatre

The Ascent of F6 by W. H. Auden and Christopher Isherwood

Directed by Rupert Doone
Music by Benjamin Britten
Costumes, masks and scene designed by Robert Medley
Musical Director: Brian Easdale
Pianists: Brian Easdale, Frida Easdale
Percussion: Phyllida Garth

MICHAEL FORSYTH RANSOM	Alec Guinness
SIR JAMES RANSOM	Gyles Isham
LADY ISABEL WELWYN	Barbara Couper
GENERAL DELLABY-COUCH	Frederick Bennett
LORD STAGMANTLE	Ronald Adam
DAVID GUNN	Arthur Macrae
IAN SHAWCROSS	Laurier Lister
EDWARD LAMP	Frederick Peisley
DR WILLIAMS	Ernest Hare
MRS RANSOM	Barbara Everest
THE ABBOTT	Francis James
AN ACOLYTE	Stephen Bate
BLAVEK	John Moody
MR A	John Moody
MRS A	Helen Horsey
AN ANNOUNCER	Stuart Latham
CHORUS	Stephen Bate
	Nella Burra
	Wallas Eaton

Group Theatre Productions Limited, 1950–6[1]

Plans to revive the Group Theatre were announced at an enthusiastic meeting convened at the ICA (Institute of Contemporary Arts) in May 1950. Two months later, Group Theatre Productions Limited (GTP) was formed with a small capital consisting of the assets of the pre-war Group Theatre and private donations amounting to some £2,500 in all.[2] Further support was promised from the ICA, which agreed to contribute up to £1,000 on condition that GTP should mount at least three productions in the course of the year.

The moving spirit behind the revival was Vera Lindsay, who (as Vera Poliakoff) had acted for the Group Theatre and for Michel Saint-Denis before the war.[3] After a period of organizational consolidation, she and Rupert Doone assumed the roles of Artistic Directors under contract to GTP.[4]

GTP had a complicated structure made up, at various times, of combinations of a Working Council, an Executive Committee, a Management Committee, a Board of Directors (later Governors), and Literary Directors (later Advisers) as well as subscriber-members who had no say in policy. One reason for the complexity of the organization was that its Articles of Association were devised with a view to putting it in the most advantageous position with regard to the Income Tax and Entertainments Duty regulations then in force, and to Arts Council patronage, without ruling out the possibility of entrepreneurial activity. Another was that honorific positions were found for a number of individuals whose fame and connections were valuable but whose interference was not wanted.[5]

The declared policy of GTP was to bring about 'new theatre' through the presentation of 'new plays, new writers and new techniques'. Practically, its emphasis was on the acquisition of the rights to produce new (or newly translated) work. Indeed, GTP became an agent of sorts for some of the works it acquired, rather than a producer, and earned income in this way.

In its first year of operation, GTP acquired the English rights to Cocteau's *Les Chevaliers de la Table Ronde* (1937); to a French dramatization of Graham Greene's *The Power and the Glory*; to Bertolt Brecht's *Mutter Courage und ihre Kinder* (1941), subject to the playwright's approval of a new translation; and to Jean-Paul Sartre's *Les Mouches* (1942), of which there was an available English version. Auden was commissioned to translate the Cocteau play and it was originally intended that it should be presented by GTP at the Edinburgh Festival in 1951.[6] To this end Rupert Doone did preparatory work on the production and John S. Woods designed settings and costumes. For financial and other reasons GTP never produced the play, though it did not abandon its intention of doing so for several years.[7] The other three plays were announced for production in 1951, along with a new translation, by R. M. Nadal and Kathleen Raine, of Calderón's *La vida es sueño*; but only *The Flies* was actually staged.

With *Mother Courage*, the initial problem was to find a suitable translator. Auden, Isherwood and others were approached and, eventually, a translation was made for GTP by James Kirkup. There was also the question of who should direct the play. Peter Brook was apparently asked and, later, Tyrone Guthrie, who expressed an interest in presenting the work in a hall rather than in a conventional theatre. After long delay, and partly because the political climate seemed unfavourable, the plans for a GTP production of *Mother Courage* were dropped.[8]

The rights to the English version of *The Power and the Glory* were eventually transferred to a commercial management by GTP, which profited from the transaction.[9] The Raine–Nadal version of *Life's a Dream* was the subject of deliberations and recriminations that went on until 1954 and resulted in the promise of a subsidy from the Arts Council, the patronage of General Franco's ambassador, personal financial guarantees and complete designs—but no production.

The first actual production by GTP was a ballet commissioned for the Festival of Britain in 1951 and performed in the Festival Gardens at Battersea. *Orlando's Silver Wedding*, as this ballet was called, was based on the story by Kathleen Hale, with music by Arthur Benjamin and choreography by Andrée Howard. *The Times* found it a 'fanciful entertainment' with a scenario 'a little too complicated for conveying in dance-mime'.[10] *Orlando* made a small profit and was useful in getting GTP started. It was followed, on 29 June 1951, by a reading of Rex Warner's new translation of *The Helen* of Euripides. Given in conjunction with the Institute of Contemporary Arts, the reading was intended to maintain the interest of the ICA and the GTP subscribers until a full production could be undertaken. This was achieved on 25 November 1951, when *The Flies* was presented for a matinée and one evening performance at the New Theatre.

This first English production of a play by Sartre was well received both for itself and because the reviewers sensed that there was a place for 'a consistent avant-garde theatre' with professional standards such as GTP hoped to be.[11] Artistically, *The Flies* brought GTP close to this objective but the production weakened its already perilous financial position. The actors were unpaid and the theatre was given rent-free but the costs were still more than double the returns.[12] It was obvious that GTP could not attempt a series of full-scale productions in regular theatres, even on Sundays, but no satisfactory alternative was found. GTP was unable to fulfil its promise of three productions for a year's subscription and consequently forfeited the £1,000 conditionally offered by the ICA.

While it was looking for ways and means of producing the plays to which it had rights, GTP took up an offer to perform at the 1952 Canterbury Festival. Its contribution was a production of Shakespeare's *The Comedy of Errors* that had already been presented at the George Inn, Southwark. Roy Walker, one of Doone's students at Morley College, and a strong supporter of GTP, was the director of this production, which was 'adopted' by GTP and, with Doone as co-director, refurbished. *The Comedy of Errors* was sufficiently successful at Canterbury for it to be transferred to London for a two-week run at the Court Theatre. GTP was able to pay its actors and make a small profit on the venture, which had, however, nothing to do with its declared aim of 'producing contemporary work in contemporary form'.

After *The Comedy of Errors* there were no full productions for more than a year, though readings of two new plays were given in conjunction with the ICA. The first of these was *The Coming of Age* by Patric Dickinson, directed by Roy Walker; the second, Herbert Read's *The Parliament of Women*, directed by Robert Speaight.[13] Among the other new plays received by GTP and seriously considered for production were *The End Begins* by R. B. Rigby and Bridget Boland's *I Confess*.[14]

The last play presented by GTP was *The Publican's Story* by Kenneth Allott and Stephen Tait. Directed by Roy Walker, *The Publican's Story* was performed at the New Theatre on a Sunday in November 1953. This depiction of the strife of a pub landlord and his wife and the ambitions and fortunes of their four daughters was seen as a 'deviation from the usual policy' of GTP and a prosaic Christmas piece.[15] Strenuous efforts were made to arrange a provincial tour for the production but they failed, partly for lack of a 'star'.

What was undoubtedly GTP's outstanding effort came last. This was *Homage to Dylan Thomas*, a programme presented in aid of Thomas's widow by GTP in collaboration with ICA and sponsored by the *Sunday Times*. Here all the old Group Theatre flair for theatrical montage and publicity was exploited. A tribute from Edith Sitwell was read, Louis MacNeice wrote and read a 'Requiem Canto', Hedli MacNeice sang poems by Thomas set by Elizabeth Lutyens and there were readings from Thomas's works by Richard Burton, Emlyn Williams and Edith Evans. Extracts from the forthcoming BBC radio production of *Under Milk Wood* were also read.[16] Artistically and financially *Homage* was a great success. GTP was well aware of the favourable publicity it earned for itself on this occasion but was in no position to take advantage of its *coup*. Planning for the long-delayed production of *Life's a Dream* dragged on amid growing frustration and rancour and, to add to GTP's difficulties, Rupert Doone was seriously ill. In effect, GTP came to a standstill in September 1954, though it was not finally wound up until 1956.[17]

GTP was in operation during a barren phase of the English theatre, when theatrical management was in a state of (partly self-induced) confusion about the relation between subsidized and strictly commercial enterprise. Preoccupied as it was with its own bureaucratic gyrations and hamstrung by a confusion of aims, it could hardly be said that GTP continued the work of the pre-war Group Theatre, whose laurels it wore. Charitably, GTP might be seen, in retrospect, as having come into being prematurely. The English Stage Company, which was formed, with very similar objectives, just as GTP expired, managed to fill the role that GTP had aspired to.

Notes

Abbreviations used in the notes

ARCHIVES AND COLLECTIONS

JJ   Collection of John Johnson
JM   Collection of John Moody
KCC/JH   John Hayward Bequest, King's College, Cambridge
KCC/JMK Keynes Papers, King's College, Cambridge
KCC/LM   MacNeice Papers, King's College, Cambridge
MBY   Collection of Michael B. Yeats
NYPL/BC Henry W. and Albert A. Berg Collection, The New York Public Library, Astor, Lenox and Tilden Foundations
NYPL/TC New York Public Library, Theater Collection
UT/HRC   Humanities Research Center, University of Texas

BOOKS AND ARTICLES

BF   Brian Finney, *Christopher Isherwood, A Critical Biography*, New York, Oxford University Press, 1979
B/M   Barry C. Bloomfield and Edward Mendelson, *W. H. Auden: a Bibliography, 1924–1969*, second edition, Charlottesville, University of Virginia, 1972
CI   Christopher Isherwood, *Christopher and his Kind 1929–39*, New York, Farrar, Straus, Giroux, 1976
EA   *The English Auden: Poems, Essays, and Dramatic Writings 1927–1939*, edited Edward Mendelson, New York, Random House, 1977
EM[1]   Edward Mendelson, 'The Auden-Isherwood Collaboration', *Twentieth Century Literature*, vol. 22, no. 3, (October 1976), pp. 276–285

EM^2	Edward Mendelson, *Early Auden*, New York, Viking Press, 1981
EMB	E. Martin Browne, *The Making of T. S. Eliot's Plays*, Cambridge, Cambridge University Press, 1969
MV	Mardi Valgemae, 'Auden's Collaboration with Isherwood on *The Dog Beneath the Skin*', *Huntington Library Quarterly*, vol. 31, (August 1968), pp. 373–383

PERIODICALS

(The place of publication is London, unless otherwise noted.)

CR	*Cambridge Review* (Cambridge)
DH	*Daily Herald*
DM	*Daily Mail*
DT	*Daily Telegraph*
DaT	*Dancing Times*
DW	*Daily Worker*
GTP	*The Group Theatre Paper*
LM	*London Mercury*
LLT	*Life and Letters Today*
LR	*Left Review*
NC	*News Chronicle*
NEW	*The New English Weekly*
NSN	*The New Statesman and Nation*
NV	*New Verse*
Obs	*The Observer*
ST	*The Sunday Times*
TAM	*Theater Arts Monthly* (New York)
TLS	*The Times Literary Supplement*
TT	*Time and Tide*

PLAYS AND PRODUCTIONS

(The editions most relevant to the Group Theatre productions are cited. The place of publication is London, unless otherwise noted. The dates of the first Group Theatre productions are added. Further details of these productions are given in Appendix D.)

Ag	*The Agamemnon of Aeschylus*, translated by Louis MacNeice, Faber and Faber, 1936. 1 November 1936
DBS	W. H. Auden and Christopher Isherwood, *The Dog*

Beneath the Skin or Where is Francis?: a play in three acts, Faber and Faber, 1935. 12 January 1936

DD   W. H. Auden, *The Dance of Death*, Faber and Faber, 1933. 25 February 1934

Del   *The Deluge* from the Chester Cycle in *English Miracle Plays, Moralities and Interludes*, edited by Arthur W. Pollard, Oxford, Clarendon Press, 1895). 25 February 1934

EL   De Haas, Arline, *East Lynne* . . . suggested by Mrs Henry Wood's famous novel, London, Dicks' Standard Plays, no. 331, n.d. [1883?]; New York, Grosset and Dunlap, [1931]. 2 August 1934

FL   Henry Medwall, *Fulgens and Lucrece*, edited by F. S. Boas and A. W. Reed, Oxford, Clarendon Press, 1926. 19 March 1933

F6   W. H. Auden and Christopher Isherwood, *The Ascent of F6: a tragedy in two acts*, Faber and Faber, 1936. 26 February 1937

HV   Jean Cocteau, *The Human Voice*, translated by Carl Wildman, London, Vision Press, 1951. 17 July 1938

Imp   Carlo Goldoni, *The Impresario from Smyrna*, translated by Clifford Bax, in *Four Comedies of Goldoni*, edited Clifford Bax, London, Cecil Palmer, 1922. 23 December, 1935

LD   *A Beautiful Play of Lancelot of Denmark* . . . translated from the Middle Dutch by Dr P. Geyl, London, Gyldendal, 1924. 24 July 1933

LP   Rudolf Besier, *Lady Patricia. A Comedy in Three Acts*, T. Fisher Unwin, 1911. Production under the auspices of the Group Theatre, 15 October 1935

OF   W. H. Auden and Christopher Isherwood, *On the Frontier: a melodrama in three acts*, Faber and Faber, 1938. 14 November 1938

PG   Henrik Ibsen, *Peer Gynt*, translated by William and Charles Archer, Walter Scott, 1892. 29 January 1933 [The translation by Randall Swingler, specially done for the Group Theatre in 1935–6, was neither staged nor published.]

Picture Louis MacNeice, *Out of the Picture*, Faber and Faber, 1937. 5 December 1937

Popomack   W. J. Turner, *The Man Who Ate the Popomack: a tragicomedy of love in four acts*, Chatto and Windus, 1929. 27 June 1932

PW   Sir John Vanbrugh, *The Provok'd Wife*, in *Sir John Vanbrugh, The Relapse . . .* , edited A. E. H. Swaen, T. Fisher Unwin, 1896. 3 April 1932

SA   T. S. Eliot, *Sweeney Agonistes: Fragments of an Aristophanic Melodrama*, Faber and Faber, 1932. 11 November 1934

Sowers   *Sowers of the Hills*. An unpublished translation by Jolliffe Metcalfe of Jean Giono's *Lanceurs de graines*. Production under the auspices of the Group Theatre, 29 October 1935

Timon   William Shakespeare, *Timon of Athens*. 19 November 1935

Trial   Stephen Spender, *Trial of a Judge*, Faber and Faber, 1938. 18 March 1938

1 Introduction

Notes to pp. 23–40

The place of publication for books cited below is London unless otherwise noted.

1 *Listener*, vol. 16 no. 398, (26 August 1936), p. 371.
2 Quoted in Allardyce Nicoll, *English Drama, 1900–1930*, Cambridge, 1973, pp. 45–6.
3 'The Possibility of a Poetic Drama', *Dial*, New York, vol. 69 no. 5 (November 1920), pp. 441–7; reprinted in *The Sacred Wood*, p. 70.
4 See Norman Marshall, *The Producer and the Play*, 1957, for an account of the emergence of the stage director.
5 *Dance-Drama: Experiments in the Art of the Theatre*, 1926, pp. 32–3.
6 *Invitation to the Ballet*, 1937, pp. 174, 179.
7 Quoted in C. Madelaine Dixon, 'Mary Wigman', *TAM*, vol. 15, January, 1931, pp. 37–42.
8 *Theatre Prospect*, 1932, pp. 58–61.
9 T. S. Eliot, 'Religious Drama and the Church', *Rep*, vol. 1 no. 6 (October 1934), pp. 4–5.
10 See Gerald Weales, *Religion and Modern English Drama*, 1961, and EMB.
11 Ness Edwards, *Workers' Theatre*, Cardiff, 1930, p. 79.
12 Rafael Samuel (ed.), 'Documents and Texts from the Workers' Theatre Movement (1928–1936)', *History Workshop*, no. 4 (Autumn 1977), p. 107.
13 Ibid., p. 131.
14 Letter to N. O. Higgins, 14 November 1937, KCC/JMK.
15 The attempt to revive the Group Theatre after the war is part of a different story. See Appendix E.

1 *Letters from Iceland*, 1937, p. 244.
2 John Ormerod Greenwood (b. 1907) took an open scholarship in History from Latymer Upper School to Jesus College, Cambridge, where he contributed to *Experiment* and succeeded Alistair Cooke as President of the Cambridge University Mummers. Unable to take up an offered apprenticeship at the Old Vic for lack of the £40 premium, Greenwood began his acting career at the Westminster Theatre where Anmer Hall offered him employment on a no-fee-no-premium basis, then, on kindlier second thoughts, at 30s (£1.50) a week. (The same offer was made to Alan Rolfe, another founder member of the Group Theatre, who was in a similar situation.)

Greenwood took part in most Group Theatre productions until 1937, playing: Fulgens and an Intruder (*FL*); Noah (*Del*); Krumpacker (*SA*); member of the Chorus (*DD*); various roles in *DBS*; and Mr A (*F6*). He was also the chief organizer for the Group Theatre Season of 1935–6. He left the Group in 1937 after being deposed as its Organizer. In 1940 he became a lecturer for the Workers' Educational Association and from 1950 to 1956 he was a producer of plays and features for the Religious Broadcasting Department of the BBC. In 1958 he became a lecturer at the Royal Academy of Dramatic Art and in 1968 founded its library, which he afterwards continued to supervise. His writings include *The Playwright* and *The Cave and the Garden*, a play produced at the Players' Theatre in 1956. Since 1930 Greenwood has been an active member of the Society of Friends.

3 Rupert Doone (Ernest Reginald Woodfield), 1903–1966. A very brief entry on Doone is to be found in *Who's Who in Dancing*, A. L. Haskell and P. J. S. Richardson (eds.); and his whole career is

surveyed by Robert Medley in *Rupert Doone Remembered by his Friends*, a pamphlet published in connection with a memorial programme presented at Morley College on 23 June 1966.

It is not easy to reconstruct Doone's early career in detail and the following list of his appearances (often in unnamed roles) and choreographic work up to 1933 is probably incomplete:

1921 *Cairo*, by Oscar Asche and Percy Fletcher, His Majesty's Theatre, 15 October; *Midnight Follies*, Hotel Metropole; *La Chasse*, a ballet danced by Astafieva's pupils, 29 November.

1922 *L'Humeur masqué*, Théâtre de la Potinière, Paris.

1923 On tour with Cléo de Mérode in the South of France; *Hassan*, by James Elroy Flecker, directed by Basil Dean, His Majesty's Theatre, 20 September.

1924 *Roméo et Juliette*, by Jean Cocteau, produced by Etienne de Beaumont, Théâtre Cigale, Paris, 2 June (Doone appeared in the preview only); *The Duenna*, by Richard Brinsley Sheridan, directed by Nigel Playfair, choreography by Doone, who also danced, Everyman Theatre, 23 October.

1925 *On with the Dance*, by Noël Coward, produced by C. B. Cochran, London Pavilion, 1 January; *Still Dancing*, by Noël Coward, produced by C. B. Cochran, London Pavilion, 19 November.

1926 *A Flutter in the Dovecot*, with Anton Dolin, London Palladium; *Aurora's Wedding*, with Vera Trefilova, Scala, Berlin.

1927 *A Riding Dance*, choreography by Bronislava Nijinska, 5 September, London Palladium; with Phyllis Bedells at the London Palladium, October.

1928: With Ida Rubinstein's company, the Opéra, Paris, 26 November.

1929: 'Play', choreography by Doone, in *Palladium Revue*, London Palladium, 18 February; with the Ballets Russes (see note 4 below).

1930: A dance recital with Phyllis Bedells, Norfolk House, 15 July (repeated St George's Hall, 30 September).

1931: *Pastorale d'Eté*, choreography by Doone, and *Straussiana* with Phyllis Bedells, Camargo Society, Savoy Theatre, 25 and 26 January; *Le Boxing*, First Ballet Club Season, Lyric Theatre, March.

1932: *The Enchanted Grove*, devised and choreographed by
Doone, Vic–Wells Ballet, Sadler's Wells, 4, 11 and 14
March, and Camargo Society, 7, 9, and 11 June; *Giselle*
and *Le Lac des cygnes*, Camargo Society. 6 June–2 July.

1933: 'The Marriage of Hebe' (an *intermède* in *Jupiter Translated*, adapted by W. J. Turner from Molière's *Amphit-
ryon*), choreography by Doone, directed by Ashley Dukes,
Mercury Theatre, 19 October; *Hansel and Gretel*,
choreography by Doone, directed by Basil Dean, Cambridge Theatre, 26 December; *The Tempest*, choreography by Doone, directed by Tyrone Guthrie, Sadler's Wells,
8 January.

Between 1934 and 1939 almost all Doone's theatrical work was
done in connection with the Group Theatre. For productions
directed by him, see Appendix D.

In 1940 he was appointed by Morley College to direct its theatre
school and he remained there until he was forced by illness to retire
in 1961. At Morley College, Doone directed many productions
including, notably, Marlowe's *Dr Faustus* (1950, 1959) and
revivals of MacNeice's version of *The Agamemnon* (1945, 1958).
With Vera Russell and others, Doone revived the Group Theatre
in 1950 and in the following year directed Jean-Paul Sartre's *The
Flies* for it. [See Appendix E.]

Doone's last months were spent in asylum for the insane, where
he died.

4 Even those who knew him are hazy about Doone's appearances
with the Ballets Russes. According to the programmes for the
1929 London season of the Ballets Russes at the Royal Opera
House, Covent Garden, Doone danced: the opening pas de trois of
Cimarosiana, 3 (matinée) and 5 July; one of Ariadne's brothers in
Aurora's Wedding, 10 July only (the role being taken by
Constantin Tcherkas in the other performances); an unnamed
role in *Baba-Yaga*, 20 and 24 July (matinée); one of the ball
players in *Les Facheux*, 22 and 24 July (matinée); one of the men in
the second scene of *Le Sacre du printemps*, 24 July.

Clearly, Doone's place in Diaghilev's company was not an
exalted one. Diaghilev appears to have found him some minor
roles and made a nonce replacement for Tcherkas. Anton Dolin
thought that Diaghilev was intent on fostering Doone's still
immature talent as a choreographer.

5 Information from the late Dame Marie Rambert.

6 See Francis Steegmuller, *Cocteau: A Biography*, 1970, p. 329n.

7 Nigel Playfair, *The Story of the Lyric Theatre, Hammersmith*, 1925, p. 210.

8 Serge Lifar, *A History of the Russian Ballet from its Origins to the Present Day*, 1954, p. 270. Doone wrote to Diaghilev on 19 February 1929, NYPL/TC.

9 Information from Robert Medley.

10 Rupert Doone, 'Petipa, Fokine, Nijinsky: their choreography compared', *Da T*, December 1931, pp. 243–45.

11 The fellow dancer was Rollo Gamble, Gillian Scaife's son, who had been in Ida Rubinstein's company with Doone. Hall went to see Doone dance at Norfolk House on 15 July 1930. Seated at the back of the room, Hall saw very little of the performance, but he engaged Doone nevertheless.

12 Isobel Scaife: a niece of Gillian Scaife, she left the stage after her marriage in 1937. Her roles with the Group Theatre included: Lucrece (*FL*); Sandareen (*LD*); Barbara Hare (*EL*); Doris (*SA*); Mrs A (*F6*). One of her infrequent appearances outside the Group Theatre was in *Children in Uniform*, Westminster Theatre, 1934.

13 'Sitter Out', *Da T*, September 1931, p. 511. Arnold Haskell would not have agreed with this assessment. When he attempted to rank the leading English male ballet dancers a few months later Doone did not appear in the first six, *NEW*, vol. 1 no. 8 (23 June 1932), p. 232.

14 *The Times*, 13 March 1932.

15 Phyllis Bedells, *My Dancing Days*, 1954, p. 177. A. L. Haskell, 'The Ballet in England', *NEW*, vol. 1 no. 8 (16 June 1932), pp. 208–9.

16 'What About the Theatre', *NV*, no. 18 (December 1935), pp. 9–10.

17 Anmer Hall (Alderson Burrell Horne), 1863–1953. A theatre manager, theatre owner, producer and (as Waldo Wright) actor, Horne was the son of a founder of the Prudential Assurance Company and an independently wealthy man. He opened the Scala Theatre in 1905 in partnership with Johnston Forbes-Robertson; in 1911 he joined the Eadie–Vedrenne management at the Royalty Theatre; during the First World War he organized theatre parties with Lena Ashwell for the YMCA; in 1923 he

took a touring company to France; and in 1929 he assumed the management of the Festival Theatre, Cambridge, where Tyrone Guthrie was his stage director and Flora Robson, resuming her interrupted career, was a member of the company. In 1931 he opened the Westminster Theatre, of which he remained the owner until 1946. Among his best-known productions were *A Month in the Country* (Royalty Theatre, July 1926), *The Lady from Alfaqueque* (Court Theatre, October 1928), and *Mourning Becomes Electra* (Westminster Theatre, November 1937).

Horne's second marriage was to Gillian Scaife (*c.* 1881–1976), with whom he had lived for many years. She made her stage début in 1901 and in her long and successful career played many roles in London productions and on tours in Australia and America. Among her notable roles were Natalia Petrovna in *A Month in the Country* (Royalty Theatre, July 1926) and Nora in *A Doll's House* (Kingsway Theatre, March 1928). Her brother, Christopher, was a close friend of Guthrie. For the Scaife family see James Forsyth, *Tyrone Guthrie: A Biography*, 1976.

18 Tyrone Guthrie, *A Life in the Theatre*, 1960, p. 55.

19 Letter to Edward Gordon Craig, 20 October 1931, UT/HRC.

20 Information from the late Selma Vas Dias. Mirko Jurak, in 'The Group Theatre: its Development and Significance . . .', refers to 'a Marxist-oriented group led by André Van Gyseghem and Selma Vas Dias' as one of the elements that split off from the incipient Group Theatre, but Van Gyseghem was never associated with the latter. Selma Vas Dias seems to have been the only politically motivated member at this stage.

21 The members of the '8 Group' were probably: Ormerod Greenwood, Rupert Doone, Isobel Scaife, John Allen, Joan White, Selma Vas Dias, Alan Rolfe and Robert Flemyng.

22 'The Thirties in Britain: the Theatre', BBC broadcast 17 November 1965.

23 John Moody OBE (b. 1906). Moody trained as a painter and, at the Webber-Douglas Academy, as a singer before becoming an actor. A founder member of the Group Theatre, his roles in its productions included: Reynald (*LD*); Archibald Carlyle (*EL*); 'Stage Manager' (*DD*); Sweeney (*SA*); Flaminius (*FL*); Shem (*Del*); Count Lasca (*Imp*); Alan Norman (*DBS*); Watchman (*Ag*); Mr A (*F6*); Oswald Vrodny (*OF*). He also acted in the Old Vic seasons of 1934 and 1937.

After the war, Moody worked mostly as a director of plays and opera and as an administrator. He was successively Director of the Old Vic School, the Liverpool Old Vic and the Birmingham Repertory Theatre. Between 1945 and 1949 he was producer for the Carl Rosa and Sadler's Wells Operas. In 1949 he was appointed Drama Director of the Arts Council. In 1954 he became Director of the Bristol Old Vic, in 1959 of the Ohel Theatre, Tel Aviv, and in 1960 of the Welsh National Opera. In the course of his career he has directed over ninety plays and more than forty operas, many of the latter with libretti translated by himself in collaboration with his wife, the singer Helen (Nella) Pomfret Burra, who was also a member of the Group Theatre.

24 Herbert Murrill (1909–1952) was educated at Haberdashers' Aske's School, the Royal Academy of Music and Worcester College, Oxford, where he was Organ Scholar. He was President of the University Musical Club at Oxford and, while he was a student there, composed the short opera (with libretto by Geoffrey Dunn), *Man in Cage*. During the early thirties he held various posts as teacher, organist and choirmaster. In 1936 he joined the BBC and, after wartime service, returned there to become, ultimately, Head of Music.

Many of Murrill's own compositions were occasional pieces. His music for the Group Theatre included: settings for interpolated songs in *FL*; incidental music for *PW*; settings for *The Group Theatre in Songs, Dances and a Play*; the score for *DD*; and the score for *DBS*.

25 The thirteen founders were probably: Ormerod Greenwood, Rupert Doone, Isobel Scaife, John Allen, Alan Rolfe, John Moody, John Gower Parks, Oliver Reynolds, Jean Shepheard, Peggy Munday-Castle, Frances Peterson, Betty Hardy and Robert Flemyng.

26 Information from Ormerod Greenwood. The New York Group Theatre had formed within the Theatre Guild and emerged as an independent entity early in 1931.

27 Draft statement of aims in the Group Theatre Archive. It is undated but certainly very early. It may have been drafted by Greenwood.

28 For cast lists of Group Theatre productions, see Appendix D.

29 Letter to Christopher Scaife quoted in James Forsyth, *Tyrone Guthrie: A Biography*, 1976, p. 125.

30 *Theatre Prospect*, 1932, p. 40.

31 Letter to Doone, 18 October 1932, NYPL/BC.

32 In an interview with the author. Robert Medley's 'The Group Theatre 1932–39' *London Magazine*, January 1981, pp. 47–60, is a valuable memoir but I believe that Medley mistakenly recalls Brecht's presence at *DD* (instead of *SA*) and one or two other details. I must immediately add that I am much indebted to Robert Medley for information about Doone and the Group Theatre.

Medley (b. 1905) attended Gresham's School, Holt, where he was Auden's close friend. He studied art at the Byam Shaw School, the Royal Academy Schools, the Slade and in Paris. From 1929 he exhibited with the London Group and his first one-man show was at the London Artists' Association Gallery in 1932. He taught at the Chelsea School of Art from 1932 to 1939, during which time much of his energy went into designing for the Group Theatre.

Medley was not, formally, one of the founders of the Group Theatre as has been supposed, nor its first designer—who was John Gower Parks—though he was involved with it, through Doone, from the beginning. His designs for the Group Theatre were: *PG*; *Sowers*; *DD*; *Sowers*; *TA*; *DBS*; *Ag*; *F6*; *LP*; *OF*; and *Danton's Death* (not produced).

Medley became an official war artist in 1940. After the war, he was visiting teacher of stage design and painting at the Slade and Head of the Art Department at the Camberwell School. A retrospective exhibition of his work was given at the Whitechapel Gallery in 1963.

33 Geoffrey Dunn (b. 1903) trained at the Royal Academy of Music and later taught there. A tenor, librettist and stage director of opera, he was co-founder in 1930 of the Intimate Opera and Herbert Murrill's collaborator in *Man in Cage*. Dunn has made English versions of many libretti.

34 See John Ormerod Greenwood, 'It was something like this' *Ark, Journal of the Royal College of Art*, vol. 15, 1955, pp. 35–38.

A good proportion of the first year's rent of £115 was paid by Constance Foljambe, the daughter of the Earl of Liverpool and one of the most dedicated members of the Group Theatre. The part of Mildred Luce (*DBS*) may have been written with her in mind.

The only amenities in the 'Rooms' when the Group Theatre took the lease were a lavatory on the landing below and a still-connected gas-ring, apparently forgotten by the gas company, which never sent a bill.

35 For a list of members, see Appendix C.

36 The singers included Ethel Lewis and Richard Wood. The former members of Pavlova's company were Mary Skeaping and Kathleen Crofton.

37 See B/M, p. 251. The piece is described as a 'Prologue' on the manuscript but it is an epilogue to *LD* as well as a prologue to the second half of the bill. None of the former members of the Group Theatre that I have interviewed, including two of those who would have played roles in the sketch (in continuation of their parts in *LD*) can remember it being used, though it is listed on the programme (as 'Epilogue'). The final lines are quoted above. The matter that precedes them in Auden's manuscript follows below. The punctuation, spelling, speech headings and layout have been regularized.

PROLOGUE
Enter KNIGHT *and Lancelot's* SERVANT.

SERVANT: Let's get back quickly. I'm dying for a cup of cocoa.

KNIGHT: I want to see —— (*the Christian name of the actress who takes the part of the* MOTHER) home first.

SERVANT: Again. Why can't you leave her alone a little? You'll be getting her into trouble. Why, during rehearsals, you were always so busy talking, she was generally late for her cues.

KNIGHT: (*Sighing*) Lucky Lancelot.

SERVANT: Well. I'm going on alone then. Give me the key, will you.

KNIGHT: Catch.

(*Exit* SERVANT. *Enter* LANCELOT.)

LANCELOT: Hullo. Not waiting for —— (*the Christian name of the actress who plays the* GIRL) I hope. The play's over now you know, and I allow no rivals off stage. Lucky devil. I wanted your part but Rupert wouldn't let me have it.

KNIGHT: Is —— coming?

LANCELOT: O, it is my wicked mama you sigh for.

KNIGHT: Of course. It is her I would gladly die for.

LANCELOT: Sweet —— is my only flame.

KNIGHT: She whom you loved and lost.

LANCELOT: The same.

> Look they come this way
> And set our hearts on fire.
> May luck be ours this day
> And give us our desire.
>
> (*Enter* MOTHER *and* GIRL.)

MOTHER: Hurry my dear or we shall be late.

> Which is the door where they said they'd wait?
> Did yours say anything very exciting?
> Let me see his note. What nice handwriting.

GIRL: Are those his flowers? He's got good taste.

MOTHER: Come we haven't got time to waste.

GIRL: Do you think that Croydon will rise to wine?

MOTHER *and* GIRL: How am I looking?

> (LANCELOT *and* KNIGHT *step forward.*)

KNIGHT: Superb.

LANCELOT: Divine.

KNIGHT *and* LANCELOT: (*Kneeling*) Ladies if you please

> We beg you on our knees
> That we may have the right
> To see you home tonight.

MOTHER *and* GIRL: I'm afraid we've been already invited.

KNIGHT *and* LANCELOT: What do you mean? Who are these men?

> (*To audience*) Go away and never come back again.

MOTHER *and* GIRL: You must not get excited

> At a moral [?]invitation
> To see us to the railway station.

KNIGHT *and* LANCELOT: But you never do this [in] London

> Croydon has turned your head.
> Croydon has us undone.
> We wish that we were dead.
>
> (*Enter* PROMPTER.)

PROMPTER: Now there. What's all this. Where are you going?

> The programme's not finished yet.

THE REST: How do you know? You're only the prompter.

PROMPTER: I know and yet the prompter knows

> Very much more than you suppose.

MOTHER *and* GIRL: But two kind gentlemen in the audience are expecting us. It'll be such a disappointment.

GIRL: The reason why you must explain.
MOTHER: And ask them nicely to remain.
PROMPTER: Ladies and Gentlemen, the play is over:
>   The story of a foolish Danish lover
>   Who lacking in himself belief
>   Took ill advice and came to grief.
>   If we have pleased you we are glad
>   For we have something more to add.
>   If not we ask you still to stay
>   For we may please you in another way.
>   Do you love music? Have you in your home
>   A piano, wireless, a harmonium?
>   Tyrone Guthrie. . . .
>   NYPL/BC. Copyright Estate of W. H. Auden.

Much later in his career, in *The Sea and the Mirror*, Auden was to use the technique of bringing characters 'onstage' after the end of the play in a highly sophisticated way.

38 Auden's list was as follows:

CLASSICAL: Aeschylus' *Agamemnon* and *Seven Against Thebes*; any plays by Aristophanes.

MEDIEVAL: Hrotsvitha's plays; *Everyman*; *The World and the Child*; *The Play of the Weather*; *The Revesby Plough Play*; *Gammer Gurton's Needle*; *Ralph Roister Doister*; the Coventry/Wakefield nativity plays; the York cycle *Harrowing of Hell*.

ELIZABETHAN: Peele's *Old Wives' Tale*; Marlowe's *Dr Faustus*, *The Jew of Malta*; Middleton's *The Changeling*; Ben Jonson's *Bartholomew Fair* and the masques (particularly *The Masque of Christmas*); Day's *The Parliament of Bees*.

EIGHTEENTH CENTURY: Lillo's *The London Merchant*.

NINETEENTH CENTURY: Part Two of Goethe's *Faust*; Ibsen's *Peer Gynt*.

MODERN: 'Various' (unspecified) plays by Brecht with music by Weill; 'various' (unspecified) plays by Cocteau; and *Marlborough Goes to War*.

The list is given in an undated letter from Auden to Doone, which was apparently written in January 1934, NYPL/BC. The categories of 'Classical', etc., are Auden's. He suggests that MacNeice be asked for a translation of a classical play, since there are no 'decent acting' versions available. As a translator for Brecht he suggests Isherwood. (The addresses given for these two, and his own, make the dating of the letter fairly certain.)

39 'The Life of Literature', Partisan Review, vol. 15, no. 11, November 1948, p. 1207.

3 *W. H. Auden and* The Dance of Death

Notes to pp. 62–7

1 *Revue Anglo-Americaine*, vol. 12, December 1934, p. 157.
2 Quoted by Anthony Blunt in Cecil Day-Lewis (ed.), *The Mind in Chains*, 1937, p. 122.
3 Quoted in EA, p. xiii. For the final version of *Paid on Both Sides* and the previously unpublished early version see EA, pp. 1–17, 409–16.
4 B/M, p. 3.
5 EA, p. 301.
6 '*Modern Poetic Drama* by Patricia Thouless', *Listener*, vol. 11 no. 278 (9 May 1934), p. 808. This review is unsigned. Edward Mendelson kindly brought it to my attention.
7 EA, p. 301.
8 See Robert Medley, 'Gresham's School, Holt' in Stephen Spender (ed.) *W. H. Auden: A Tribute*, pp. 37–43.
9 See EM[1] and BF, pp. 158–61.
10 See EM[1], *The Fronny* was apparently sent to Eliot, who was inclined to publish it.
11 'The Theatre of Ideas', *Theatre Newsletter*, vol. 6, 29 September 1951, p. 54.
12 Undated letter from the Downs School, NYPL/BC.
13 Undated letter from the Downs School, NYPL/BC. Medley notes that the composer referred to was Tippett.
14 Information from Hedli (Anderson) MacNeice. Hedli Anderson was shaken by events in Germany. In her pension the son of the family committed suicide and the daughter sold herself to a business man. Some time after she joined the Group Theatre, Britten and Auden, she recalls, set out to put her 'on the map', the former working very hard with her on the development of her voice. Britten wrote for her and frequently accompanied her in performances given for parties or fund-raising activities associated with the political Left. Through the Group Theatre, also, she met Louis MacNeice whom she married in 1942.

15 C. H. Waddington, 'Specialisation in Poetry', *CR*, vol. 55, 1 December 1933, p. 148.

16 Mendelson (EA, p. 270) quotes Auden's inscription in a copy of the play, 'The communists never spotted that this was a nihilistic leg-pull.' This was apparently written after 1940 and so after Auden had radically changed his views about political poetry. It tells us more about that change than about Auden's attitude in writing *DD*.

17 *TLS*, 15 March 1934, p. 190.

18 Thomas Greenidge, *Socialist Review*, vol. 5, January 1934, pp. 58–9.

19 Edwin Berry Bergum, 'Three English Radical Poets', *Masses*, vol. 2, 3 July 1934, p. 33.

20 See Richard Buckle, *Diaghilev*, 1979, p. 445.

21 The Ballets Jooss was presented by Cochran at the Savoy Theatre for a two-week run beginning 12 June 1933. See *The Times*, 13 June 1933, p. 12.

22 *Anna, Anna* was part of the programme presented by George Balanchine's *Les Ballets 1933* which followed the Jooss company at the Savoy. *The Times*, 1 July 1933, p. 10. In 1959 an English version of *Anna Anna* or *The Seven Deadly Sins of the Lower Middle Class*, was made by Auden and Chester Kallman for the New York City Ballet production. See B/M, p. 255.

23 W. J. Turner, *NSN*, 21 July 1934.

24 Letter quoted by Naomi Mitchison, *You May Well Ask: A Memoir 1920–1940*, 1979, p. 125.

25 Quotations are from John Moody's prompt copy; page references are to the 1933 edition from which the prompt copy was made up. The same prompt book was used in 1934 and 1935 and it is impossible to deduce from it what modifications were made for which performance.

26 Sir Thomas More, *The Four Last Things*, D. O'Connor, ed., 1935, p. 19.

27 A manuscript copy of Murrill's score survives. John Glofcheski at the piano very kindly accompanied John Allen, Ormerod Greenwood and Alan Rolfe in a reconstruction of the songs for me.

28 Moore made three designs for the mask. The simplest of these, now in NYPL/BC was chosen. The other two are in the possession of Robert Medley.

29 'Auden, Bottrall and Others', *Scrutiny*, vol. 3, June 1934, p. 80.

30 Reprinted in *History Workshop*, no. 4 (Autumn 1977), pp. 137–42.

31 The description of the Communist 'intruders' comes from George W. Bishop, 'Plays by Modern Poets', *DT*, 2 October 1935, p. 10.

32 John Allen recollects that the lyric went something like this:

> *Good morning to you master,*
> *Good morning to you mistress dear,*
> *We've been wandering in the fields*
> *And at last we are assembled here*

> *. . . this day,*
> *And we bring to you a branch*
> *Of the snowy buds of May.*

33 Charles Lindbergh's solo flight over the Atlantic was made in May 1927; 3,726 miles in 37 hours. Rear-Admiral Murray F. Sneter in his *Airmen or Noahs* (1928) wrote of how 'the loneliness of Lindberg's flight fires the imagination'. Brecht's play on the theme, *Der Flug der Lindberghs* (*Der Lindberghflug*), was performed in Berlin in December 1929.

34 Johnson and mysticism are similarly satirized in 'A Communist to Others', EA, p. 120.

35 *NV*, no. 7 (February 1934), pp. 21–2.

36 F.C. in *Granta*, vol. 43, 29 November 1933, p. 170. For other comparisons between Auden and Coward see, for examples *Week-End Review*, 16 December 1933, p. 6; *ST*, 6 October 1935, p. 4; *Spectator*, 11 October 1935, p. 545.

37 *Revue Anglo-Américaine*, vol. 12 December 1934, p. 157.

38 'Recent Verse', *NEW*, vol. 4, 12 April 1934, p. 617.

39 W. J. Turner, *NSN*, new series, vol. 7, 3 March 1934, p. 303.

40 MacDiarmid's 'A Prayer for a Second Flood' appeared in his *First Hymn to Lenin and other Poems*, 1935. In Lawrence's *The Rainbow*, 1915, a modern flood divides the old rhythmical life from the new industrialism; Shaw's *Heartbreak House*, 1919, is an ark with a drunken Noah (Captain Shotover), heading for the rocks; in Yeats's *The Player Queen*, 1922, the playing of an old play of Noah is the setting for a modern revolution; Day-Lewis's *Noah and the Waters*, 1936, is a politicization of the biblical story. For Brecht's unfinished attempt on the theme see *Collected Plays*, vol. 2, John Willett and Ralph Manheim, eds., 1979, pp. viii, 101.

1 T. S. Eliot, *The Rock*, 1934, p. 46.

2 See Hallie Flanagan, *Dynamo*, New York, 1942, pp. 82–4, 159; also *New York Herald Tribune*, 7 May 1933, p. 22. The Vassar production opened on 6 March 1933. E. Martin Browne (EMB, p. 38) was mistaken about the date of the Group Theatre production and in supposing that it was the first.

3 With Margaret Ellen Clifford at Briarcliff College, New York, in March 1931. *Paid on Both Sides* was also presented at the Festival Theatre, Cambridge, 12–17 February 1934, i.e., a matter of weeks before the first Group Theatre production of *DD*. See B/M, p. 4.

4 See Appendix A. Eliot was indebted to Francis M. Cornford's *The Origin of Attic Comedy* for his schema and he told Hallie Flanagan that Cornford's book was essential reading in connection with *SA*.

5 Compare 'The Lake Isle' in Pound's *Personae*, New York, 1926, p. 117, with 'The Lake Isle of Innisfree' in Yeats's *Collected Poems*, 1950, p. 44.

6 EMB, p. 8.

7 T. S. Eliot, *On Poetry and Poets*, 1957, p. 91.

8 Letter to Hallie Flanagan, 27 February 1934, NYPL/TC.

9 Letter to Hallie Flanagan, 20 March 1934, NYPL/TC.

10 T. S. Eliot, *The Use of Poetry and the Use of Criticism*, 1933, p. 154; *Selected Essays*, 1951, p. 451.

11 Introduction to Charlotte Eliot, *Savonarola*, 1926. p. xii.

12 EMB, p. 9.

13 EMB, p. 10.

14 *The Rock*, pp. 43–4.

15 Derek Verschoyle, 'The Theatre', *Spectator*, vol. 152 no. 5527 (1 June 1934), p. 851; T. S. Eliot, 'The Rock', letter to the editor, *Spectator*, vol. 152 no. 5528 (8 June 1934), p. 887.

16 'The Possibility of Poetic Drama', in *The Sacred Wood*, 1920, p. 70.

17 Jane Dudley, 'The Mass Dance', *New Theatre*, vol. 1, December 1934, pp. 17–18.

18 *The Rock*, p. 46.

19 *On Poetry and Poets*, p. 91.

20 Letter from Eliot to Doone, 25 May 1934, NYPL/BC.

21 See EMB, p. 43.

22 On 9 February 1934, Eliot wrote to Hallie Flanagan (NYPL/TC), 'I cannot tell you when or whether there will be more of *Sweeney* but in any case I hope to begin something new of the same kind as soon as I have finished with a dramatic pageant which is to be produced in the early summer.'

It is reasonable to assume that Eliot did not intend to write a play about the patron saint of Canterbury *before* the matter of the commission for the Canterbury Festival was broached and that *Murder in the Cathedral* was therefore not the 'something of the same kind' as *SA*.

Browne thought that in his letter to Doone of 25 July 1934 (NYPL/BC, reproduced in EMB, p. 39), Eliot must have been referring to *Murder in the Cathedral* but this is scarcely possible. Eliot tells Doone that he cannot 'definitely promise a play at a particular time' and that it is 'extremely unlikely' that he could 'even think of finishing it until next summer'. Had he been referring to a play he was writing for the Canterbury Festival, he would have had to be definite about finishing it at 'a particular time' and before the next summer at that. And, of course, there would have been no point in allowing Doone to suppose that the Group Theatre would receive the play first if Eliot had already accepted the Canterbury commission.

Eliot felt that he had committed himself to the Group Theatre in some way and later obtained from the organizers of the Canterbury Festival their agreement to a first performance of *Murder in the Cathedral* at the Mercury Theatre by the Group Theatre. This was in connection with the Poets' Theatre (see Appendix B).

23 See Appendix A.

24 *The Superior Landlord*, f.3, KCC/JH.

25 Letter from Eliot to Doone, 25 July 1934, NYPL/BC; reproduced in EMB, p. 39.

26 Letter from Auden to Doone and Medley, 5 August 1934, NYPL/
   BC.
27 Letter from Doone to John Johnson, 18 December 1934, JJ.
   Yeats had enquired from Margot Ruddock about 'the Eliot
   dance play' in November. See R. McHugh (ed.), *Ah! Sweet
   Dancer: W. B. Yeats—Margot Ruddock: A Correspondence*,
   1970, p. 24. (McHugh is clearly mistaken in supposing this a
   reference to *The Rock*, which had closed over four months
   before the letter was written.) Before Yeats saw a performance of
   SA, on 16 December 1934, he was inclined to think that Eliot
   had thrown out the poetic baby with the dirty bathwater in *SA*
   (ibid., p. 27).
   The play offered by Brecht (unnamed in Doone's letter) had
   music by Paul Hindemith. It was probably *Der Badener
   Lehrstück vom Einverständnis* (*The Didactic Play of Baden: On
   Consent*) or *Der Lindberghflug* that was offered. After 1934,
   disagreement between Brecht and the composer prevented
   productions of the first of these and that may have been a reason
   for Brecht to have dropped the idea of a Group Theatre
   production.
28 Letter from Eliot to Auden, 6 December 1934. Valerie Eliot
   kindly supplied the quotation.
29 Desmond MacCarthy, 'Sweeney Agonistes', *Listener*, 9 January
   1935.
30 The other records include photographs and the prompt book
   made up from a copy of the first, 1932, edition, NYPL/BC; JM.
31 'A Modern Use of Masks', *GTP*, no. 5 (November 1936), p. 3.
   The article is unsigned but the editor, John Johnson, is certain
   that Auden was the author and it is so attributed in B/M, p. 184.
32 'My production is concerned with morals as well as aesthetics. I
   have sought to criticize the conventionalities of modern
   behaviour with its empty codes and heartiness—immoral but
   never immoral enough—decaying but so long in dying. I see
   Sweeney himself as a modern Orestes (the only three-dimensio-
   nal character in the play). The rest are conventionalized
   conventional characters—the Eumenides or Bogies of Sweeney's
   persecution.' From the 'Producer's Note' by Doone in the
   programme for 16 December 1934, Group Theatre Rooms.
33 'Sweeney Agonistes (An anecdote or two)', in *T. S. Eliot: A
   Symposium*, compiled by R. March and Tambimuttu, 1948,

p. 84. Coghill refers to Doone as playing Snow. Doone spoke the line but Snow and Schwartz were not represented as characters in the production.

34 Eliot noted the discrepancy between the meaning of the production and his intended meaning in letters he wrote to Auden and Yeats on the same day, 6 December 1934 (information from Valerie Eliot), and to John Johnson on 1 April 1935, VT/HRC, as well as to Coghill.

35 Eliot's influence over Doone apparently extended to religious matters but was counteracted by Medley's. After the war, Doone was on the verge of converting to Christianity but—just as he had once restrained Medley from joining the Communist Party—Medley dissuaded him.

A story told of him by the late Roy Walker puts Doone in an Eliotesque light. One night he was walking home in the small hours after a dinner party. It was wet and he was wearing a raincoat lent to him by his much taller host. A policeman accosted Doone and questioned him closely about the coat. Doone got on his high horse and demanded to know if the officer was accusing him of theft. 'Well,' said the constable, 'if you're not guilty, why are you getting so upset?' 'Because I am guilty,' cried Doone, 'we're all guilty.'

1 'Religious Drama and the Church', *Rep*, vol. 1 no. 6, (October 1934), pp. 4–5.
2 From a broadsheet appeal for subscriptions, dated 1 February 1935, printed by the Group Theatre. This is the second of two stanzas. The first reads:

> *Poor and Prosperous, Pert and Proud*
> *Living in our land and loving laughter*
> *Ever so often we have asked your help*
> *Anxiously We ask for we have had no answer*
> *Send us your* SUBSCRIPTION *as swift as the swallow*
> *Easing our overdraft: They're our only income*

The initial letters of each line are printed in red. Doubtless the verse was dashed off by Auden. It amplifies a message, signed by Isobel Scaife, about the urgent need for subscriptions. I am indebted to Edward Mendelson for a copy of this item.
3 From a professionally printed flyer, headed 'The Group Theatre Rooms', n.d., JM.
4 Information from Ormerod Greenwood.
5 *Theatre: The Rediscovery of Style*, 1960, p. 43.
6 Irving Wardle, *The Theatres of George Devine*, 1978, pp. 50–1.
7 Ibid., p. 56.
8 Doone had used this title, before Auden, for a dance item (itself derived from an interpolated dance in *FL*) in *The Group Theatre in Songs, Dances and a Play*.
9 This performance was a contribution to a 'Garden Party and Exhibition' in aid of the Fulham Housing Association, held on Saturday, 9 June 1934.
10 Information from Group Theatre circulars: 'Autumn Announcements 1934', n.d., probably printed in September; 'Announce-

ments', n.d., obviously printed 1 December 1934, and a Group Theatre 'Calendar', n.d., printed in 1935, NYPL/BC.

11 Educated at the universities of Manchester and Munich, Dukes (1885–1959) was a dramatic critic for various periodicals before and after the First World War. His writings on the theatre included: *Modern Dramatists*, 1911; *The Youngest Drama*, 1923; *Drama*, 1926; and *The World to Play With*, 1927. *The Scene is Changed*, 1942, is a memoir of his theatrical activities. Among his many adaptations of German, French and Italian plays were: *From Morn to Midnight*, 1920; *Elizabeth of England*, 1932; *Mandragola*, 1929; and *The Broken Jug*, 1958. *The Man with a Load of Mischief*, 1924, was his most successful original play.

He married Marie Rambert in 1918. In 1930 he acquired the premises in Notting Hill Gate that became her ballet studio and a stage for the Ballet Club. As the Mercury Theatre it was licensed for dramatic performances in 1933. The records of the Mercury have apparently disappeared.

12 Letter from Yeats to Edmund Dulac, 19 March [1935], UT/HRC.

13 'English Theatre Organization', *Reale Academia d'Italia, Fondazione Alessandro Volta 4, Convegno di Lettere 8–14 Ottobre 1934, XII*, Rome, 1935, pp. 404–7.

14 *TAM*, vol. 19 no. 2 (February 1935), p. 110. The article was written in November 1934.

15 'I had meant to go on producing plays by poets at the Mercury and to build up a repertory which could be cast from a regular company.' *The Scene is Changed*, 1942, p. 212.

16 See R. McHugh, ed., *Ah, Sweet Dancer*, 1970, p. 34.

17 See Appendix B.

18 The book Yeats sent to Doone was *Wheels and Butterflies*, (1934). The quoted phrase is reprinted in Yeats's *Explorations*, p. 400.

19 W. B. Yeats, *Collected Plays*, pp. 63–9. Allison Armstrong has suggested to me that *The Herne's Egg* also implies some such setting as the Group Theatre Rooms.

20 Auden's enthusiasm for *Magnificence* was evident in his review of a new edition of Skelton's poems, appearing in *Criterion*, vol. 11 no. 43 (January 1932), pp. 316–19. His later and heavily qualified reference to the stageworthiness of the play appeared in his contribution to Katherine Garvin (ed.), *The Great Tudors*.

The contrast in the two views shows how rapidly Auden's views of the theatre changed. In the first he wrote:

> I believe *Magnificence* to be an excellent acting play. The subject is of topical interest to any age, the verse easy to understand, an important advantage in poetry to be heard; a great deal of scope is left for action . . . (p. 318).

In the second:

> Its fault, a fatal one in drama, is its prolixity but cut by at least two thirds it might act very much better than one imagines (p. 67).

21 The adaption of *Edward II* by Brecht and Feuchtwanger, first staged in 1924 (Munich), was revived in 1927 (Hamburg) and 1928 (Leipzig). See John Willett, *The Theatre of Bertolt Brecht*, pp. 24–5.

22 Toller's *No More Peace!* was produced by Scobie Mackenzie at the Gate Theatre on 11 June 1936 (just after the end of the Group Theatre season). The translation was by Edward Crankshaw. Auden made the English versions of the lyrics and Murrill set them. Auden and Murrill may have done this work in the expectation of a Group Theatre production.

23 Letters from Greenwood to Shaw, 12 August 1935, and Shaw to Greenwood, 15 August 1935, UT/HRC.

24 Letter from Cocteau to Doone, October 1935, NYPL/BC. *La Machine infernale*, directed by Louis Jouvet, had opened on 10 April 1934 at Théâtre Louis Jouvet, with Cocteau himself as narrator.

25 *ST*, 25 August 1935, p. 4. There was a similar notice in *The Times*, 26 August 1935, p. 8.

26 Group Theatre flyer, headed '1st Group Theatre Season', n.d. printed by the Westminster Press, JM. The flyer also advertised vacancies for 'students' who would 'help in any capacity as required' without pay—a less generous arrangement than some of the founders of the Group Theatre had themselves enjoyed a few years earlier at the Westminster.

27 Letter to Craig, 23 January 1935, UT/HRC.

28 'A Reformer in the Theatre' and an unsigned editorial, *The Times*, 17 August 1935, pp. 11–12. A letter on the subject from Craig appeared on 9 September 1935.

29 Greenwood's letter to the editor, dated 11 September 1935, was not printed, but he sent a copy to Craig, UT/HRC.

30 Letter to Greenwood, 3 November 1935, UT/HRC. Part of Craig's answer was to refer Greenwood to a footnote in his article 'The Russian Theatre Today'. The direct quotation is taken from this footnote.

31 Letter to Craig, 16 October 1935, UT/HRC.

32 Letter to Greenwood, 13 November 1935, UT/HRC. This letter may not have been sent.

33 Letter to Craig, 7 November 1935, UT/HRC.

34 Ibid.

35 Ibid.

36 *A Life in the Theatre*, 1960, p. 61.

37 Ibid., pp. 61–2.

38 Ibid., p. 62.

39 Letter to Craig, 16 October 1935, UT/HRC.

1 E. C. Large, 'The Pleasures of the Pit', *NEW*, 30 January 1936, p. 309.

2 Jean Scott Rogers, who prepared the prompt copy, notes that additions and corrections were still being typed on 18 September.

3 'The Theatre', *Spectator*, 11 October 1935, p. 547.

4 'The Dance of Death', *Obs*, 6 October 1935.

5 'At the Play', *Punch*, 9 October 1935, p. 412.

6 Programme for *DD and SA*, Westminster Theatre, October 1935. In Auden's holograph, NYPL/BC, the word 'compressed' (which makes better sense) appears where the published version has 'confessed' and the word 'directly' after 'deals'.

7 *NEW*, 10 October 1935, pp. 435–6.

8 A. Desmond Hawkins, 'The Group Theatre', letter to the editor, *NEW*, 24 October 1935, pp. 39–40. Cf. his review of the 1934 performance quoted in chapter 3 (p. 88 and note 38).

9 E.L., 'Group Theatre at the Westminster', *Drama*, vol. 14 no. 29 (November 1935), pp. 20, 23.

10 *The Times*, 2 October 1935, p. 12.

11 *NV*, no. 18 (December 1935), p. 9.

12 A. V. Cookman, *LM*, vol. 33 no. 193 (November 1935), p. 56. *Drama* thought *SA* overproduced; George W. Bishop called it 'obscure' and 'pretentious' in his reviews in *DT*, 2 October 1935, p. 10 and *ST*, 6 October 1935, p. 4; the *NSN*, 5 October 1935, p. 446 dismissed *SA* as a 'macabre trifle'.

13 *The Times*, 23 March 1911, p. 10.

14 Programme for *LP*, Westminster Theatre, November 1935.

15 Sydney W. Carroll, *DT*, 17 October 1935, p. 20; a shorter notice by D.D. had appeared the previous day.

16 *Obs*, 20 October 1935, p. 19.

17 From a flyer headed 'Programme Announcement for Group Theatre', UT/HRC. It appeared between 18 and 29 October 1935.

18 The first performance of *Les Lanceurs de graines* was given in Geneva in 1932. It was also performed at the Théâtre de l'Atélier in October 1932. The Quinze presented the play at Wyndham's Theatre on 3 July 1933. The first English adaptation opened at the Arts Theatre on 14 May 1933.

19 See A. V. Cookman, 'The Theatre', *LM*, vol. 33 no. 194 (December 1935), p. 192; *DT*, 30 October 1935, p. 10; *The Times*, 30 October 1935, p. 12.

20 'The New Poetic Drama', letter, *TLS*, 31 January 1935, p. 62. Doone was responding to an article in the previous issue in which the word 'disciples' was used. A. V. Cookman made the same statement in *LM*, vol. 33 no. 193 (November 1935), p. 56.

21 There were four statements in the series. The one that appeared in the programme for *LP* consisted of an excerpt from the article (quoted in chapter 5 above) by Craig in the *The Times*, 17 August 1935, p. 12. Craig expressly, but too late, withheld permission for the quotation, which was juxtaposed with previously published statements of the Group Theatre's aims. A contribution by W. J. Turner appeared in the programme for *TA*. Turner professed himself strongly antagonistic to group efforts of all kinds. After this, the series was abandoned.

22 Doone's statement appeared in the programme for *Sowers*. The last part of it reads:

> Art should serve life. Life is creative: the author creates, the actor creates. There is no such thing as interpretive art. Art is man creating.
>
> Authors should not live in their studios or musicians in the concert halls, or the painters in the studios. They should return. The theatre needs them.
>
> Theatre art is the art of co-operation. I want the theatre to be a social force, where the painter and the author and the choreographer and the machine and the business man and the actor and the illusionist and the stage producer combine with the audience to make realism fantasy and fantasy real.

23 The first reference to the Group Theatre's belief 'in the theatre as a social force' appears to have been made in an undated

flyer, UT/HRC, printed shortly before the opening of the Group Theatre season in October 1935.

24 Programme for *TA*, Westminster Theatre, 19 November 1935.

25 Britain went off the Gold Standard on 21 September 1931.

26 A. V. Cookman, *NY Times*, 15 December 1935, pp. xi, 5. He also reviewed the production in *LM*, vol. 33 no. 195 (January 1936), p. 324. *NSN*, vol. 10 no. 248 (23 November 1935), p. 771 referred to Milton's 'ranting'; Henry K. Fisher in *LLT*, vol. 14 no. 3 (Spring 1936), p. 155, said Milton made Shakespeare's verse sound 'more like plumbing than poetry'.

27 *NSN*, vol. 10 no. 248 (23 November 1935), p. 771; *Obs*, 24 November 1935, p. 17.

28 Programme note by Monck. The speed of playing and delivery, characteristic of Monck's productions, was partly achieved by cutting. See Una Ellis Fermor, *English*, vol. 1 (1936), p. 64; and Nugent Monck, 'The Maddermarket Theatre and the Playing of Shakespeare', *Shakespeare Survey*, vol. 12 (1959), pp. 71–5.

29 There is a set of photographs of the production in the Group Theatre Archive, NYPL/BC. Brown called the design 'miminy piminy'. The *NSN* described the costumes as 'over-fanciful'; Agate mocked them as 'haphazard' and effeminate.

30 James Agate, 'Hurly Without Burly', *ST*, 24 November 1935, p. 6.

31 Carlo Goldoni, *Four Comedies of Carlo Goldoni*, Clifford Bax, ed., 1922, p. 143.

32 *NV*, vol. 18, (December 1935), p. 1.

33 'Theatre Now', *LR*, vol. 2 no. 3 (October 1935), pp. 105–7.

34 Information from Robert Medley on himself and Doone, and from John Allen on himself. For Britten and Marx see DM, p. 46.

35 D[ilys] P[owell], *ST*, 2 February 1936.

36 'A Year in the Theatre', *Criterion*, vol. 15 no. 61 (1936), p. 658.

37 'It was something like this.'

38 See note 1 above. Professor Alan Heuser has pointed out several other articles by E. C. Large on social and economic subjects. Otherwise I would have suspected that the name was a pseudonym for Louis MacNeice.

39 'I hear Wystan's new play is going to be all about mountaineering. A grand subject for him.' From a letter from MacNeice to Doone, 8 February [1936], NYPL/BC.

1 [W. H. Auden], '*Modern Poetic Drama* by Patricia Thouless', review, *Listener*, vol. 11 no. 278 (9 May 1934), p. 808.

2 The description of *The Chase* is based on the 'working copy' sent to Doone and Medley, which forms part of the Group Theatre Archive, NYPL/BC. See B/M, 252–3.

3 See MV. The Gate Theatre production opened 2 June 1930.

4 The 'Sermon . . .' had been published in *LLT*, vol. 10 no. 53 (May 1934), pp. 164–7.

5 On the collaboration of Auden and Isherwood on the play see: MV; B/M, pp. 15–16; EM[1]; and BF, pp. 158–61.

6 Baroness Conyers was the mother of Augusta Byron. The story of the miraculous *post mortem* voyage of the actor Charles Coghlan is told by Sir Johnston Forbes-Robertson in *A Player Under Three Reigns*, 1905, pp. 165–6. Isherwood (CI, p. 3) recalled 'the delicious nausea of initiation terror which Christopher felt as Wystan pulled back the heavy leather door curtain of a boy bar called the Cosy Corner and led the way inside'. Inside, Isherwood found Bubi whose name was adopted for the female cabaret singer in *DBS*. For 'Mother Hubbard's', the night-club run by the notorious Kate Meyrick, see James Laver, *Between the Wars*, 1961, p. 100. Auden reviewed H. Bolitho's biography of Lord Melchett, *Alfred Mond*, in *Scrutiny* vol. 2, December 1933, pp. 307–10. T. R. Barnes assumed that the Curate represented 'Anglo-Catholicism in general and Mr Eliot in particular'. (See note 19 below.)

7 Quotations from *DBS* are from the first (London, 1935) edition, unless otherwise noted.

8 'German Literature in England', *New Republic*, nos. 98–9 (5 April 1939), p. 255.

9 See Klaus Volker, *Brecht Chronicle*, trans. Fred Wieck, New York, 1975, p. 79.

10 See MV.

11 *The Moon in the Yellow River, and The Old Lady Says 'No!'.*
   Johnston's scene was itself derived from the Nighttown episode
   in Joyce's *Ulysses*.

12 *Bertolt Brecht Collected Plays*, vol. 2 no. 3, 1979, p. 11.

13 See MV. The source cited by Isherwood is J. R. Ackerley's
   Prisoners of War. Ackerley's play was extraordinarily bold for
   its time in representing the homoerotic relationships in a group
   of captured officers.

14 Eric Walter White, 'Bertolt Brecht', *LLT*, vol. 13 no. 1
   (September 1935), p. 75.

15 CI, p. 195.

16 Ibid., p. 316.

17 'The Muse's Off Day', *NSN*, 8 February 1936, p. 188.

18 I. M. Parsons, 'Poetry, Drama and Satire', *Spectator*, no. 154 (28
   June 1935), pp. 1112–13; T. R. Barnes, 'Poets and the Drama',
   Scrutiny, vol. 4, September 1935, pp. 189–95; D. G. Bridson,
   'Recent Poetry', *TT*, vol. 16, 17 August 1935, p. 1204; Donald
   Davidson, 'Six Poets: A Study in Magnitude', *Southern Review*,
   vol. 1, Spring 1936, pp. 884–6; Montagu Slater, 'The Fog
   Beneath the Skin', *LR*, vol. 1 no. 10 (July 1935), pp. 425–30;
   John Garrett, *Criterion*, vol. 14 no. 57 (July 1935), pp. 687–90.

19 The plans for an autumn production were announced on the
   flyleaf of the first edition and in a flyer inserted in some copies of
   it. A brochure described as the 'First Announcement' of the
   Group Theatre Season, probably printed in August or September
   1935, did not include *DBS* in the regular programme but as the
   first (it was in fact the *only*) 'special Sunday performance' for
   subscribers and members. Although the play appeared on
   Doone's list of proposed plays sent to Anmer Hall in July, the
   decision to give it a regular place in the season may not have been
   firm when the season opened. Whether this or some other matter
   was at issue, Doone announced the cancellation of the
   production in November 1935, after a quarrel with Hall.
   Information from Jean Scott Rogers.

20 Information on Auden's revisions from Jean Scott Rogers.

21 'Drama', *NEW*, vol. 8, 13 February 1936, pp. 354–5.

22 *ST*, 19 January 1936, p. 6; a cut and revised copy of the first
   edition, marked '2nd Copy', was licensed by the Lord
   Chamberlain on 22 December 1935, BL/LCCP. A two-page

typescript of further 'Alterations and Cuts' may have been submitted later. It includes the cutting of most of pp. 44–5 where there is a reference to public mourning.

23 Eliot to Doone, 5 March 1936; MacNeice to Doone, 8 February 1936, NYPL/BC. For MacNeice's use of liturgical music in *Out of the Picture* see Chapter 10.

24 Prompt copy, NYPL/BC. See B/M, pp. 15–16. Copyright Estate of W. H. Auden.

25 Prompt copy, NYPL/BC. Copyright Estate of W. H. Auden.

26 The *Daily Express*, 31 January 1936, and the *News of the World*, 9 February 1936, used a picture John Moody (as Alan) in a dressing-gown leaning over Carmen Wincelma (as Lou Vipond) recumbent in a frilly négligé. Kenneth Allott, in a very antagonistic review, remarked that the 'substitution of a woman for a dummy . . . spoilt the point of the scene'. See note 31 below.

27 Letter from Eliot to Doone, 5 March 1936, NYPL/BC. For Britten's opinion see Donald Mitchell, *Britten and Auden in the Thirties*, 1981, pp. 119–20.

28 Prompt copy, NYPL/BC, Copyright Estate of W. H. Auden. The image of the swallows at dawn on the frontier had appeared in Auden's *Poems* (1928). See EA, p. 440.

29 For Connolly see note 17 above; Ivor Brown, *Illustrated London News*, 15 February 1936, p. 23.

30 'Not So Hot', NV, no. 19 (February–March 1936), p. 15.

31 *Punch*, vol. 190, 12 February 1936, p. 189.

32 Mitchell, loc. cit. The song set by Britten was 'Now through night's caressing grip . . .', included in *On this Island*, p. 11. See B/M, p. 283.

33 E. D. Randall, 'Speaking Personally', *Action*, vol. I, 21 February 1936, p. 10.

34 'Theatre', *Jewish Chronicle*, 7 February 1936.

35 D. H. in *Colosseum*, vol. 3 no. 9 (March 1936), pp. 81–2, thought the production 'admirable'. *Play Pictorial*, February 1936, found it 'often beautiful and always stimulating' and illustrated the comment with photographs. Harold Conway, *DM*, 31 January 1936, thought the staging 'brilliantly' executed; and *DH*, 31 January 1936, also found it successful. W. H. Darlington had praise for play and production in *DT*, 31 January 1936. Roger Roughton in *DW*, 24 January 1936, thought the production the Group Theatre's best to date.

Charles Morgan, 'A Leftist Dance by the Thames', *NY Times*, 23 February 1936, x, p. 1, had specially high praise for the Lunatic scene. Derek Verschoyle, *Spectator*, vol. 156, 7 February 1936, p. 211, thought the staging a great improvement on that of *DD*. It was 'less inclined to force after freakishly nervous effects', he said.

1 *Letters from Iceland*, p. 246.
2 From 'How To Join The Group Theatre', a flyer printed at the Group Theatre Rooms on brown wrapping paper, late 1936.
3 *GTP*, no. 1 (June 1936), p. [4].
4 Programme for 'Left Theatre Review', Phoenix Theatre, 25 April 1937.
5 Paul Rotha, *Documentary Diary: An Informal History of the British Documentary Film*, 1973, pp. 188–91.
6 *NC*, 23 October 1937.
7 John Louis Beddington (1893–1959) was educated at Wellington and Balliol College, Oxford. He served in the army during the First World War and was wounded. In the twenties he worked for Shell-Mex in China. During the thirties he was able to provide, through Shell, commissions for a number of artists in various media. In 1940 he became Director of the Films Division of the Ministry of Information and was made a CBE in 1943. See Rotha, *Documentary Diary*, pp. 164–5 and *The Times*, 15 April 1959, p. 15c.
8 Auden's remark appeared in his review of Rotha's *Documentary Film*, EA, p. 355. See also *World Film News*, vol. 1 no. 1 (April 1936), p. 13. For Auden and the GPO Film Unit see EM[2], pp. 190–1 and 281–2.
9 Calder-Marshall's remark comes from Cecil Day-Lewis (ed.), *The Mind in Chains*, 1936, p. 59. Hallie Flanagan's hope of making a film of *DBS* is mentioned in her correspondence, 16 July 1936 with Emmett Lavery of MGM, NYPL/TC. That Auden knew of her intention is not certain.
10 *GTP*, no. 2 (August 1936), p. 2.
11 'Selling the Group Theatre', *GTP*, no. 1 (June 1936), p. 2.
12 See Michael Yates, 'Iceland 1936' in *W. H. Auden: A Tribute*, Stephen Spender, ed., 1975, p. 65.
13 *GTP*, no. 4, (October 1936), p. 1.
14 *GTP*, no. 6 (December 1936), p. 4.
15 Group Theatre flyer headed 'Three New Plays', n.d., JM.

16 *GTP*, no. 4 (October 1936), p. 1.

17 Theatre programme for *The Agamemnon*, Westminster Theatre, 1 November 1937.

18 A notice of the Laver occasion appeared in the *Sketch*, 28 October 1936, and of the party at which Eliot spoke in the *Star*, 3 November 1936.

19 See *TAM*, vol. 21 no. 7 (July 1937), p. 534 and vol. 21 no. 10 (October 1937), p. 773.

20 *TAM*, vol. 21 no. 1 (January 1937), p. 26.

21 *TAM*, vol. 21 no. 10 (December 1937), pp. 772–4. The auspices Dukes had in mind were doubtless his own but Doone made some effort to get more business out of *DBS* when he broached with Yeats the idea of a performance in Dublin. Yeats was quite sure that the play was not suitable for the Abbey, where the traditions were 'popular and Irish' but thought that it might find an audience at the Dublin Gate Theatre. Letter from Yeats to Doone, 18 March [1937], NYPL/BC.

22 Letter from Dukes to L. Bertram, 4 June 1938, UT/HRC.

23 Ibid.

24 *GTP*, no. 7 (January 1937), p. 4.

25 *TAM*, vol. 21 no. 12 (December 1937).

26 Day-Lewis had offered his *Noah and the Waters* to Doone already (see p. 89 above); Dylan Thomas had written to John Johnson on 15 July 1936, JJ, that he would 'start a play quite soon' with a view to having it performed by the Group Theatre, though no play was forthcoming; and Spender had asked George Barker for a play early in 1937. Letter from Spender to Barker, n.d. [early 1937], UT/HRC.

27 *Fact*, no. 4 (1937), pp. 37–8.

28 The questionnaire is a two-page typescript beginning, '1. What sort of a Theatre do you want, if any?' This question is followed by twenty-one others, JM and NYPL/BC.

29 Letter from Spender to Lady Ottoline Morrell, 22 October [1937], UT/HRC. Spender briefly describes the forthcoming programme of the Group Theatre and asks Lady Ottoline to join.

30 See *The Times*, 4 November 1937. The Nijinsky exhibition was held at the Storran Gallery, 5–27 November 1937.

31 *CR*, 19 November 1937, p. 104.

32 Theatre programme for 'Group Theatre', 17 July 1938, Westminster Theatre. The printed programme included transla-

tions of the songs sung by Oswald.

33 'The Directors of the Group Theatre feel that the moment has arrived when we must take action and try to become more active in order to establish our aims. We now have a strong production unit of composers, designers, writers, etc., and also a nucleus of good actors and actresses who wish to co-operate with us more or less permanently in order that we may get a permanent company working together. My idea is that we can do this eventually; but in order to do this, I think we need a theatre school, with actors and actresses whom we have to teach in the school. This would be practical financially, as the actors and actresses could do their ordinary jobs in the meantime. Of course they would be paid an average fee for their work in the school, but I hope to discuss this more fully later on . . .

'This idea of having a school is not an excuse to find a way out. But we have come to the conclusion that it is a necessity to our development. The students whom we train could become part of the company, or form a nucleus of actors and actresses, who would wish to co-operate with us in the school.

'The production unit would teach in the school and would, I think, be a great attraction to it. I also think we should be able to maintain a distinguished list of lecturers for each term, which would also be an attraction. . . .

'The position of the building itself will depend, of course, on circumstances. But it should be in a place like Soho, if not in Soho itself in a central part of London in a poor district and accessible. There should be a large enough stage and auditorium to allow us to give our own public shows. And the auditorium should contain not less than 250 people, and the stage be large enough to give the plays a proper showing. But such details must be finally settled in view of practical achievement.'

From a letter from Doone to Keynes, 3 May 1938, KCC/JMK. Keynes was unwell and apparently unresponsive to the idea of a school. Nothing more was heard of it.

34 See *ST*, 14 November 1937, p. 9.

35 The party is described in P. N. Furbank's *E. M. Forster*, vol. 2, 1979, p. 223. The phrase quoted is from an interview with Hedli (Anderson) MacNeice.

36 See Humphrey Carpenter, *Auden: A Biography*, 1981, p. 245.

37 CI, p. 289.

1 W. H. Auden and Christopher Isherwood, *The Ascent of F6*, 1937, p. 70. Other page references to this, the second English edition, are given in the text in square brackets.

2 Letter to Rupert Doone, 8 February 1936, NYPL/BC. See chapter 6, note 39.

3 EA, p. 61.

4 EA, pp. 28, 149.

5 Cecil Day-Lewis, *Collected Poems*, 1954, pp. 85, 97, 109.

6 EA, p. 105.

7 'Speaking Personally', BBC Television, 12 October 1938.

8 *Listener*, vol. 7, 26 June 1935, p. 1110.

9 T. S. Eliot, *Murder in the Cathedral*, 1937, pp. 83–4.

10 The given page reference is to the London 1937 edition but here and elsewhere I have actually quoted from the prompt copy in the Group Theatre Archive, NYPL/BC. This prompt copy was used for the Old Vic production of 1939 and, as well as the 'new' final scene it contains, according to Robert Medley's accompanying note, 'other interpolations based on previous performances'. The copy is made up of a disbound copy of the fourth impression of the second edition pasted into a manuscript book. I have not been able to discover the prompt copy used for the first production but the copy sent to the Lord Chamberlain for licensing was the first English edition very heavily revised. The resultant text of this copy is very close to that of the second English edition, with the exception of the last scene.

11 In his earlier 'Dante' essay Eliot defended philosophical poetry and quoted the passage about virtue and knowledge from the *Convivio*: 'The principal design [of the odes] is to lead men to knowledge and virtue, as will be seen in the progress of the truth of them.' *The Sacred Wood*, 1920, p. 164.

In his later 'Dante' (1929) essay Eliot quoted the passage from the *Inferno* that begins Ransom's speech: 'O brothers! who through a hundred thousand dangers have reached the West . . . you were made not to live like beasts but to pursue virtue and knowledge.' *Selected Essays*, 1951, p. 249. The translation used by Ransom is Eliot's but his view of Dante is essentially that found in Yeats's poem 'Ego Dominus Tuus'.

12 EA, p. 321.

13 CI, pp. 242, 106.

14 The descriptions of Lawrence by Ralph Fox and Winston Churchill are quoted in Samuel Hynes, *The Auden Generation*, p. 190.

15 Ibid.

16 See below p. 197.

17 G. W. Stonier, 'The Ascent of F6', *NSN*, vol. 18 no. 436 (1 July 1939), p. 13.

18 EA, p. 321.

19 'T. E. Lawrence' in Christopher Caudwell, *Studies and Further Studies in a Dying Culture*, p. 20.

20 In a review of *T. E. Lawrence. By his Friends, Listener*, 9 June 1937, p. 1160.

21 'Chormopuloda', *Listener*, 14 October 1936, supplement, p. 7.

22 Auden declared that the first edition *F6* was published 'early' and against the authors' will by Faber and Faber. See B/M, p. 23.

23 *The Ascent of F6*, first edition, 1936, pp. 74–5.

24 D.W., 'At the Play', *Punch*, vol. 192, 10 March 1937, p. 272.

25 CI, pp. 240–1. See also EM[1]; and BF, pp. 162–7.

26 See MV.

27 *The Ascent of F6*, first edition p. 123.

28 This was the first American edition. See B/M, pp. 22–3. The original last scene was not included in the second English edition of 1937.

29 P. N. Furbank, *E. M. Forster*, vol. 2, 1979, p. 214.

30 A. R. Humphreys, 'The Ascent of F6', *CR*, vol. 58, 30 April 1937, p. 35. See also BF, p. 127.

31 Furbank, *E. M. Forster*, vol. 2, pp. 213–14.

32 Letters from Yeats to Doone, 13 and 18 March 1937, NYPL/BC. The spelling has been normalized.

33 Auden's revision for a production at Swarthmore College, 19–21 April 1945. E. F. Von Erffa, 'Auden at Swarthmore', *National Theatre Conference Bulletin*, vol. 7, [November 1945], pp. 27–32; and B/M, p. 21. For the 1939 Old Vic production a last broadcasting studio scene was used. It was very close to the original scene of 1936 though it was publicized as being 'new'.

34 F. R. Leavis, 'Mr Auden's Talent', *Scrutiny*, vol. 5, December 1936, pp. 323–7.

35 *GTP*, no. 7, p. 4.

36 Cecil Day-Lewis, 'Paging Mankind', *Poetry*, vol. 49, January 1937, pp. 225–8.

37 G. M. T[revelyan], 'Poetry and Revolution', *Colosseum*, vol. 3 no. 12 (December 1936), pp. 312–14.

38 *The Ascent of F6*, first edition, 1936, p. 68.

39 See BF, p. 163.

40 Stephen Spender, 'Fable and Reportage', *LR*, vol. 2 no. 14 (November 1936), pp. 779–82.

41 'Speaking Personally', BBC Television, 12 October 1938.

42 'Audiences, Producers, Plays, Poets', *NV*, no. 18 (December 1935), pp. 3–4. See also Eliot's letter to Doone quoted in chapter 5, note 28.

43 'The Ascent of F6', *Twentieth Century Verse*, vol. 3, April – May 1937, p. 59. A. V. Cookman, on the other hand, found Devlin 'simple and persuasive', *LM*, vol. 25, April 1937, p. 619.

44 See above, chapter 7, pp. 158–9.

45 CI, p. 241. See also BF, p. 162.

46 Among those who referred to the play as a tragedy were Forster and Trevelyan in the reviews cited above and Dilys Powell in 'Heroic Tragedy', *LM*, vol. 34, October 1936, p. 561.

47 'The English Scene: Tragedy Returns', *TAM*, vol. 21, February 1937, p. 356.

48 CI, p. 268; *NSN*, vol. 13 no. 315 (6 March 1937), p. 368.

49 For quotations from the diaries of Benjamin Britten I am indebted to Donald Mitchell. These quotations are the copyright of the Britten Estate and are not to be reproduced without written permission.

50 Derek Verschoyle, 'The Theatre', *Spectator*, no. 158 (5 March 1937), p. 403; Hugh G. Porteus, 'F6', *NEW*, vol. 10, 11 March 1937, p. 433.

51 For Verschoyle, see note 50 above. Yeats gave his opinion in a
    letter to Doone of 13 March [1937], NYPL/BC.
52 Letter from Keynes to Eliot, 29 July 1936, KCC/JMK.

1 *Modern Poetry*, 1938, p. 196.
2 Louis MacNeice, *The Dark Tower and Other Radio Scripts*, 1947, pp. 14–15.
3 Ibid., p. 13.
4 'In Defence of Vulgarity', *Listener*, vol. 18 no. 468 (29 December 1937), p. 1408.
5 *The Dark Tower . . .* , 1947, p. 21.
6 *Modern Poetry*, 1938, p. 193.
7 Letter to Anthony Blunt, 9 February 1934, KCC/LM. The books were: a collection of poems, a novel, a play, a collection of Latin humour and an analytic autobiography.
8 Letters to Blunt, 5 January 1934, 3 March 1934, and 8 June 1934, KCC/LM; and to Doone, 22 July [1934], NYPL/BC.
9 Letter to Blunt, 8 June 1934, MacNeice reports that he has recently heard about 'a thing called, I think, the Group Theatre'.
10 Letter to Doone, 22 July [1934], NYPL/BC. *Station Bell* was eventually performed by the Unnamed Society of Manchester in December 1936. There is an incomplete typescript of the play in UT/HRC and a complete stage version in BL/LCCP.
11 MacNeice sent a draft of *Ag* to Doone about 13 March 1936 and at that time mentioned his plan for a prologue. He made revisions after he returned to England late in April. In the Group Theatre Archive there is a typescript of the translation. It is very close to the published text except for the notes on staging added by MacNeice in green ink. The typescript is accompanied by an untitled four-page holograph note which is, in effect, a prologue, apparently written to be spoken. It begins, 'Before this play starts there are several things to be said. . . .' Letters from MacNeice to Doone, 13 March 1936 and April 1936, NYPL/BC.
12 Draft 'prologue', f.4, NYPL/BC.
13 *The Agamemnon of Aeschylus*, translated by Louis MacNeice,

1936, p. 8. (Subsequent page references to this edition are given in the text.)

14 Letter to Blunt, 3 April 1936, KCC/LM.

15 The salute was mentioned in the review in *TT*, 7 November 1936, p. 1562.

16 Henry Adler, *New*, 11 November 1935, p. 95.

17 Draft 'prologue', f.3, NYPL/BC.

18 This chorus does not appear in the published text. It was reproduced in *GTP*, no. 4, p. 13.

19 From the 'Translator's Note' in the theatre programme, Westminster Theatre, 1 November 1936.

20 Letter MacNeice to Doone, 13 March 1936.

21 Ibid.

22 MacNeice's note on the typescript of *The Agamemnon*, f.70, NYPL/BC.

23 Letter, 23 July 1936.

24 *TT*, 7 November 1936, p. 1562.

25 Letter to the editor, *TT*, 21 November 1936, p. 1632.

26 'A Modern Use of Masks: An Apologia', *GTP*, no. 5 (November 1936), p. 4. The article was reprinted in part in *The Times*, 27 October 1936, p. 12. See B/M, p. 184.

27 *Stage*, 5 November 1936, p. 42.

28 See: *Era*, 4 November 1936; *DH*, 2 November 1936; *Obs*, 8 November 1936, p. 17; *NSN*, 7 November 1936, pp. 709–10; *The Times*, 2 November 1936, p. 12.

29 *Missing Persons*, 1968, p. 132.

30 Letter to Doone, 23 June 1936, NYPL/BC.

31 'An *Agamemnon* for an Age of Dictators', *New Republic*, 19 May 1937, p. 52.

32 Yeats's remark on this occasion was reminiscent of the one he made after the first production of Alfred Jarry's *Ubu Roi* in 1896: 'After us the savage god.' See his *Autobiographies*, 1956, p. 349. Yeats's *Purgatory* and *The Death of Cuchulain* were approximations to tragedy that imply the impossibility of the genre.

33 See EMB, pp. 90–1, 117.

34 Information from letters to Blunt and Doone previously cited. In *Blacklegs*, NYPL/BC, Jack, who is scabbing out of uxoriousness and against his own principles, is shot dead by his brother. In the same kangaroo court two other blacklegs are 'acquitted',

one because he is working on principle and the other because he has no principles.

35 Letter from Keynes to Eliot, 7 March 1937, KCC/JMK.

36 *LM*, vol. 37 no. 219 (January 1938), p. 331.

37 Letter from Eliot to Keynes, 7 May 1937, KCC/JMK.

38 Letter to Blunt, 10 November 1935, KCC/LM.

39 Prompt copy of *Out of the Picture*, ff.13–14, NYPL/BC. In this prompt book from the Group Theatre Archive many pages of a copy of the London 1937 edition are replaced by typescript sheets pasted in. The pagination of the printed copy is preserved except in that for extra typescript sheets alphabetical sequences are used to supplement the page numbers as required.

40 Ibid., f.22.

41 Ibid., f.76.

42 Ibid., f.54.

43 Ibid., f.53B.

44 Ibid., ff.116–17.

45 *The Times*, 6 December 1937, p. 18.

46 Letter to the editor, *NV*, no. 28 (January 1938), p. 18.

47 K[enneth] A[llott], 'MacNeice, MacLeish, and Young', *NV*, no. 28 (January 1938), p. 18; D[ilys] P[owell], *ST*, 12 December 1937, p. 4.

48 The 'First Chorus' appeared in *Poetry* (London), no. 2 (April 1938), pp. 8–9.

49 The typescript of *Eureka*, UT/HRC, is dated '11 December 1945'. The play is about the 'brave new world' of a Fascist British state in which a happiness serum is used to tranquillize political opponents. *Traitors in our Way*, otherwise known as *Another Part of the Sea*, was produced by the Belfast Group Theatre under the first title and on BBC television, in 1960, under the second. The theme of the play is spying and betrayal. It was partly inspired by the repercussions from the defection of Guy Burgess, a matter in which (as it would later appear) MacNeice's close friend Anthony Blunt was implicated. See Barbara Coulter, *Louis MacNeice in the BBC*, 1980, pp. 122, 178–9.

   One for the Grave was first published in 1967, in the *Massachusetts Review*, as *One for the Dead*.

50 *One for the Grave*, 1968, p. 13.

51 Ibid., p. 13.

52 Ibid., p. 87.

1 *On the Frontier*, 1938, p. 41.

2 *Forward from Liberalism*, 1937, p. 198.

3 Louis MacNeice, *The Strings are False*, 1965, p. 114; Stephen Spender, 'Oxford to Communism', *NV*, nos. 26–7 (November 1937), p. 10.

4 Page references are to the London 1938 edition. I have not been able to discover a prompt copy for the Group Theatre production.

5 The scene occurs in a manuscript version of the play, described as 'original manuscript', now in UT/HRC.

6 'The Poetic Dramas of W. H. Auden and Christopher Isherwood', p. 103.

7 See Andrew Forge, (ed.), *The Townsend Journals: An Artist's Record of His Times, 1928–51*, 1976, p. 44; and S. John Woods, *John Piper: Paintings, Drawings and Theatre Designs, 1932–54*, 1955.

8 Letter from Spender to Lady Ottoline Morrell, 10 January 1936, UT/HRC.

9 'Poetry and Expressionsim'.

10 *The Times*, 19 March 1938, p. 10; 'Two Views of a Play', (one of them by Gavin Ewart, the other anonymous), *Twentieth Century Verse*, no. 10 (May 1938), pp. 522–54. See also Nevill Coghill, 'Odin Meets with the Wolf', *Spectator*, 18 March 1938, pp. 483–4; *DW*, 21 March 1938, p. 7; *Jewish Chronicle*, 25 March 1938, p₁ 57; Desmond MacCarthy's review, *NSN*, vol. 15, 26 March 1938, pp. 523–4; Janet Adam Smith's review, *Criterion*, no. 17 (July 1938), pp. 730–4; H. A. Mason, 'Mr Spender's Play', *Scrutiny*, no. 7 (September 1938), p. 222; K. A[llott], 'Play for Puritans', *NV*, no. 30 (Summer 1938), p. 20; Philip Toynbee, 'Too Good for the World', *Town Crier*, 19 December 1938, p. 2. Michael Roberts was one reviewer who

found that, despite the fault of excessive abstraction, 'the characters are credible as human beings, the situations are genuinely dramatic, and the argument is poetically convincing', 'The Tragedy of Justice', *LM*, vol. 37 no. 222 (April 1938), p. 652. An anonymous reviewer in the *Listener*, 30 March 1938, p. 2, described Spender's Judge as 'genuinely tragic' and the 'nearest approach to a universal figure incarnating the conflicts of the age that the modern drama has yet thrown up'.

11 'Politics on the London Stage', *New Writing*, vol. 2, (Spring 1939, pp. 103–12.

12 See the letter from the directors of the Group Theatre, *NSN*, vol. 15, 26 March 1938; and the letter from Doris Thelluson, *Weekly Review*, 21 April 1938.

13 MacNeice, *The Strings are False*, 1965, p. 168.

14 Medley's detailed sketches for a series of stage settings for *Danton's Death* are in the Group Theatre Archive, NYPL/BC.

12 On the Frontier

Notes to pp. 239–44

1 'The Public v. the Late Mr William Butler Yeats', EA, p. 393.
2 Unsigned review, 'The Arts Theatre: *On the Frontier*', CR, vol. 60, 25 November 1938, p. 134. Other reviews that made similar observations about the untimeliness of OF were by Cecil Day-Lewis, *Listener*, vol. 20, 24 November 1938, p. 1145; by P.T., *NEW*, vol. 14, 23 February 1939, p. 302; and in *Gownsman*, 19 November 1938, p. 29.
3 NC, 19 March 1937.
4 Isherwood was engrossed in his efforts to snatch Heinz from the maw of the German authorities and was forcing himself to finish *Lions and Shadows*; and he also managed to fit in a film script in the early part of the summer. Auden spent the summer term teaching at the Downs School and had the *Oxford Book of Light Verse* to be getting on with.
5 Letters from Isherwood to Doone, 1 September [1937], NYPL/BC; and from Keynes to Auden, 6 October 1937, KCC/JMK.
6 Letter from Auden to Keynes, 9 October 1937, KCC/JMK.
7 Quoted in the *Star*, 14 November 1938.
8 Letter from Keynes to Auden, 14 November 1937, KCC/JMK.
9 Letters from Keynes to Auden, 22 November 1937; to George Rylands, same date; and to Doone, 23 July 1938, KCC/JMK.
10 Letter from Keynes to Auden, 22 November 1937, KCC/JMK.
11 Letter from Isherwood to Doone, 1 September 1937, NYPL/BC.
12 Letter from Keynes to N. O. Higgins, 20 July 1938, KCC/JMK; and information from Robert Medley.
13 CI, p. 317; chapter 8, p. 181 above.
14 Letter from Keynes to Isherwood, 5 October 1938.
15 Page references are to the first (London, 1938) edition. I have not been able to discover a prompt copy of the play. The copy submitted to the Lord Chamberlain for licensing shows that the published text was revised for performance chiefly to avoid

giving political offence. In the passage quoted, the Third Prisoner's lines were at first censored but later permitted. For the new interlude see note 32 below.

16 Letter from Eliot to Keynes, 15 November 1938, KCC/JMK.

17 CI, p. 328.

18 In an interview with the author, 17 July 1976.

19 *Criterion*, vol. 18 no. 71 (January 1939), p. 323.

20 Letter from Isherwood to Doone, 1 September 1937.

21 'The Theatre', *Spectator*, no. 161 (18 November 1938), p. 858.

22 CI, p. 288 and EA, pp. 136–8.

23 P. T., *New*, vol. 14, 23 February 1939, p. 302, observed that 'Ostnia [is] presumably England since its monarch broadcasts in exact imitation of George V in his Christmas speeches.'

24 A. N. Green-Armytage, 'A Valuable Failure', *Colosseum*, vol. 5 no. 20 (January 1939), pp. 66–7.

25 *Stage*, 17 November 1938.

26 Julian Symons, 'About Frontiers', *Twentieth Century Verse*, nos. 15–16 (February 1939), p. 164; Kenneth Allott, 'A Tract', *NV*, vol. 1 no. 1 (January 1939), p. 25.

27 *NEW*, vol. 14, 23 February 1939, p. 302.

28 Tom Paine, 'On the Frontier', *NSN*, vol. 16, 19 November 1938, pp. 26–7.

29 CI, p. 324.

30 *France–Grande Bretagne*, no. 188, (Juillet–Août 1939), p. 233.

31 Louis Bonnerot, 'On the Frontier', *Etudes Anglaises*, vol. 4, January–March 1940, p. 78.

32 The new interlude was inserted into the Lord Chamberlain's copy of the play in the form of a three-page typescript with corrections from which the following quotations are made. Copyright, Estate of W. H. Auden.

33 Letter from Keynes to Herbert Farjeon, 24 November 1938, KCC/JMK.

34 A typescript carbon copy was submitted on 11 October for licensing by the Lord Chamberlain, and Doone consulted with Major Gwatkin, the censor, at the Lord Chamberlain's office a week or so later. (Letter from Doone to Keynes, 19 October 1938, KCC/JMK.) The BL/LCCP copy bears four kinds of notations: those in pencil, which seem to be a censor's first queries; those in blue pencil representing cuts required for political reasons; those in red ink, which may represent a second

censor's (Major Gwatkins's?) views and the substitutions he has negotiated or suggested; and one cut made in green pencil, apparently indicating censorship on moral grounds. The main changes and annotations are recorded below, with page references to the first, 1938, edition:

'Stahl' is changed to 'Alving'; 'Leader' is changed to 'Guidanto' (here and throughout); and 'Storm-Trooper Grimm' is changed to 'Cpl. Grimm' (p. 9).

The admonition 'but not too pansy' is added to the description of Lessep; the phrase 'wears a beard' in the description of the Leader (Guidanto) is annotated 'suggested alteration to "The Master"' (p. 12). ('The Master' probably refers to Keynes.)

The paragraph of Valerian's speech beginning 'No, not by you, dear Leader . . .' is cut (p. 25).

A censor queries 'England doomed, Germany bankrupt, and the United States . . .' with 'Leave?' (in pencil) and is answered (in red ink): 'This points away from Germany' (pp. 27–8).

The passage 'Though really . . . National Academy of Art' is annotated: 'obviously suggested by Hitler's desiring to be a super art-critic'. 'National Academy of Art' is changed to 'National Salon' (p. 28).

'Culture House' is changed to 'Agricultural Institute' (p. 29).

The reference to 'the labour camps' is blue-pencilled but a marginal notation, 'left', appears in red ink, presumably cancelling the excision. 'Shock Troops' in the same speech is censored (in blue) and 'Blue Guards' is substituted for it in red (p. 30). See the similar, and annotated, change on p. 61.

The sentences 'In Russia, yes. In Spain, yes.' are censored in blue but the red-ink note reads 'I don't see much harm in naming these countries.' 'When the old Emperor abdicated' is censored and 'When the old King abdicated' is supplied in red (p. 31).

The allusion to the Leader's (i.e., Guidanto's) 'fancy-dress' uniform is censored (p. 32).

The stage direction 'giving Westland salute' is annotated (in red): 'not a recognized salute' (p. 33).

The passage 'He is no longer . . . cities and men . . .' is questioned by the (first?) censor and the question is answered, in red: 'If "The Leader" is changed and wears a beard into the bargain does this matter?' (p. 34).

The blue-pencilling of the mentions of 'Europe and America' and 'England' are apparently cancelled (p. 37).

The word 'fieldboot' is censored. 'They talk of the mystical value of blood' is censored (in blue) but apparently allowed by the note (in red) 'Most Dictators say this!' (p. 41).

The word 'European' is censored from the title of Eric's essay 'The chances of European peace'. The name 'Blutstein' is annotated 'alter, too German' but then allowed with 'leave', both instructions being in red ink (p. 46).

In the phrase 'Europe's a powder-magazine', 'Europe' is censored (blue) and 'The Continent' substituted (red). Against the two-speech passage 'After the last war . . . last time' are two annotations. The first (in red) reads: 'This won't do. It is much too near the truth. Sending in alterations to this passage.' The second (also in red) reads: 'Cut. Mrs Thelluson telephoned 3.30 11 Nov 38.' The cut recorded by Mrs Thelluson (the Group Theatre's secretary) may have been of the last sentence of the offending passage, since this sentence only is shown as cut (p. 47).

A note, in red, against 'shock-troop' (which is cancelled in blue) reads: 'All shock troops become Blue Guards. "Shock" out' (p. 61).

'European' is censored (p. 62).

In 'The unceasing struggle of my life . . .', the word 'struggle' is censored. The red-ink annotation identifies the objection as being to a possible allusion to *Mein Kampf* and records 'efforts' as an alternative (p. 64). In the phrase 'Westland stands in Europe . . .', 'in Europe' is censored. The first red-ink suggestion was 'The continent or leave out' but this was deleted and 'The World' recorded as the acceptable alternative (p. 65).

The stage direction 'The wireless-sets play their respective national anthems' is censored (p. 66).

'Hammel' is changed to 'Rubek' (p. 78). (On p. 90 there is a red-ink annotation that the name 'Hammel' is 'Too German'.)

The passage 'I never wished . . . dear country' was censored but later annotated in red: ' "If the cap fits" but it doesn't. It isn't true of any dictator and they are anxious to leave it in' (p. 81).

With respect to the phrase 'in England and France and America', which is censored, the first red-ink annotation is 'add Germany' but this is deleted. 'Germany' appears again in red, however, and so does the word 'abroad'. The last is obviously a possible substitute for the whole of the offending phrase (p. 83).

The stanza 'The Colonel . . . underclothes' is censored in green pencil (p. 99).

'Alter all these' is the requirement, in red ink, noted against the censored names 'Kurt', 'Fritz' and 'Karl'. The names 'Jon', 'Lars' and 'Carl' are marginally noted in red. (p. 100).

'Tarnberg' is censored, but a note in red says 'leave' (p. 102).

'Frommer' is censored and 'Krog' substituted. 'Route army' becomes 'army route'. The allusion to 'civil' war is consored (p. 105).

The name 'Schwartz' is changed to 'Ragnar' and 'Kurt' to 'Knud' (p. 107).

35 Letter from Keynes to Doone, 30 November 1938, KCC/JMK.
36 Joseph Gordon Macleod, 'To-day's "Non-Commercial" Theatre: Notes on the Frontier', *Townsman*, vol. 2 no. 5 (January 1939), p. 22.

13 Conclusion

Notes to pp. 257–60

1 Unsigned review of *Modern Poetic Drama* by Patricia Thouless, *Listener*, vol. 11 no. 278 (9 May 1934), p. 808.
2 *France–Grande Bretagne*, no. 188 (Juillet–Août 1939), p. 230.
3 Ibid., p. 233.
4 From 'The Last Twenty-Five Years of English Poetry', KCC/JH, a lecture prepared by Eliot in 1939 to be delivered in Italy under the auspices of the British Council. The lecture series was cancelled.
5 'Speaking Personally', BBC Television, 12 October 1938.
6 'The Poetic Dramas of W. H. Auden and Christopher Isherwood', pp. 106–7.

A The Superior Landlord

Notes to pp. 263–4

1 I am grateful to Valerie Eliot for allowing me to examine and quote from the Eliot papers in the library of King's College, Cambridge, and to the college librarians for their helpfulness.
2 Robert Sencourt, *T. S. Eliot: A Memoir*, p. 122.

1 Letter to Doone, NYPL/BC. The invitation was for Monday, 22 October.

2 Letter to George Yeats, Saturday, [27 October 1934], MBY.

3 At this time, Margot Ruddock (1907–1951) used her first married name, Collis, as an actress, and her maiden name, Ruddock, as a poet. In private life she was Mrs Lovell, having married Raymond Lovell, an actor, in 1932.

   See Roger McHugh's Introduction to his edition of the correspondence of Yeats and Margot Ruddock, *Ah, Sweet Dancer*, 1970, pp. 9–15; and *Uncollected Prose* by W. B. Yeats, John P. Frayne and Colton Johnson (eds.), vol. 2, 1975, pp. 501–6.

4 Letter to George Yeats, Tuesday, [30 October 1934], MBY. Yeats reports that Dukes 'has undertaken all expenses'.

5 McHugh, *Ah, Sweet Dancer*, p. 27.

6 See note 4, above. Sir Frederick Ashton tells me that Yeats was very interested in his work at this time and may have seen him as De Valois's successor at the Abbey Ballet School. At Yeats's request, Ashton and Dulac spent some time training Margot Collis to speak verse, with mixed results according to Yeats's own account.

7 Letter from Eliot to Lady Ottoline Morrell, 29 October 1934.

8 Letters from Yeats to George Yeats, [30 October 1934], and to Dobbs, 19 December [1934], MBY.

9 Letter from Edmund Dulac to Yeats, 16 March 1935, UT/HRC.

10 See EMB, p. 39. Browne's account mistakenly conflates the plans for the Poets' Theatre with what actually happened. That the first plan was, in fact, for Browne to direct a Group Theatre production of *Murder in the Cathedral* at the Mercury *before* the Canterbury performance, is indicated by the dates for the proposed Poets' Theatre season and Eliot's letters to Doone of 20 February and 30 April 1935, NYPL/BC. In the second, he writes:

As for the play, please don't think that there is no chance of my ever letting you do it if you wanted to. It was only that Yeats' season having fallen through, I felt obliged to refer the matter again to the Canterbury people, and as they definitely felt that their production would have a better chance if not preceded by another one in London, I thought I should defer to their wishes.

In a letter to the editor, *Obs*, 22 December 1935, p. 7, Dukes was quite definite about the fact that 'it was at one time arranged, with the author's consent, to give *Murder in the Cathedral* at the Mercury before the Canterbury production'.

11 Letter from Yeats to Dobbs, Sunday, [22 December 1934].
12 Ibid.
13 Letter from Dulac to Yeats, 16 March 1935, UT/HRC.
14 Letter to Dulac, 19 March [1935], UT/HRC.
15 Letters from Doone to Dulac, 18 March 1935, and from Dukes to Doone, 19 March 1935, UT/HRC.
16 20 March 1935, NYPL/BC.
17 *Letters of W. B. Yeats*, Allan Wade, ed., 1954, p. 835 and *Ah, Sweet Dancer*, p. 44.
18 See *Ah, Sweet Dancer*, pp. 51–2, 54–7; and *Uncollected Prose*, pp. 501–3.

E Group Theatre Productions Limited, 1950–6
Notes to pp. 299–300

1 This account is based largely on the minutes and memoranda of GTP, NYPL/BC and JM, which are referred to in these notes as MM, followed by the date of the item. I am also indebted to Robert Medley, John Moody, Audrey Russell, Vera Russell, and the late Roy Walker for recollections of GTP.

2 Gifts from the Elmhirst Trust and Roy Walker totalling £750 were later added.

3 Vera (Poliakoff) (Lindsay) Russell (b. 1911, St Petersburg) was educated in England, studied at the Royal Academy of Dramatic Art and made her first stage appearance in 1929. During the thirties she acted in a number of London productions as well as with the Compagnie des Quinze. During the war she joined the BBC and after the war was active in the promotion of theatre and the arts generally.

4 The contracts secured the positions of the two Artistic Directors for seven years and provided, *inter alia*, that each should receive a retainer of £10 per annum and 25 per cent of the first £2,000 of surplus monies. There never was a surplus.

5 In July 1952, the Literary Directors, T. S. Eliot, Graham Greene, Herbert Read and John Lehmann wanted clarification of their function. Letter from Eliot to Doone, 29 July 1952, NYPL/BC. As a result their title was changed to 'Literary Advisers', (MM, 15 November 1952), but Graham Greene immediately resigned, (MM, 20 November 1952).

6 T. S. Eliot had no enthusiasm for the play, in which, he thought, 'the people were too unreal, and the ideas . . . too obscure to attract an ordinary English audience'. Letter from Eliot to Doone, 8 December 1951, NYPL/BC. Lord Duncannon, a prospective Governor of GTP objected so violently to it that it was assumed that he would not wish to associate himself with GTP, as had been proposed, (MM, 12 February 1952).

7 *The Knights of the Round Table* was produced by BBC Radio on 22 May 1951 and by the repertory company of Salisbury Playhouse in May 1954. Auden's translation was published in *The Infernal Machine and Other Plays by Jean Cocteau*, New York, 1963, where it is described as having been made for the BBC. Auden made the translation with both the prospective stage production by GTP and a broadcast production (for which he wrote alternative passages) in mind, as his letter to Doone of 19 March 1951, NYPL/BC, makes clear.

8 Robert Medley recalls that Auden was asked to undertake the translation. Isherwood wrote to Doone on 12 September 1950 praising the play but declining the task, NYPL/BC. MM, 18 October 1950 and 24 November 1950, indicate that J. B. Priestley and Henry Reed were to be approached. In December 1952 the search for a translator was continuing and James Kirkup was suggested.

The remark on the play's unsuitability given the political climate occurs in MM, 1 February 1954. The first English production of the play was given in June 1955 at the Taw and Torridge Festival, Devon, under the direction of Joan Littlewood. How the production rights came to be transferred from GTP to the actual producers remains obscure, as does the translation used on this occasion. See Nicholas Jacobs and Prudence Ohlsen, *Bertolt Brecht in Britain*, 1977, p. 35.

9 GTP received at least one payment (of £300) on account of its interest in *The Power and the Glory*, (MM, 15 February 1954). It was due to receive £100 per month as a percentage of Donald Albery's management fee for Greene's *The Living Room*, (MM, 28 September 1953).

10 *The Times*, 20 July 1951, p. 8e.

11 T. C. Worsly, 'Ustinov and Sartre', *NSN*, 1 December 1951, pp. 621–2. See also Worsly's 'Two plays of Ideas', *Britain Today*, no. 190 (February 1952), pp. 28–31; Ivor Brown, 'Old Worlds for New', *Obs*, 2 December 1951, p. 6; *The Times*, 26 November 1951, p. 8e; *Picture Post*, 19 January 1952; and Harold Hobson, *The French Theatre Today: an English View*, 1953, p. 89.

12 The production costs were over £800, the box office returns somewhat less than £350. The use of the New Theatre was made possible by Donald Albery, Managing Director of Wyndham's Theatres and Executive Director of the GTP.

13 *The Coming of Age* was read on 18 January 1953 at the Institut Français; *The Parliament of Women* on 14 June at the ICA.

14 Bridget Boland's play was eventually staged and she offered GTP a share of her royalties in recognition of its help, (MM, 13 August 1954 and 4 December 1954). She later offered *Masquerade* for the consideration of GTP but this was rejected. Mervyn Peake also offered at least one unnamed play, (MM, 1 March and 15 March 1954).

15 *The Times*, 23 November 1953, p. 2e; MM, 14 December 1953, 18 and 26 January 1954.

16 The proceeds from *Homage*, which was presented on 14 January 1954, were over £1,000, (UT/HRC).

17 MM, 8 May 1956.

Index